THE LORDSHIP OF DENBIGH
1282–1543

by

D. HUW OWEN

UNIVERSITY OF WALES PRESS
2024

© D. Huw Owen, 2024

All rights reserved. No part of this book may be reproduced in any material form (including photocopying or storing it in any medium by electronic means and whether or not transiently or incidentally to some other use of this publication) without the written permission of the copyright owner. Applications for the copyright owner's written permission to reproduce any part of this publication should be addressed to the University of Wales Press, University Registry, King Edward VII Avenue, Cardiff CF10 3NS.

www.uwp.co.uk

British Library CIP Data

A catalogue record for this book is available from the British Library

ISBN   978-1-83772-174-0
eISBN   978-1-83772-175-7

The right of D. Huw Owen to be identified as author of this work has been asserted in accordance with sections 77 and 79 of the Copyright, Designs and Patents Act 1988.

Typeset by Richard Huw Pritchard
Printed by CPI Antony Rowe, Melksham, UK.

SERIES EDITORS' FOREWORD

Since the foundation of the series in 1977, the study of Wales's history has attracted growing attention among historians internationally and continues to enjoy a vigorous popularity. Not only are approaches, both traditional and new, to the study of history in general being successfully applied in a Welsh context, but Wales's historical experience is increasingly appreciated by writers on British, European and world history. These advances have been especially marked in the university institutions in Wales itself.

In order to make more widely available the conclusions of original research, much of it of limited accessibility in postgraduate dissertations and theses, in 1977 the History and Law Committee of the Board of Celtic Studies inaugurated this series of monographs, *Studies in Welsh History*. It was anticipated that many of the volumes would originate in research conducted in the University of Wales or under the auspices of the Board of Celtic Studies, and so it proved. Although the Board of Celtic Studies no longer exists, the University of Wales Press continues to sponsor the series. It seeks to publish significant contributions made by researchers in Wales and elsewhere. Its primary aim is to serve historical scholarship and to encourage the study of Welsh history.

I Mary a Hywel gyda diolch
ac er cof am Tomos

CONTENTS

SERIES EDITORS' FOREWORD v
PREFACE ix
LIST OF ILLUSTRATIONS xiii
LIST OF ABBREVIATIONS xv
GLOSSARY xvii

Introduction 1
1 Geographical Context and Political Background 7
2 Social and Economic Background 21
3 Political Control of the Lordship, 1282–1344 31
4 Administration of the Lordship, 1282–1334 47
5 Society and Economy, 1282–1334: Seigneurial Revenue, Escheat and Exchange 57
6 Society and Economy, 1282–1334: An English Colony, Predominant Members of Settler Families 77
7 The Boroughs of the Lordship, 1282–1334 95
8 Political Control, 1344–1382 112
9 Political Control, 1382–1425 127
10 The Land Market, 1334–1437 139
11 The Economy, 1334–1425 161
12 Administration, 1334–1543 175
13 Political Control and Land Tenure, 1425–1485 187
14 Political Control and Land Tenure, 1485–1543 201
15 Boroughs, 1334–1543 213
Postscript 227
Conclusion 231

APPENDIX	237
BIBLIOGRAPHY	239
INDEX	269

PREFACE

The text of this volume has been in the pipeline for many years, and is based partly on my thesis 'The Lordship of Denbigh, 1282–1425', for which I was awarded a PhD in 1967. My research was undertaken at the University College of Wales under the supervision, initially, of Professor T. Jones Pierce and, later, following Professor Jones Pierce's death in 1964, by the late Professor J. Beverley Smith, whose constant and careful guidance, combined with friendly encouragement and inspiration, is fully acknowledged by me. I have also benefitted over the years from the support of Professor Smith and Dr Llinos Beverley Smith, who for a long time were my neighbours in Aberystwyth, and I look forward with eager anticipation to the publication of Dr Smith's proposed volume on society in the Welsh March in the later Middle Ages.

While preparing my thesis I also benefitted from the immense interest taken in my research work by the late Professor Glanville R. J. Jones, University of Leeds, who readily provided me with valuable information on specific aspects, something that I valued greatly. I also acknowledge the kindly and unceasing assistance of Clare Talbot, librarian at Hatfield House, and the staff of the Public Record Office, Chancery Lane, London and the National Library of Wales, Aberystwyth.

Further work on a proposed volume based on my thesis was undertaken while I was employed at the College of Librarianship Wales, Aberystwyth and then at Cardiff University. At Cardiff University considerable interest was shown in my research project by my heads of department, the late Professors Stanley B. Chrimes and Gwynedd O. Pierce, as well as by the late Professor William Rees, formerly head of the departments of history and

Welsh history. I also benefitted from my contacts with members of staff in various departments, and especially the daily meetings with the late Professor J. Gwynfor Jones, my friend and colleague in the department of Welsh history.

A number of warm working relationships were again developed while I was employed in the department of pictures and maps at the National Library of Wales, and I greatly appreciate the support and friendship of four national librarians and members of staff, especially in the above department. However, I must confess that in this period only a limited amount of time was available for research and I tended to give priority to publications that were more closely related to my curatorial responsibilities relating to the library's visual and cartographic collections.

Another factor contributing to the delay in proceeding with my proposed Denbigh volume was the possibility that one day another person would embark on a volume that would concentrate on the period 1425–1543. Unfortunately, that volume did not materialise, and I gradually reached the decision that I should undertake the work.

In completing the text of the present volume, I again wish to thank the members of staff of the various administrative, curatorial, reprographic and technical departments of the National Library of Wales, and especially the staff of the reading room for their patience and co-operation in dealing with my numerous requests. Also, similarly, my thanks to the staff of the library at Aberystwyth University, where I have been a regular reader in recent years. Thanks too to the staff at the National Archives in Kew, the libraries at Bangor University and Cardiff University, the Denbighshire Record Office, Ruthin, and the Flintshire Record Office, Hawarden

In addition to those named in the first paragraph, I have valued greatly the support of a number of individuals. These include Dr Susan Davies, whom I thank in Chapter 1, and Cledwyn Fychan, whose valuable contributions on the history of Denbighshire include those listed in the Bibliography. I am grateful for the guidance and advice on specific aspects provided by Professors Ralph A. Griffiths, the late A. D. Carr, R. R. Davies and Glanmor Williams: certain publications by them, and also by those persons mentioned above, proved to be extremely valuable and are specified in the Introduction. I also greatly appreciate the constant encouragement expressed over many years by my friend Professor David Howell, Swansea. I wish to thank Dr Llion Wigley and Dr Dafydd Jones of the University of Wales Press for their guidance and assistance. I am also grateful to my wife Mary and son Hywel, who read various drafts of the text, for their valuable comments and technical help. It is a pleasure to dedicate this volume to them and in memory of my late son Tomos.

LIST OF FIGURES

1 North-east Wales in the later Middle Ages, based on map in A. D. Carr, *The Gentry of North Wales in the Later Middle Ages* (opp., p. xvi)

2 The *cantrefi* of Rhos and Rhufoniog: administrative divisions

3 Aerial view of Denbigh castle and town walls, by kind permission of Cadw '© Crown copyright (2023), Cadw'

4 The dispersal of the Welsh population at the time of the Conquest

5 The Englishry: townships subject to the *Ballivus Anglicorum*

6 Part of map, Humphrey Llwyd, *Cambriae Typus* (1573)

7 Part of map, John Speed, *Denbigh* (1610)

LIST OF ABBREVIATIONS

Arch. Camb.	*Archaeologia Cambrensis*
BBCS	*Bulletin of the Board of Celtic Studies*
BPR	*Register of the Black Prince*
CAC	*Calendar of Ancient Correspondence concerning Wales*
C. Charter R.	*Calendar of Charter Rolls*
CCR	*Calendar of Close Rolls*
C. Fine R.	*Calendar of Fine Rolls*
Cal. Inq. Misc.	*Calendar of Inquisitions Miscellaneous*
Cal. Inq. P.M.	*Calendar of Inquisitions Post Mortem*
CMCS	*Cambrian Medieval Celtic Studies*
CPR	*Calendar of Patent Rolls*
CWR	*Calendar of Welsh Rolls, Calendar of Chancery Rolls Various*
DWB	*Dictionary of Welsh Biography*
EHR	*English Historical Review*
History Gwydir	*History of the Gwydir Family*
JMHRS	*Journal of the Merioneth Historical and Record Society*
LlC	*Llên Cymru*
NLW	National Library of Wales
SC	*Studia Celtica*
SD	*Survey of the Honour of Denbigh, 1334*
TCHS	*Transactions of the Caernarfonshire Historical Society*

TDHS	*Transactions of the Denbighshire Historical Society*
THSC	*Transactions of the Honourable Society of Cymmrodorion*
TNA	The National Archives, Kew
WG	*Welsh Genealogies*
WHR	*Welsh History Review*

GLOSSARY

alnetus: alder tree
affirmari: to hold land at farm. See also 'firma'
amobr: payment made by a female on marriage or for loss of virginity
[ad] approvandum: for profit, source of revenue
ardreth: tax, duty, toll
assart: plot of land converted from forest for arable use
borough: town or urban community with special privileges, normally granted by charter
bovate: unit of land (technically, land that may be ploughed in one season by an ox)
burgage: unit of land held according to customs of a borough
burgess: member of borough/urban community
cantref (plural ***cantrefi***): territorial unit, normally comprising two or more commotes
commote: territorial unit, normally comprising number of *trefi* ('townships')
commutation: process changing a legal obligation or entitlement to a cash payment
enfeoff: grant in fee
escheat: reversion of property to state or lord, normally following owner's involvement in rebellion, failure to pay rent or death of person without legal heirs
farm (***firma***): fixed payment
fee: feudal service
feodum (**fief**): land held in return for service or fixed payment
fine: sum of money exacted as a penalty by court of law or other authority
gafael: unit of land occupied by lineage group

gwely: descent group in occupation of plot of land
hereditario: entitlement/involvement in an inheritance by hereditary title
inquisition post mortem: subject of research or investigation into cause of sudden death
lease: a contract by which one party/person (the lessor) conveys land/property/service to another party/person for a specific period
maerdref: main township in commote; originally the lord's home farm
messuage: house, normally with outbuildings and land
pannage: payment from tenants to allow their pigs to forage for food in lord's forest
prid: see ***tir prid*** below
quo warranto: by what authorisation/guarantee
raglot (***rhaglaw***): predominant local official in commote
ringild (***rhingyll***): local official, normally subordinate to raglot
tir cyfrif: reckon-land, land held by bondmen
tir prid: land held by tenure to allow means of avoiding prevention of alienation of clan land
township: territorial unit, district
tref (***trefi***): township (townships) occupied by clansmen
twnc: rent paid as commutation of traditional due
uchelwr: person of noble stature
vaccary: pasture or farm where cows raised, dairy farm or herd of cows
vill: settlement consisting of buildings with associated lands

SOURCES

Concise Oxford Dictionary (Oxford, 2011)

Richard Ashdowne, David Howlett and Ronald Latham (eds), *Dictionary of Medieval Latin from British Sources*, 3 vols (Oxford, 2018)

Geiriadur Prifysgol Cymru, A Dictionary of the Welsh Language (University of Wales Press, online)
The Oxford English Dictionary, 2nd edn, 20 vols (Oxford, 1989)
T. M. Charles-Edwards, *Early Irish and Welsh Kinship* (Oxford, 1993)

INTRODUCTION

The history of the medieval lordship of Denbigh has attracted considerable attention over an extended period, even though it has not been the subject of a substantial scholarly study. Humphrey Llwyd, born at Denbigh in 1527, and Member of Parliament for the Denbigh boroughs, has been considered to have been 'among the most gifted and provocative scholars of his generation', with Gruffudd Hiraethog, the eminent contemporary Welsh poet, praising him as a pearl in the House of Commons: 'perl mewn Ty Parlment yw hwn'.[1] Llwyd described the Vale of Clwyd as 'one of the fayrest valleyes within this Ile' and the lordship of Denbigh as 'one of the greatest and best lordships in Englande'.[2] Significant nineteenth- century sources included Richard Newcombe's *An Account of the Castle and Town of Denbigh*, published in 1829; and John Williams (Glanmor)'s two volumes, *Ancient and Modern Denbigh* (Denbigh, 1856, reprinted Mold, 1989) and his *The Records of Denbigh and its Lordship* (Wrexham, 1860). The latter two volumes include transcripts and translations of early documents relating to the early history of the lordship of Denbigh created in 1282 in the territory previously forming the *cantrefi* of Rhos and Rhufoniog, with the area also known as Gwynedd Is Conwy, lying to the east of the river Conwy.[3]

A study of the nature and extent of earlier settlement patterns in this area is dependent largely on the detailed evidence presented in the comprehensive *Survey of the Honour of Denbigh, 1334*, edited by Paul Vinogradoff and Frank Morgan (1914), with the active support of a number of scholars who contributed to the series of sections comprising the introduction.[4] In his preface, Vinogradoff paid tribute to Frederick Seebohm's awareness of the significance of the survey, his discussion of its contents and inclusion of extracts in his volume *The Tribal System in Wales* (1891; 1904).[5] The 1904 edition had contained a reference to the survey as being in Seebohm's possession and included his tribute to its detailed description of 'survivals of the tribal system actually at work throughout a considerable district at the time of the English conquest of North Wales'.[6]

A recent study has praised Seebohm for his 'highly original contribution, unprecedented in its scale and systematic approach, to the study of medieval Welsh society' and for drawing attention to 'the remarkable longevity of the "tribal system" down to the late thirteenth century'.[7] William Rees referred to the influence of Seebohm and Vinogradoff in his preface to *South Wales and the March* (1924), stating that they 'have laid the foundations for all future research in this direction'.[8] Significant advances in the study of aspects of land tenure and the rural economy characterised the publications of T. Jones Pierce, in the volume *Medieval Welsh Society*, edited by J. Beverley Smith (1972), and those by R. R. Davies, noted below and including *Lordship and Society in the March of Wales 1284–1400* (1978).[9]

Vinogradoff referred to Seebohm's presentation of one of the extant copies of the survey, which he received from Colonel Howard of Wigfair, to the Maitland Library at All Souls College, Oxford University. He also drew attention in his introduction to other copies of the survey, and especially the one housed in the National Archives among the Land Revenue Records Miscellaneous Books, no. 232.[10] Supplementary material presented by Vinogradoff and Morgan in their volume included two genealogical tables that listed the kindred associations of numerous individuals; a map locating a number of the more significant places mentioned in the text; and, finally, three indices of places, subjects and persons.[11] At the outset, the survey was described as being the work of Hugh Buckley – '*facta per Hugonem de Beckele*' – and represented one of a number of assessments of the resources of a lordship in north-east Wales, with other examples being the surveys of Bromfield and Yale, Chirk and Ruthin or Dyffryn Clwyd.[12]

Numerous instances were provided, as in the very first entry in the survey, of the contrast between the position before and after the Edwardian conquest, with this entry also referring to the order in which the text would be presented, with the commote of Ceinmeirch, noted as being 'propius Anglie' ('near to England');[13] followed by the commotes of Is Aled, Uwch Aled, Is Dulas and Uwch Dulas. Each account for the five commotes concluded with details of customary payments, rents and dues, and valuations; with the latter varying from the highest sum of £394 17s. 6¼d recorded for Is Aled, and the lowest amount £139 11s. 9½d for Uwch Aled.[14] The total valuation of the lordship of Denbigh, including a sum of £10 0s. 5¼d for the townships of Penmaen and Llithfaen, listed separately at the end, amounted to the considerable sum of £1,101 7s. 1¾d.[15]

The data contained in the 1334 survey was profitably compared with earlier financial accounts, especially those accounts compiled in 1297 and 1305, the 1330 rental and 1331 view of account.[16] These clearly reflected the administration's efforts to obtain maximum amounts of revenue from the lordship, with an evaluation provided on the various sources of seignorial revenue. Payments to the central receiver were also revealed by a series of receivers and ministers' accounts in the period extending from 1345 to the sixteenth century.[17] At the same time, determined efforts were made to ensure the physical removal of many local inhabitants from their traditional homes and to attract English settlers to the lordship; additional information has been provided on the estates of several of the more prominent families.[18] Significant changes in the tenurial framework were reflected in a series of detailed financial surveys, with the rentals of 1437 concentrating on data relating to the commotes of Ceinmeirch and Is Aled;[19] and those for 1450–1,[20] 1476–7,[21] and 1491–2[22] providing comprehensive coverage for all five commotes in the lordship.

Publications by individuals named in the opening paragraphs of the Preface to this volume that proved to be of considerable value include J. Beverley Smith's contributions to the *Welsh History Review* in 1966 and 1976 and his *Llywelyn ap Gruffudd, Prince of Wales* (1998); Llinos Beverley Smith's studies of the gage of land (1976 and 1977) and the history of women (2000); and together their joint editorship of, and contributions to, the *History of Merioneth: The Middle Ages* (2001). Also, Glanville Jones's articles in the *Welsh History Review* in 1961 and 1964, and chapter in *The Agrarian History of England and Wales, Volume 1, Part. 2, A.D. 43–1042* (1972); Gwynfor Jones's *Early Modern Wales, c. 1525–1640* (1994); and studies of the Wynn family of Gwydir (1995) and (in Welsh) the poets of the nobility (1997). [23]

Close contacts were also developed over the years with scholars based at various institutions, and I benefitted from meetings with them and as well as from their various publications. These included A. D. Carr's, *Owen of Wales: The End of the House of Gwynedd* (1991), and *The Gentry of North Wales in the Later Middle Ages* (2017); R. R. Davies's *Lordship and Society in the March of Wales 1284–1400* (1978), *The Revolt of Owain Glyn Dwr* (1995), and *The Age of Conquest: Wales, 1063–1415* (2000); R. A. Griffiths's, *The Reign of King Henry VI* (1981), *Conquerors and Conquered in Medieval Wales* (1994); R. R. Davies's and R. Schofield (eds), *Wales and the Welsh in the Middle Ages* (2011); and Glanmor Williams's *The Welsh Church from Conquest to Reformation* (1962, 1976), *Recovery, Reorientation and Reformation: Wales c.1415–1642* (1987), and *Wales and the Reformation* (1997).[24]

Also appreciated have been the publications of T. M. Charles-Edwards, especially his *Early Irish and Welsh Kinship* (1993), whose discussion of the lineage terms *gwely* and *gafael* in Chapter 4 proved to be extremely valuable, with numerous references cited from the Survey of Denbigh, as noted in Chapters 5 and 6. Other influential publications have included M. Lieberman, *The March of Wales, 1067–1300* (2008), and *The Medieval March of Wales* (2020); *The Acts of Welsh Rulers, 1120–1283*, edited by Huw Pryce

(2005), and Huw Pryce, *Writing Welsh History: From the Early Middle Ages to the Twenty-First Century* (2022); A. C. Reeves's, *The Marcher Lords* (1983); David Stephenson's *Political Power in Medieval Gwynedd: Governance and the Welsh Princes* (2014) (previously published as *The Governance of Gwynedd* (1984) but with a new introduction), and *Medieval Wales c. 1050–1332: Centuries of Ambiguity* (2019); and Matthew Frank Stevens's *Urban Assimilation in Post-Conquest Wales: Ethnicity, Gender and Economy in Ruthin, 1282–1348* (2010), and *The Economy of Medieval Wales, 1067–1536* (2019).[25]

Notes

1 Humphrey Llwyd, '*The Breviary of Britain*', *with Selections from 'The History of Cambria'*, ed. by Philip Schwyer (London, 2011), pp. 1–2; D. J. Bowen, 'Gruffudd Hiraethog ac Argyfwng Cerdd Dafod', *Llên Cymru*, 2 (1952–3), 154.
2 Huw Pryce, *Writing Welsh History: From the Early Middle Ages to the Twenty-First Century* (Oxford, 2022), p. 132; Humphrey Llwyd, *Cronica de Wallia and Other Documents from Exeter Cathedral Library, MS. 3514*, ed. by Thomas Jones, *BBCS*, 12 (1946–8), 29–41.
3 Richard Newcombe, *An Account of the Castle and Town of Denbigh* (Denbigh, 1829); John Williams (Glanmor), *Ancient and Modern Denbigh* (Denbigh, 1856, reprinted Mold, 1989); and John Williams (Glanmor), *The Records of Denbigh and its Lordship* (Wrexham, 1860).
4 P. Vinogradoff and Frank Morgan, *Survey of the Honour of Denbigh 1334* (London, 1914).
5 *SD*, v; F. Seebohm, *The Tribal System in Wales* (London, 1895, 1904).
6 Seebohm, *The Tribal System in Wales* (London, 1904), p. xxxviii.
7 Pryce, *Writing Welsh History*, p. 323.
8 William Rees, *South Wales and the March* (Oxford, 1924), p. vii.
9 T. Jones Pierce, *Medieval Welsh Society*, ed. by J. Beverley Smith (Cardiff, 1972); R. R. Davies, *Lordship and Society in the March of Wales 1284–1400* (Oxford, 1978).
10 *SD*, pp. v–vi, cxxiii.
11 *SD*, Tables 1 and 2, and map, pages following pp. cxxiv, 324–47.
12 *SD*, pp. 1–2; T. P. Ellis (ed.), *The First Extent of Bromfield and Yale, A.D., 1315* (London, 1924); G. P. Jones (ed.), *The Extent of Chirkland (1391–1392)* (Liverpool, 1933); R. I. Jack, 'Records of Denbighshire Lordships: The Lordship of Dyffryn Clwyd in 1324', *TDHS*, 17 (1968).
13 *SD*, p. 1.
14 *SD*, pp. 46–50; 148–54; 208–10; 268–71; 313–16.
15 *SD*, pp. 316–23.

16 TNA DL 29/1/1; TNA/*DL* 29/1/2; Hatfield House Library, Cecil Papers, 28; TNA SC 6/1182/1.
17 TNA SC 6/1182/2; 4980.
18 *Infra*, pp. 83–90.
19 NLW Wynnstay, 86.
20 NLW MS 12647 F.
21 NLW MS 163 B.
22 TNA SC 12/27/24.
23 For further information on references cited in this paragraph see Bibliography.
24 For further information on references cited in this paragraph see Bibliography.
25 For further information on references cited in this paragraph see Bibliography.

1
GEOGRAPHICAL CONTEXT
AND POLITICAL BACKGROUND

The lordship of Denbigh was created in 1282 when Edward I granted to Henry de Lacy, Earl of Lincoln, an extensive territory that had previously formed part of a region known as *Y Berfeddwlad* ('the Middle/Heart of the Country'). This represented a descriptive term for an area lying between the rivers Conwy and Dee, comprising the four *cantrefi* of Rhos, Rhufoniog, Dyffryn Clwyd and Tegeingl ('Englefield'). The possession of this territory was contested initially by the rulers of Powys and Gwynedd, where viable units of government had been established, and later by the princes of Gwynedd and the king of England. The term *Y Berfeddwlad* itself represents an apt comment on the area's attraction to the powerful *gwledydd*, the units of government established by the rulers of Gwynedd in the west and those of Powys in the south-east. For long periods, the territory forming *Y Berfeddwlad* was considered to be an out-lying appendage of Gwynedd, and this was reflected in its other designation, that is Gwynedd Is Conwy.

The territory that came to form the lordship of Denbigh may be defined as a multi-featured region influenced largely by topographical factors and traversing three regional divisions of Wales.[1] The greater part of the western frontier was formed by the Conwy valley, and similarly the northern boundary consisted of a fairly broad coastal belt. This continued into the Vale of Clwyd that, on the eastern flank of the lordship, represented the floor of a rift valley. A fertile region, its soils contained medium and medium-heavy loams. To the west of the vale stands a limestone escarpment that varies in altitude from 300 feet in the north and east, to 1,048 feet at Tre Prys Llygod in the west. It is dissected by numerous rivers: the most significant of which are the Aled and Elwy, which flow northwards to meet at Fron Fawr. To the southwest of this escarpment lies Mynydd Hiraethog, rising to a height of 1,742 feet 'at Mwdwl Eithin, and another mountain range, with a peak of 2004' at Foel Goch, which dominates the southern extremity of the lordship (see Figures 1 and 2). A considerable area of the lordship therefore consisted of upland terrain that was avoided by invading armies who chose as their routes either the coastal plain of the north, or, in the south, the Alwen, Ceirw or upper Conwy valleys.[2] The utilisation of these entry routes was largely responsible for the political instability of this region in the period preceding the creation of the lordship.

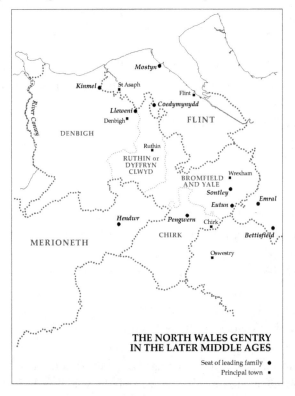

Figure 1: North-east Wales in the later Middle Ages, based on map in A. D. Carr, *The Gentry of North Wales in the Later Middle Ages* (opp. page xvi)

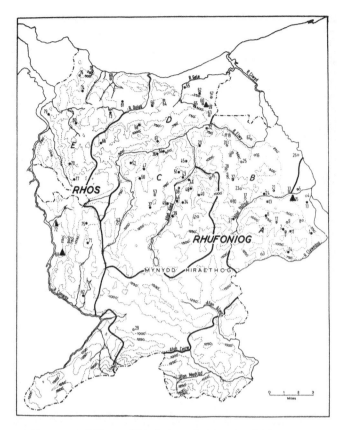

Figure 2: The *cantrefi* of Rhos and Rhufoniog, administrative divisions

This area, together with its immediate vicinity, is of considerable historical significance in that it contains evidence of the earliest known human activity/settlement in Wales. The earliest recorded site in Wales, the Pontnewydd Cave, has been dated to *c*. 230,000 BCE, late in the Lower Palaeolithic period (Old Stone Age), with its inhabitants sustaining themselves by hunting animals and gathering plant materials and using various stone weapons and tools. The cave, probably used for storage and protection in difficult weather conditions, was located within limestone cliffs on a south-western slope high on the side of the Elwy Valley.[3] Other important prehistoric sites in this area include

Boncyn Crwn, Llansannan, dated to the second millennium BCE;[4] the Brenig Archaeological Trail, forming a cemetery occupying much of the upper area of the valley containing Llyn Brenig, which had been in use for approximately 500 years, extending from *c.* 2000 BCE to 1,500 BCE;[5] and the Parc-y Meirch hoard, buried near to the hill fort of Dinorben, dated from the Late Bronze Age, 1150–1100 BCE.[6]

The Capel Garmon firedog, partly cow and partly horse, dating from the period 50 BCE–75 CE, is considered to be an early blacksmithing masterpiece.[7] Other significant Iron Age sites in this area include the hill forts of Bryn Euryn, Colwyn Bay; Mynydd y Gaer, Llanefydd; and the Old Foxhall-Enclosure, Henllan: the three occupied in the late first millennium BCE. Bryn Euryn was probably refortified and re-occupied in the fifth and sixth centuries.[8] The same period witnessed the memorial inscriptions on standing stones at the Gwytherin churchyard and the possible continued use of the hillfort of Dinorben.[9] It has been suggested that the *cantref* of Rhos, probably including the fortress of Degannwy – which had been associated with the Roman period, and with the reign of Maelgwn Gwynedd in north Wales in the first half of the sixth century – was the background territory of Hywel Dda, the ruler of Dyfed and Gwynedd in the tenth century and the person traditionally associated with the codification of Welsh law: *cyfraith Hywel* ('the law of Hywel).[10] Also, memorial stones at Llangernyw churchyard are considered to date from the ninth and tenth centuries.[11]

The Domesday survey of 1086 recorded that the Norman lord, Robert of Rhuddlan, was in possession of the castle, borough and manor of Rhuddlan, together with an area termed 'Nortwales', which was defined as measuring 'twelve leagues long and four wide', with land for only twenty ploughs with the remainder being 'unploughable woodland and swamp'.[12] Robert's conquest of the *cantref* of Tegeingl and construction of the castle of Rhuddlan in 1073 had been followed by his success in capturing Hywel ap Ithel, the hereditary lord of the *cantrefi* of Rhos and Rhufoniog in

1081, and building the castle of Degannwy.[13] It is probable that the lands actually occupied by the Normans formed only part of the forementioned *cantrefi*; namely, the coastal belt of Rhos and an area within the lowland Vale of Clwyd in Rhufoniog. Hywel ap Ithel had been forced to flee to Ireland in 1099 but was allowed to return and govern the area that was not in Norman hands, largely through the patronage of the lords of Powys.[14]

In 1118 he waged war on rivals, but although successful at the battle of Maes Maen Cymro fought near Ruthin, he was wounded severely and his death resulted in the annexation of his two *cantrefi*, not by the rulers of Powys – whose power was by now on the wane – but by the sons of Gruffudd ap Cynan of Gwynedd.[15] However, the name 'Gwynedd Is Conwy' reflected the frequent association of *Y Berfeddwlad* with Gwynedd in the twelfth and thirteenth centuries. For certain periods, following successful incursions against the rulers of Gwynedd, this area was subject to royal control, but Welsh successes in the late twelfth century under Owain Gwynedd led to the ruler of Gwynedd asserting mastery over the lands east of the river Conwy.[16]

A significant development influencing the later territorial composition of the lordship of Denbigh was the grant to the abbey of Aberconwy of certain lands, previously located in the *cantrefi* of Rhos and Rhufoniog. These had been conveyed in a charter purportedly issued in 1199 by Owain Gwynedd's grandson, Llywelyn ap Iorwerth, 'Llywelyn the Great', who had succeeded in gaining possession of the two *cantrefi*. The abbey had initially been founded on 24 July 1186 on a site in Rhydynog felen and then moved to Aberconwy, located near to the estuary of the river Conwy.[17] Whereas the original and the secondary sites of the abbey were located in the area that later formed Caernarfonshire, some of the lands held by the abbey were in localities that later formed the lordship of Denbigh. These included the grange of Foelas, Ceirniog and Llanfair Rhyd Castle, located partly in Rhos and partly in Rhufoniog, on lands amounting to 8,200 to 8,300 acres, 16 miles south of the abbey, with the river Conwy as their southern boundary.[18] Also, in the same area, but entirely within the commote of Rhufoniog, the abbey held two territories: one known as Llyn Cymer, comprising 2,400 to 2,500 acres, part of which now constitutes Llyn Alwen; and the other Llechwedd Cryn Llwyn, occupying 1,300 to 1,400 acres. Both these localities were known as Tir yr Abad Ucha, in contrast to the more westerly holding, which identified as Tir yr Abad. In time, all the lands of the abbey in this locality became known as 'Hiraethog'.[19] Other lands held by the abbey, amounting to 1,200 to 1,300 acres at the southern end of the Creuddun peninsula, together with the remainder of the commote of Creuddun, were excluded from the lordship of Denbigh, and incorporated in Caernarfonshire.[20] This was also the case with the Eirias-Penmaen-Llysfaen area, which would seem to have been an administrative unit separate from the commote of Rhos in the pre-conquest period.[21] Another locality in this neighbourhood, the Rhos Fynach Weir, near Llandrillo yn Rhos, has been occasionally associated with the abbey of Aberconwy, but it is very doubtful whether it was actually part of the abbey's property.[22]

By 1199 Llywelyn ap Iorwerth was possibly in full control of north Wales and his supremacy was celebrated by several poets, including Llywarch ap Llywelyn, 'Prydydd y Moch', for whom he was a generous patron.[23] A significant military reverse in 1211 resulted in this whole area being yielded to King John. Sir John Wynn's *History of the Gwydir Family*, written after 1580, recorded the tradition that two kinsmen – the cousins, Owain ap Dafydd and Gruffudd ap Rhodri – had in 1212 been granted by King John the three *cantrefi* of Rhos, Rhufoniog and Dyffryn Clwyd.[24] Llywelyn ap Iorwerth's control over the four *cantrefi* was restored that year and his possession of the area was confirmed in the Treaty of Worcester in 1218.[25]

Gruffudd ap Rhodri seems to have been a prominent figure in Llywelyn's administration in the 1220s and 1230s.[26] On the other hand, his kinsmen Gruffudd ap Caradog and his brother Einion were opposed to Llywelyn ap Iorwerth towards the end of his life, and also his designated heir, Dafydd.[27] Their sister Senana was the wife of Llywelyn's illegitimate son, Gruffudd. His mother Tangwystl was the daughter of Llywarch Goch, a resident of the *cantref* of Rhos, and, according to the 1334 Survey of Denbigh, she had received from Llywelyn property in the township of Dincadfel, in the commote of Is Aled, which she had then sold to Cynan ap Llywarch, whose kinsmen continued to occupy the land.[28] Following Llywelyn's death, Gruffudd and Einion ap Caradog fled Dafydd's lands and sought to be sheltered by Llywelyn ap Gruffudd in the Perfeddwlad.[29]

Following the death of Llywelyn ap Iorwerth in 1240, his son Dafydd was forced the following year to appear before the king at Gwerneigron, in the *cantref* of Rhos on the bank of the river Elwy, and required to concede Degannwy, Rhuddlan and the *cantref* of Tegeingl, with the latter placed under the control of the Justice of Chester and a new castle, Diserth, built near Rhuddlan.[30] Royal forces marched through the *cantref* of Rhos to Degannwy in the summer of 1245, and in the autumn the king prepared to withdraw from north-west Wales. However, following Dafydd's death in February 1246, royal forces again advanced to Degannwy. In the following year, his two nephews, Owain and Llywelyn ap Gruffudd, who had succeeded Dafydd as rulers of Gwynedd, yielded their claims to the four *cantrefi* at the Treaty of Woodstock. The river Conwy therefore again formed the boundary between Gwynedd and the royal lands in north-east Wales, which were now placed firmly under the control of the Justice of Chester.[31]

The financial account of John de Grey, Justice of Chester, covering May 1247 to July 1250, provided valuable information on the *cantrefi* of Rhos and Rhufoniog, even though the main emphasis was on the *cantref* of Tegeingl, which appears to have been more Anglicised than the other three *cantrefi*. The rent for the *cantref* of Rhos was £28 8s. 6d for a period of three-and-a-quarter years; and the total rent from Rhos, Rhufoniog and Dyffryn Clwyd for the same period amounted to £60 19s. 4½d. Further revenue was provided by the manors, and a tallage account compiled by Alan la Zusche – de Grey's successor as Justice of Chester in 1251 – indicated payments for Dinbych ('Denbigh') of £6 13s. 4d, and £2 from the manor of Ystrad.³²

Alan la Zusche, who had paid 1,000 marks for the right to hold this office, twice the amount paid by de Grey, was accused of extortion, and the chronicler Matthew Paris expressed sympathy for local inhabitants. The four *cantrefi* were granted in 1254 to the lord Edward, heir to the English throne, and within two years complaints against the oppression by his officials led to an uprising inspired by Llywelyn ap Gruffudd.³³ As a result, the Perfeddwlad was again attached to Gwynedd, and this action spurred on Llywelyn to establish himself as the supreme Welsh lord, with his recognition as Prince of Wales in 1267 by Henry III at the Treaty of Montgomery.³⁴

Llywelyn was based at Denbigh when he sent a letter to the king in May 1269, and his high regard for his status as prince of Wales, while staying at Dinorben (the *maerdref* in the *cantref* of Rhos), was well illustrated by his response to the letter that he received from the king's chancery in June 1273. Llywelyn asserted in his reply that the king, who at this time was absent from his kingdom, was probably unaware of the contents of this letter, as he knew that the rights (*'iura'*) of Llywelyn's principality were entirely separate from the rights of the king's realm, even though Llywelyn held his principality under the king's royal power (*'potestas'*), a response described as being 'among the most notable statements of his [Llywelyn's] view of his status as prince of Wales'.³⁵ Llywelyn's triumph, however, was short-lived, and he was defeated in the war of 1277, described as 'the greatest military undertaking to confront a king of England for many years'.³⁶ The damage caused during the military campaign waged in 1277 was reflected in the complaint expressed by Bishop Anian of St Asaph that English troops had desecrated churches and ecclesiastical property in his diocese.³⁷ Hostilities were concluded by the Treaty of Aberconwy, signed on 9 November 1277, whereby Llywelyn was stripped of his power and territorial acquisitions, including Gwynedd Is Conwy, which was divided into two portions: the *cantrefi* of Rhos and Tegeingl, which would be administered by the Justice of Chester; and the *cantrefi* of Rhufoniog and Dyffryn Clwyd, granted to Dafydd ap Gruffudd.[38]

Discontent with the new arrangements was expressed in both units, and in 1281 lists of grievances were presented on behalf of Dafydd, the men of Rhos and Goronwy ap Heilyn, who had hitherto participated in the royal administration of this area. Dafydd's complaints included the seizure by royal officials of the three townships held in dower by Gwenllian de Lacy, the illegitimate daughter of Llywelyn ap Iorwerth and the forementioned Tangwystl, which he claimed should have reverted to him after her death. It has been suggested, based on the sixteenth-century use of the term 'Llys Gwenllian', that one of these townships may possibly have been located on the banks of the Ystrad stream at the manor of Ystrad Owain.[39] The inhabitants of Rhos complained that they had been governed contrary to the law and custom of the land, and their grievances, which had also been expressed in 1256, included a reference to the substitution of English for Welsh law.[40]

Goronwy ap Heilyn, the grandson of Cynwrig ap Heilyn and nephew of Ednyfed Fychan, and therefore a member of one of the predominant families in north Wales, was significantly involved as one of Llywelyn's main representatives in the negotiations culminating in the Treaty of Aberconwy.[41] Having been a member of the royal commission established in 1278 to resolve matters arising from the implementation of this treaty, he had served as bailiff of the *cantref* of Rhos and *rhaglaw* of Dinorben in the period after 1277, but had been removed from these offices, probably as a result of Reginald de Grey's appointment as Justice of Chester.[42]

On Palm Sunday 1282, Dafydd ap Gruffudd attacked Hawarden and afterwards considerable damage was caused to a number of churches, including Dinorben (Cedigog), Abergele, Dineirth (Llandrillo yn Rhos), Eglwysbach, Betws yn Rhos,

Llangernyw, Llansanffraid and Llanddulas.⁴³ Dafydd's brother Llywelyn soon committed himself in opposition to the royal forces and one report referred to the summoning of a 'parliament' to Denbigh.⁴⁴ Edward I responded by mobilising his army, and a fairly similar policy to that of 1277 was adopted, with the royal army seeking to advance towards the river Conwy.⁴⁵ However, greater opposition seems now to have been encountered and the progress of Edward's army, illustrated by the record of payments issued at Llandyrnog on 22 August and again probably on 21 September, with the king present there on 2 October.⁴⁶ The royal army's military success was illustrated in October 1282 by the creation of a series of lordships in north-east Wales: Chirk, Bromfield and Yale, Dyffryn Clwyd and Denbigh: the latter, formed by the amalgamation of the greater part of the *cantrefi* of Rhos and Rhufoniog, granted on 16 October to Henry de Lacy, Earl of Lincoln.⁴⁷ Edward was based in Denbigh from 22 October until 5 November when he returned to Rhuddlan. An infantry force led by Richard Bruce was located at Denbigh by 11 November and continued to be present there until 1 December. A further contingent comprising twenty-five crossbowmen, fifteen archers and six masons was based there by 18 November, as was a force of 578 archers commanded by William le Vavasour from 30 November until 6 December, with a group of 115 archers from 1 to 7 December. A fairly large force was located at Denbigh for the greater part of December, with Richard Ashbourn commanding twenty-six or twenty-seven crossbowmen and 300 infantry men from 2 to 6 December, and 627 infantrymen from 14 to 20 December 1282.⁴⁸ In the same month, on 11 December, Llywelyn was slain, and was succeeded by his brother Dafydd. Following the capture and death of Dafydd in June 1283, and the probable death also at this time of Goronwy ap Heylin, who had served as Dafydd's *distain*, the Welsh uprising was finally crushed, with the newly formed lordship of Denbigh one of the significant features of the post-conquest settlement of Wales.⁴⁹

Notes

1. These have been defined, by map, in E. G. Bowen, *Wales: A Physical, Historical and Regional Geography* (London,1957), p. 268.
2. G. R. J. Jones, 'The Military Geography of Gwynedd' (unpublished MA thesis, University of Wales, 1949).
3. Helen Burnham, *A Guide to Ancient and Historic Wales: Clwyd and Powys* (London, 1995), pp. 4, 9–10; D. Browne and S. Hughes (eds), *The Archaeology of the Welsh Uplands* (Aberystwyth, 2003), p. 21; Mark Redknap, *Discovered in Time: Treasures from Early Wales* (Cardiff, 2011), pp. 10–11.
4. Burnham, *A Guide to Ancient and Historic Wales*, pp. 23–5.
5. Burnham, *A Guide to Ancient and Historic Wales*, pp. 25–8; Browne and Hughes, *Archaeology*, pp. 116, 126.
6. Redknap, *Discovered in Time*, pp. 64–5.
7. See *https://museum.wales/articles/1340/Stunning-ironwork-firedog-uncovered-in-farmersfield* (accessed 7 March 2024).
8. Burnham, *A Guide to Ancient and Historic Wales*, pp. 53–6, 167.
9. W. Gardner and H. N. Savory, *Dinorben: A Hill Fort Occupied in Early Iron Age and Roman Times* (Cardiff, 1964), p. 98; Wendy Davies, *Wales in the Early Middle Ages* (Leicester, 1982) pp. 24, 44, 89; A. D. Carr, 'The Medieval *Cantref* of Rhos', *TDHS*, 41 (1992), 7; Burnham, *A Guide to Ancient and Historic Wales*, pp. 90, 95; David Longley, 'The Royal Courts of the Welsh Princes in Gwynedd', in Nancy Edwards (ed.), *Landscape and Settlement in Medieval Wales* (Oxford, 1997), p. 46.
10. Davies, *Wales in the Early Middle Ages*, pp. 24, 98–9, 110; T. M. Charles-Edwards, *Wales and the Britons, 350–1064* (Oxford, 2014), pp. 267–73, 510–13.
11. Burnham, *A Guide to Ancient and Historic Wales*, p. 94.
12. A. Farley and H. Ellis (eds), *Domesday Book*, vol. 1 (London, 1783), 269b; Philip Morgan (ed.), *Domesday Book, 26: Cheshire* (Chichester, 1978), 269b; Davies, *Wales in the Early Middle Ages*, p. 12.
13. J. E. Lloyd, *A History of Wales from the Earliest Times to the Edwardian Conquest*, vol. 2, (London, 1939), pp. 381–4; K. L. Maund, *Ireland, Wales and England in the Eleventh Century* (Woodbridge, 1991), p. 113.
14. *Brut y Tywysogion, or The Chronicle of the Princes, Peniarth Ms Version*, trans. with introduction and notes by Thomas Jones (Cardiff, 1952), pp. 21, 46.
15. Lloyd, *History of Wales*, pp. 416, 465–6; R. R. Davies, *Conquest, Coexistence and Change, 1063–1415* (Oxford, 1987), p. 75.
16. J. Beverley Smith, 'Owain Gwynedd', *TCHS*, 32, (1971), 8–17.
17. Colin Gresham, 'The Aberconway Charter', *Arch. Camb.*, 94 (1939), 123–63; Colin Gresham, 'The Aberconway Charter: Further Consideration', *BBCS*, 30 (1982–3), 111–47; Rhys W. Hays, *The History of the Abbey of Aberconway* (Cardiff, 1963), pp. 4–7; Charles Insley, 'Fact and Fiction in Thirteenth-Century Gwynedd', *SC*, 33 (1999), 235–50; David Stephenson, *The Governance of Gwynedd* (Cardiff, 1984), re-issued as *Political Power in Medieval Gwynedd, Governance and the Welsh Princes* (Cardiff, 2014), (hereafter, *Political power*), pp. xliv–xlvi.
18. Hays, *History of Aberconway*, pp. 14–15.

19 Hays, *History of Aberconway*, pp. 15–16.
20 Hays, *History of Aberconway*, pp. 11–12.
21 Stephenson, *Political Power*, Appendix VII, 'Eiryoes', pp. 238 239.
22 Hays, *History of Aberconway*, pp. 16–17.
23 *SD*, pp. 213–14; Lloyd, *History of Wales*, pp. 588–90, 612–13; Davies, *Conquest, Coexistence and Change*, pp. 239, 241; Roger Turvey, *Llywelyn the Great, Prince of Gwynedd* (Llandysul 2007), pp. 34–41; A. D. Carr, 'Prydydd y Moch, Ymateb hanesydd', *THSC*, 161–80; Elin M. Jones (ed.), *Gwaith Llywarch ap Llywelyn, Prydydd y Moch* (Aberystwyth, 1991), pp. 180, 224; *SD*, pp. 213–14.
24 *Brut*; J. Beverley Smith, 'Magna Carta and the Charters of the Welsh Princes', *EHR*, 99 (1984), 361–2; Sir John Wynn, *The History of the Gwydir Family and Memoirs*, ed. with introduction and notes by J. Gwynfor Jones (Llandysul, 1990), pp. 4–5, 87–8; see below pp. ** for information on lands later held by Rhodri's descendants in the lordship of Denbigh.
25 Lloyd, *History of Wales*, pp. 636–54; Davies, *Conquest, Coexistence and Change*, pp. 241–3; J. Beverley Smith, *Llywelyn ap Gruffudd, Prince of Wales* (Cardiff, 1988), pp. 16–24; Turvey, *Llywelyn the Great*, pp. 56–75.
26 Stephenson, *Political Power*, pp. 116, 215.
27 Wynn, *History of the Gwydir Family*, pp. 10–11; Stephenson, *Political Power*, p. 117.
28 Wynn, *History of the Gwydir Family*, pp. 9, 96; J. E. Lloyd, 'The Mother of Gruffudd ap Llywelyn', *BBCS*, 1/4 (1923), 335; *SD*, pp. 127–8.
29 Wynn, *History of the Gwydir Family*, p. 10; Stephenson, *Political Power*, p. 117.
30 Smith, *Llywelyn ap Gruffudd*, pp. 29–39; Huw Pryce, *The Acts of Welsh Rulers, 1120–1283* (Cardiff, 2005), pp. 466–74.
31 *Brut*, p. 107; C. W. Lewis, 'The Treaty of Woodstock, 1247: Its Background and Significance', *WHR*, 2 (1964–5), 37–65; Smith, *Llywelyn ap Gruffudd*, pp. 49–67, 70, 78, 86; Pryce, *Acts of Welsh Rulers*, pp. 483–5.
32 A. J. Roderick, 'The Four Cantreds: a study in adminstration', *BBCS*, 10, (1939–41), 246–56; Smith, *Llywelyn ap Gruffudd*, pp. 78–80.
33 R. Luard (ed.), *Matthaei Parisiensis Monachi Sancti Albani Chronica Majora*, vol. 5 (1872–83), pp. 592–3; Roderick, 'Four Cantreds', 248, 252; Smith, *Llywelyn ap Gruffudd*, pp. 80–6.
34 J. Goronwy Edwards (ed.), *Littere Wallie preserved in Liber A in the Public Record Office* (Cardiff, 1940), (hereafter, *Lit. Wall.*), 2; *Brut*, p. 115; Smith, *Llywelyn ap Gruffudd*, pp. 178–86; Pryce, *Acts of Welsh Rulers*, pp. 536–42.
35 J. G. Edwards (ed.), *Calendar of Ancient Correspondence Concerning Wales* (Cardiff, 1935), p. 86; Smith, *Llywelyn ap Gruffudd*, p. 360; Pryce, *Acts of Welsh Rulers*, pp. 548–9, 553–4.
36 Smith, *Llywelyn ap Gruffudd*, p. 414.
37 A. W. Haddan and W. Stubbs (eds), *Councils and Ecclesiastical Documents relating to Great Britain and Ireland*, vol. 1 (Oxford, 1869), pp. 522–3; Smith, *Llywelyn ap Gruffudd*, p. 428.
38 Edwards (ed.), *Lit. Wall.*, pp. 118–22; *CPR, 1272–81*, pp. 231–2; Stephenson, *Political Power*, pp. 9, 213; Smith, *Llywelyn ap Gruffudd*, pp. 438–44; Pryce, *Acts of Welsh Rulers*, pp. 589–98.

39 C. T. Martin (ed.), *Registrum Epistolarum Fratris Johannis Peckham Archiepiscopi Cantuariensis*, vol. 2, Rolls Series (London, 1882–6), pp. 460, 445–7; *Calendar of Ancient Correspondence Concerning Wales*, pp. 73–4; J. E. Lloyd, 'Who was Gwenllian de Lacy?', *Arch. Camb.*, 6/19 (1919), 292–8; Smith, *Llywelyn ap Gruffudd*, pp. 461–2, 468, 505–8.
40 *Registrum Epistolarum Fratris Johannis Peckham Archiepiscopi Cantuariensis*, vol. 2, pp. 447–51, 454–8, 460–3; Smith, *Llywelyn ap Gruffudd*, pp. 454–6, 462–4, 466, 577.
41 Edwards (ed.), *Lit. Wall.*, pp. 118–22; Stephenson, *Political Power*, 9; Smith, *Llywelyn ap Gruffudd*, pp. 437–8.
42 *Registrum Epistolarum Fratris Johannis Peckham Archiepiscopi Cantuariensis*, vol. 2, pp. 450, 459–60; J. Conway Davies (ed.), *The Welsh Assize Roll, 1277–1284* (Cardiff, 1940), pp. 116–17; Stephenson, *Political Power*, pp. 42, 104, 214; Smith, *Llywelyn ap Gruffudd*, pp. 454–5, 464–6; Carr, 'Medieval Cantref', 11–12.
43 *Brut*, p. 227; Smith, *Llywelyn ap Gruffudd*, pp. 460–3, 465–8; Edwards (ed.), *Lit. Wall.*, p. 63, 70, 86, 88, 128, 130, 134, 135; Carr, 'Medieval Cantref', 12.
44 Smith, *Llywelyn ap Gruffudd*, pp. 465–7, 509–10, 522–3; J. E. Morris, *The Welsh Wars of Edward I* (Oxford, 1901), p. 153.
45 Morris, *The Welsh Wars of Edward I*, pp. 154–63, 173–78.
46 TNA E 101/4/1. (Wardrobe and Household Records 1282–4; Main Cavalry Payroll). See Preface, p. 2, for statement recording my appreciation to Dr Susan Davies for providing me with this reference compiled as part of her valuable research work on the information provided by the Wardrobe and Household records for 1282–4 on Edward I's Welsh campaign leading to the conquest of Wales and castle building programme.
47 *CWR*, 243.
48 *CWR*, 243.
49 *Brut*, pp. 120–1; A. D. Carr, 'The last days of Gwynedd', *TCHS*, 43 (1982), 7–22; Smith, *Llywelyn ap Gruffudd*, pp. 550–2, 561–7, 571, 576–9; *SD*, p. 297, for reference to the death of Gronw ap Heilyn.

2

SOCIAL AND ECONOMIC BACKGROUND

An understanding of the organisation of society in the area that came to form the lordship of Denbigh is dependent largely on the detailed surveys compiled in the early fourteenth century as a direct result of the Edwardian conquest, as was that of other areas of north Wales. The value of these surveys is enhanced in that a retrospective as well as a current assessment is provided of the resources of a specific locality. As previously noted, an extremely valuable historical source, compiled in 1334, is the detailed survey of the lordship, constituted in 1282 and comprising an extensive area lying to the east of the river Conwy.[1] The main components were the commotes of Is Dulas and Uwch Dulas in the *cantref* of Rhos, and the commotes of Is Aled, Uwch Aled and Ceinmeirch in the *cantref* of Rhufuoniog, which contained a number of *trefi*, or townships, which were surveyed in considerable detail in 1334. No information was provided on those townships that were in monastic or episcopal possession, and they seem to have been occupied largely by bondmen.[2]

A plot of land in the vicinity of Maenan, amounting to approximately 3,500 acres on the east bank of the river Conwy, was on 23 October 1284 granted to the Cistercian community formerly located at Aberconwy.[3] Another area of monastic land, known as Tir yr Abad, was located to the south of Mynydd Hiraethog. The townships of Henllan, in Is Aled, Llansannan in Uwch Aled, and Llangernyw in Is Dulas, formed part of the estates of the Bishop of St Asaph,[4] while the tenants of Llanrhaeadr and Llech, in Ceinmeirch, held their lands of the Bishop of Bangor.[5]

In contrast, the lay townships were described in detail in the 1334 survey. The extentor, Hugh Buckley, seeming to have been anxious to extract as much revenue as possible, therefore specified various sources of revenue that, although formerly operative, had become obsolescent by this time. The inclusion of this information enhances the value of the survey as a source for an understanding of the social framework of this area in the period immediately before the establishment of the lordship.

An examination of the Survey of Denbigh enables one to appreciate the impact of the policies of the rulers of Gwynedd on this territory, which was governed by them for a considerable period in the thirteenth century. The survey records that relatively few townships were occupied entirely by bondmen. In the whole lordship, which consisted of eighty-one lay townships, only twelve were occupied entirely by persons of bond status, while another twenty-one contained both bond and free elements. A significant feature was that a number of the bond townships were located in the vicinity of *maerdrefi*, which were certainly the oldest institutions recorded in the survey. The *maerdref* was traditionally located near the *llys* ('court') of the commotal lord and contained substantial areas of *tir bwrdd* or demesne land whose produce provided for the maintenance of the court. An exclusively bond population, residing in the *maerdref* or in the nearby townships, would labour on the *tir bwrdd* under the supervision of an officer designated the *maer*.[6]

This pattern was evidently a feature of the four *maerdrefi* whose existence is indicated by the evidence of the survey, and which were located at Cilcennis, Dinorben, Dinbych and Ystrad Owain. The only render contributed in kind at the *maerdref* of Cilcennis was a substantial butter rent, for which a render of 30s. 3d was paid, and the nature of this payment reflected the pastoral economy of Uwch Dulas.[7] Dinorben, located in a favourable position,[8] was a demesne centre in the commote of Is Dulas, and the focal point of a locality populated largely by bond communities. Situated in its vicinity were the bond township of Talgarth and the mixed townships of Dinorben Fychan, Meifod and Cegidog, with the latter two being predominantly of bond status. The survey recorded that the bondmen of Dinorben Fychan, Meifod and Cegidog were responsible for ploughing and harrowing duties at the *maerdref*.[9] The extent of manorial activities at the neighbouring township of Wigfair in the immediate post-conquest period suggests that it had previously been a subsidiary of this *maerdref*.[10] The *maerdref* at Dinbych, in the commote of Is Aled, was maintained by the exclusively bond population of this township,[11] and the *maerdref* of Ystrad Owain was located near the stronghold of Llys Gwenllian in the bond township of Ystrad in the commote of Ceinmeirch.[12] Therefore, four of the five commotes under consideration, with Uwch Aled representing a sole exception, contained a *maerdref*, populated by persons of bond status.

Bond communities may also be observed along the valleys and on the coastline. The coastal townships of Mochdre, Rhiw and Colwyn were inhabited largely by bondmen.[13] Other bond townships, such as Llech Talhaearn and Caledan, in Uwch Aled, were situated in favourable locations along river valleys, and these trends were also reflected in the coastal and valley sites of a number of mixed townships that seem to have been of bond origin. The territorial extent of Segrwyd was not specified,[14] but in view of the amount of land, 51.9 per cent, which escheated to the lord, amounting to 818.5 acres, it is probable that this township originally contained about 1,700 acres. Prion consisted of 1,208.5 acres[15] and the entry for Postyn suggests that in that township and in the townships of Kilford and Cilcedig there was a bond 'clan' or descent-group agglomeration, comprising twenty-three *gafaelion*.[16] Ceinmeirch differed from the other commotes in that the distinctive *gwely* did not appear here at all, and that both bond and free groupings held their land in *gafaelion*. This was in sharp contrast to the position in the other commotes that were characterised by a widespread interspersal of *gwelyau* and *gafaelion*. This expansion of free descent-groups was probably a comparatively recent development and suggests that the extensive bond townships of Ceinmeirch in 1334 represented distinctive features of the commote's earlier social structure, and that in the eleventh century, before *gwelyau* had emerged, society in this area was overwhelmingly bond in character.[17]

The 1334 survey also recorded the continued occupation of land by descent-groupings, with extensive lands held by members of the Hedd Molwynog, Marchweithian, Braint Hir and Marchudd ap Cynan kinship groups that were later regarded as constituting four of the fifteen 'Royal Tribes of Wales'.[18] A distinction may be immediately drawn between those groupings that were dispersed over a wide territorial area and those that were concentrated in one locality. The former feature tended to predominate and the settlement of the Hedd Molwynog descent-group along the river Aled was an exception to the general rule, with the lands held forming a solid block of territory in the parish of Llansannan in Uwch Aled. Several entries state that *pastus* payments were rendered at Deunant, which seems to have been the location for the initial settlement, and that his descendants were later able to spread into various townships alongside the river Aled.[19] This occupation of a fairly compact territorial entity, however, was an exception and it was far more common for kinship members to move further afield from the original settlement.[20]

It is more difficult to determine the original location of the powerful Marchweithian and Braint Hir descent-groups. The naming of three *gwelyau* in the township of Prŷs after Runon ap Cadwgan, Ithel ap Cadwgan and Cynddelw ap Cadwgan, prompts one to endorse T. P. Ellis's suggestion that Prŷs was the original settlement of the Marchweithian kindred. This township was located in an upland area on Mynydd Hiraethog in the commote of Is Aled, and it seems to have represented a strategic military vantage point overlooking one of the best inland routes leading towards Gwynedd Uwch Conwy; this route is today represented by the A5 road. It was from Prŷs that Marchweithian's descendants established themselves in secondary settlements further afield, including the township of Garthgyfannedd near the Conwy river in Uwch Dulas.[21]

The evidence suggesting that Prŷs was a primary settlement for the Marchweithian kindred may also indicate that it was in this township that Ithel and Cynon ap Llywarch, founders of the Braint Hir descent-group, originated, and then extended into various other townships, including Ystrad Cynon, where the *pastus principis* due was rendered, and Nantglyn Cynon.[22] Land was also held by this grouping in Nantglyn 'Sanctorum' and Gwytherin, and references in these townships to the payment of the *abbadaeth* due suggest that members may have been originally ecclesiastical tenants.[23]

The largest and most influential kindred in the area that later formed the lordship of Denbigh was that of Edrud ap Marchudd, described by Paul Vinogradoff, as 'the most perfect example of the complicated ramifications of a progeny'.[24] Abergele, in Is Dulas, and Llwytgoed, in Uwch Dulas, were probably the initial settlements from which members spread to other townships.[25] The descent-group of Edrud ap Marchudd was not only the largest one in the two *cantrefi*, with lands also held in Gwynedd Uwch Conwy, but it was also extremely powerful with members holding significant positions in the administration of the Welsh princes, as illustrated by the careers of Ednyfed Fychan, his two sons Goronwy and Tudur, and grandson Goronwy ap Heilyn.[26] Plots of land were held by a privileged tenure and while no dues were demanded of them, their only obligation was that of rendering military service to the lord.

The failure of the determined effort made by the thirteenth-century rulers to strengthen their authority and create what has been described as a strong feudal state had significant implications for the lords of Denbigh in a later period.[27] Various legal devices had been employed in the pre-conquest period to evade the traditional restrictions imposed by Welsh land law to prevent the disposal of land outside the kindred grouping. One of these was *tir prid*, which represented, in theory, a temporary alienation from the territorial holding but which was in fact a perpetual mortgage. Examples of its application in this area were recorded in the 1334 survey. The entry for Denbigh recorded that Dafydd ap Bleddyn Saer held one-third of one gafael in *tir prid*, and therefore land formerly occupied by bond *gafael* tenure had passed out of the possession of the kindred group and into the hands of an individual; and also one-third of Twynnan, in Uwch Dulas, had been held by Gronw ap Heilyn ap Ken, who, as noted above, was probably the individual who had played a prominent role in the crucial events of the period 1277–83. One of the methods by which he had assumed possession of these lands was by way of *Tir Prid: per viam de Tyrpride*. Two-thirds of the township was held by the privileged *Wyrion Ednyfed*, the clan of Cynddelw ao Iorwerth ap Gwgan, who was probably the 'Ken' included in the name of Gronw ap Heilyn ap Ken: if this is correct, it confirms that Gronw was a member of the *Wyrion Ednyfed* 'clan' grouping.[28]

Moreover, the entry for Dincadfel, to the north-west of Llanefydd in Is Aled, reveals Iorwerth ap Iorwerth as an active participant in a transfer of land that had formerly belonged to a kindred. Hoedlyw ap Ithel had mortgaged to Llywelyn ap Iorwerth the rights that he held in a portion of land belonging to the clan of Ithel ap Cadwgan ab Ystrwyth. Llywelyn had then handed over the mortgage to Tangwystl Goch, the mother of his eldest son Gruffudd, and she in turn had sold the rights to Cynan ap Llywarch, a member of the Braint Hir kindred. Not only had Llywelyn granted the land to Tangwystl but he had also allowed her to sell it illegally; '*minus iuste*', and thereby had been involved directly in the alienation of 'clan' land.[29]

Parallel to these changes in land tenure, attempts were also made to establish a money economy, with certain dues, previously paid in kind, now commuted into cash renders. The survey reveals that by 1334 commutation in the lordship was complete but a careful assessment of this document provides an indication of the extent of commutation at the time of the conquest. A study of Gwynedd Uwch Conwy has shown that *twnc* represented cash renders at the time of the conquest, and that other payments in cash represented subsequent commutations of dues and services.[30] Therefore, a study of the varying ratios of *twnc* payments, as recorded in the survey, enables one to assess the extent of commutation in the five commotes in the pre-conquest period.

First, it is clear that the extent of commutation in this area increased in the pre-conquest period as one moved from east to west. Therefore, whereas the *twnc* ratio in Ceinmeirch stood at 9.2 per cent, those for Is Aled and Uwch Aled were 9.9 per cent and 11.3 per cent, respectively, and were even higher in Is Dulas at 12.6 per cent and at 17.7 per cent in western-most Uwch Dulas. The variations could probably be explained by the relative proximity of the five commotes to Gwynedd Uwch Conwy, with the progressive cash-raising policies of the princes of Gwynedd influencing neighbouring Uwch Dulas to a greater extent than the comparativel remoter Ceinmeirch. A high level of commutation also characterised the payments of those major free clans that held land in Rhos and Rhufoniog, and this again may well illustrate the economic policies of the Gwynedd princes. It has been argued that commutation 'had enabled the incipient State to drive a powerful wedge into the quasi-autonomous organisation of the clan',[31] and the evidence presented by the 1334 survey confirms this view.

The creation of a borough also represented another aspect of the attempt to establish a money economy in pre-conquest Gwynedd Is Conwy. Despite the absence of concrete evidence, the information provided by the 1334 survey suggests that the native princes had founded a borough at Llanrwst. The survey identified three boroughs in the lordship – namely, Abergele, Denbigh and Llanrwst – and a significant contrast was drawn, on the one hand, between Abergele and Denbigh, which constituted centres of English influence, and Llanrwst with its predominantly Welsh population. The aggregation of property in Llanrwst, in 1334, as noted in Chapter 7 of this volume, suggests that this borough had existed for a period greater than the half-century following the formation of the lordship, and that its origins may be traced back to the pre-conquest period.[32]

Notes

1. See pp. 1–3 and p. 5 for details of the manuscript copy of the survey discussed in this volume.
2. See Figure 2, The *cantrefi* of Rhos and Rhufoniog, administrative divisions; G. R. J. Jones, 'The Distribution of Bond Settlements in North-West Wales', *WHR*, 11 (1964), 26. This omission must be borne in mind when the evidence of the Survey is assessed.
3. R. W. Hays, *The History of the Abbey of Aberconway, 1186–1537* (Cardiff, 1963), pp. 70–4.
4. TNA SC 6/1143/23.
5. TNA SC 6/1143/25.
6. For a detailed discussion of the administrative framework of the royal courts of the thirteenth-century rulers of Gwynedd, see David Langley, 'The Royal Courts of the Welsh Princes of Gwynedd, A. D. 400–1283', and Neil Johnstone, 'An Investigation into the Location of the Royal Courts of Thirteenth-Century Gwynedd', in Nancy Edwards (ed.), *Landscape and Settlement in Medieval Wales* (Oxford, 1997), pp. 41–69.
7. *SD*, p. 275. The full significance of this payment of a butter rent at a *maerdref* was emphasised by G. R. J. Jones, 'The Tribal System in Wales', *WHR*, 1/2 (1961), 119–22, with reference to bondmen exploiting for their lord, at the *maerdref*, the arable land that was usually the most suitable for cultivation within the commote.
8. G. R. J. Jones, 'The Military Geography of Gwynedd' (unpublished MA thesis, University of Wales, 1949), pp. 57–8, for a statement that the major environmental factor responsible for the location of this *maerdref* on a limestone ridge was aspect rather than soil fertility; *SD*, pp. 222–33.
9. *SD*, pp. 210–22.
10. *SD*, pp. 52–6.
11. *SD*, pp. 2–3, 44–5.
12. *SD*, pp. 306–15.
13. *SD*, 306–13.
14. *SD*, pp. 7–20.
15. *SD*, pp. 25–7, 43–4; T. M. Charles-Edwards, 'A Note on Terminology', in *Early Irish and Welsh Kinship* (Oxford, 1993), pp. xiv–xvi, referred to his adherence to the terminology favoured by Robin Fox, *Kinship and Marriage* (Harmondsworth, 1967), with an avoidance of the word 'clan' and tendency to favour the term 'descent grouping'.
16. Jones, 'Tribal System', 111–32; and T. Jones Pierce, *Medieval Welsh Society*, ed. by J. Beverley Smith (Cardiff, 1972), pp. 254–83, 333–7 for a discussion on origin, nature and expansion of *gwely* ('resting place') and '*gafael*' ('holding') settlements.

17 P. C. Bartrum, 'Pedigrees of the Welsh Tribal Patriarchs', *NLW Journal*, 13 (1963–4), 129, 132, 133.
18 *SD*, pp.157, 172, 182 where the clan holding was undivided and termed Wyrion Rand; T. P. Ellis, *Welsh Tribal Law and Custom in the Middle Ages*, vol. 1 (Oxford, 1926), p. 130, where Asser was described as the son of Gwrgi, one of the three sons of Hedd Molwynog, who was stated to be a contemporary of Henry II. See Charles-Edwards, *Early Irish and Welsh Kinship*, pp. 239–42 for a detailed discussion of the progenies of Hedd's great grandson Rhahawd ab Asser, with Table 4.4 (p. 240) recording Hedd's lineage.
19 *SD*, pp. 167–85, 206–8; Ellis, *Welsh Tribal Law*, p. 133.
20 *SD*, pp. 96–107, 279–80; Ellis, *Welsh Tribal Law*, pp. 121–6; *SD*, pp. 96–107, 279–80; Jones, 'Distribution of Bond Settlements', 26, confirmed that Prŷs was a long-established township. In a valued discussion with Glanville Jones, while emphasising the relatively unattractive character of Prŷs compared with lowland townships for agricultural activities, he also suggested the possibility that freemen may well have been encouraged to settle here for military purposes at a time when the defences of Gwynedd were being organised. This settlement, largely funded by military considerations, could have formed the basis for the extension of prominent clans, as previously outlined; Charles-Edwards, *Early Irish and Welsh Kinship*, pp. 232–3, 235, with Table 4.2 (p. 232) recording Marchweithian's descendants, pp. 436–43.
21 *SD*, pp. 80–5, 91–3; N. Neilson 'Rents and Services', in *SD*, p. lxiv.
22 *SD*, pp. 94–6, 192.
23 Ellis, *Welsh Tribal Law*, p. 106 described this clan as the 'largest of all the free clans of north Wales'; P. Vinogradoff, 'Kindreds and Villages', in *SD*, p. xxxii.
24 *SD*, pp. 245–51, 299–304, 275, 262, 197, 294, 261, 297, 227, 205; Charles-Edwards, *Early Irish and Welsh Kinship*, pp. 233–9, with Table 4.3 (p. 234) recording Marchudd's descendants.
25 *SD*, pp. 245–59, 299–306;, Ellis, *Welsh Tribal Law*, p. 107 for details of the extensive lands occupied by this clan in localities sited within the present-day shires of Anglesey and Gwynedd.
26 See Jones Pierce, *Medieval Welsh Society*, p. 38, for a statement that the territory governed by the Welsh princes 'had developed in every direction all the characteristics of a feudal state in miniature'; Susan Reynolds, *Fiefs and Vassals: The Medieval Evidence Reinterpreted* (Oxford, 1994), p. 391; *Statutes of the Realm*, vol. 1 (London, 1810–28), p. 55; Stephenson, *Political Power*, pp. 193–7.
27 D. Jenkins (ed.), *Llyfr Colan, Y Gyfraith Cymreig yn ôl hanner cyntaf Llawysgrif Peniarth 30* (1963, 158: mae'n glir, oddi wrth Rheol S607, na ellir gwerthu tir yn rhydd ['It is clear, on the basis of regulation S607, that land could not be freely sold']); Jones Pierce, *Medieval Welsh Society*, p. 236, for a description of conversion of tribal holdings from '*tir priod* to *tir prid*'; Llinos Beverley Smith, 'The Gage and the Land Market in Late Medieval Wales', *Economic History Review*, 2/29 (1976), 537–50; Llinos Beverley Smith, '*Tir Prid*: Deeds of Gage of Land in Late Medieval Wales', *BBCS*, 27 (1977), 263–77.

28 *SD*, pp. 53, 297, 127–8; Smith, *Llywelyn ap Gruffudd*, pp. 12–13; Charles-Edwards, *Early Irish and Welsh Kinship*, pp. 435–6.
29 Jones Pierce, 'The Growth of Commutation in Gwynedd in the Thirteenth Century', *Medieval Welsh Society*, pp. 103–25.
30 *SD* for details of payments of *twnc* in the various townships of the lordship, including those in the townships of Segrwyd [9], Ystrad Cynon [83], Deunant [161], Wigfair [213] and Erethlyn [287].
31 Jones Pierce, *Medieval Welsh Society*, p. 124.
32 *SD*, pp. 280–2; *infra*, pp. 104–6.

3
POLITICAL CONTROL OF THE LORDSHIP, 1282–1344

In the period following the Edwardian conquest, political and military considerations dictated the distribution of lands located between the rivers Conwy and Clwyd. Edward I seems initially to have been anxious to retain in his own hands a large part of this area, comprising the four *cantrefi* of Rhos, Rhufoniog, Dyffryn Clwyd and Tegeingl, known as the Perfeddwlad. On 29 September 1281, he included the *cantref* of Rhos in his grant of the justiciarship of Chester to Reginald de Grey.[1] Further information on this development was provided in a letter patent dated 8 October 1283, which offered De Grey a rebate of 300 marks on an agreed payment of 1,000 marks. This would represent compensation for the failure to honour an earlier agreement conferring on him the county of Chester and the castles of Chester and Flint. Also, very significantly, in relation to the later creation of the lordship of Denbigh, the *cantref* of Rhos in addition to the *cantref* of Tegeingl, a reduction in the farm of the new county of Flint in 1284 may be explained by the transfer of the *cantref* of Rhos to the new lordship of Denbigh.[2] There was no suggestion in this proposed transaction of the creation of a marcher lordship but the position was drastically changed after the hostilities of 1282.

Following a series of attacks launched in the summer and autumn of 1282, Edward I rewarded his commanders by allowing them to retain possession of the lands that they had conquered.[3] The earl of Lincoln, who had been a close associate of Edward I, was the first witness to Edward I's grant of the lordship of Chirk, on 2 June 1282, to Roger Mortimer, the *younger* son of Roger

Mortimer of Wigmore, who had actively prosecuted the war in the middle March.[4] As a result of a successful onslaught on the Vale of Clwyd in the late summer, Reginald de Grey, moving from Hope, occupied Ruthin, and Edward, aided by Lincoln, conquered other lands lying between the rivers Conwy and Clwyd. Following these actions, Denbigh capitulated in early October, and Dinas Bran, in Powys Fadog, was captured by John de Warenne, the earl of Surrey, who, on 7 October, received the confiscated lands of Maelor and Ial, which then formed the lordship of Bromfield and Yale.[5] This was followed on 16 October by the grant to Lincoln of the lordship of Denbigh, comprising the *cantrefi* of Rhos and Rhufoniog and also the commote of Dinmael, traditionally associated with the *cantref* of Edeyrnion, but specifically excluding the commote of Creuddun, to the north-west; and also the land of Faenol, on the north-eastern flank.[6]

A considerable part of the area that constituted the newly created lordship of Denbigh had formerly been held by Reginald de Grey, who, on 23 October 1282, received the lordship of Ruthin, constituting the *cantref* of Dyffryn Clwyd.[7] He also received lands previously belonging to the forementioned Gwenllian de Lacy.[8] Military service was demanded of the four recipients of the territories that respectively formed the lordships of Chirk, Bromfield and Yale, Denbigh, and Ruthin. Of these lordships, Denbigh was the largest and most valuable, with Lincoln required to provide the service of six knights, in contrast to the four, three and two knights, respectively, demanded for the possession of Bromfield and Yale, Ruthin, and Chirk. The four recipients were allowed to retain rights traditionally associated with the commote, with Denbigh to be held 'with all things pertaining to those cantreds and commotes'.[9] This territorial re-adjustment made in 1282 clearly disfavoured Reginald de Grey, and the rebate on 8 October 1283 of 700 marks of a payment of 1,000 marks due to the king probably represented compensation for the abrogation of the earlier concession.[10]

There was no traditional relationship between the *cantrefi* of Rhos and Rhufoniog, and the commote of Dinmael, whose lords, the descendants of Owain Brogyntyn, the illegitimate son of Madog ap Maredudd, ruler of Powys who had died in 1160, were tenants in chief by military service of the lord of Denbigh. Throughout the period under review, the commote was never considered an integral part of the lordship, and the probable explanation for its association was that de Lacy had been personally responsible for its conquest. The surviving Welsh lords of Dinmael, holding their lands by the distinctive *pennaeth* (Welsh barony) tenure, were allowed to retain the privileged status by which they held their lands.[11] In 1285, the king commanded Lincoln to allow Gruffydd ap Owain ap Bleddyn to hold his lands of him by military service, as Gruffydd had done homage to the king for them.[12]

On the other hand, the omission of Creuddun and Faenol perhaps reflected Edward's awareness of the necessity to secure areas of key importance to counter any possible future Welsh resistance.[13] He may also possibly have been aware of the potential danger of extending the Welsh March, which, comprising lordships in south Wales and along the eastern boundary with England, had been established as a result of a series of conquests completed by Norman lords.[14] In contrast, the four lordships in north-east Wales that came into existence in 1282, were created by royal charter. In each case, the new lordship being created was to be held by knight's service, with the earl of Lincoln required to provide the service of six knights, and in this respect again the four lordships differed from the older marcher lordships.[15] Also, this grant contained no reference to a relationship between the new lordship and the land to the west of the river Conwy forming the Principality of Wales. However, in due course, it was argued on historical grounds that the lordships should be intendent to the Principality of Wales, created in 1301, and not to the Crown.[16]

The military requirements of the period immediately following the creation of the lordship involved the building of castles. Preparation for the construction of the royal castle of Conwy resulted in the relocation of the abbey of Aberconwy, whose foundation and property have been traced above.[17] The abbey was physically moved to a new site at Maenan in the Conwy valley, and the possession of the land in the immediate vicinity of the re-sited abbey was transferred from the lordship of Denbigh to the shire of Caernarfon.[18]

Use also seems to have been made of royal resources to assist with the initial construction stages of Denbigh castle and town walls, which commenced soon after the grant of the lordship, on 16 October 1282, to Henry de Lacy, earl of Lincoln, with both the earl and the king present at Denbigh during the final ten days of October. The intention seems to have been to set as much as possible of the castle and town on the summit of a hill, with the castle sited on the highest and most impregnable part.[19] The castle has been described as 'the most celebrated of the baronial castles', and as 'one of the outstanding architectural creations of the Welsh conquest'.[20] Its semi-circular towers and gatehouses formed

Figure 3: Aerial view of Denbigh castle and town walls, by kind permission of Cadw '© Crown copyright (2023), Cadw'

both the outer wall of the castle and town defences and the three-towered gatehouse has been described, even in its present-day ruined condition, as a 'wonder of medieval construction': this was considered by John Leland to have possibly been, if completed, 'among the most memorable peaces of workys yn England'.[21]

In the immediate post-conquest period, the keeper of the Wardrobe's accounts recorded a payment of £22, of which the greater amount – £19 18s. 0d – was spent on the purchase of more than 1,200 'clays' for the building of the castle, and most of the remainder on carrying 184 cartloads of timber from nearby woods to the castle.[22] Many payments were authorised by Henry of Greenford, who served as constable of Criccieth after 14 March 1283.[23] Master James of St George, the king's master of works, was present during the early construction stages, and, as was also the case in other localities in north Wales, the castle was only one feature of a plan that provided for the military stronghold and urban centre.[24] Groups of carpenters and diggers were moved from Rhuddlan in the late summer and autumn to embark on the construction of Denbigh castle.[25] Another immediate task was the construction of town walls, and these were further strengthened after the Madog uprising in 1294–5.[26]

In 1282, Edward I would have had few qualms concerning the fidelity of the earl of Lincoln, who had proved himself to be a successful military commander and an able diplomat. After being granted the lordship, Lincoln distinguished himself in military offensives against the Scots and the French, as well as in diplomatic campaigns to those lands.[27] Despite his prominence on the English political stage, he seems to have had an uneasy relationship with two of the other beneficiaries in 1282. It is possible that he, the prominent courtier and diplomat, would have had difficulty tolerating the considerable influence wielded by the locally dominant Reginald de Grey, lord of Ruthin and justice of Chester.[28] He was also involved in a long-standing dispute with John de Warenne, earl of Surrey and lord of Bromfield and Yale. The two had engaged in 1269 in a private war, which was terminated only by the personal intervention of the king, Henry III. The passage of time clearly did not soothe feelings, and in May 1317 Surrey aided in the abduction of Lincoln's daughter, Alice, the wife of Thomas, earl of Lancaster, the second lord of Denbigh, and who, it has been suggested, may well have been a more than willing victim.[29]

An even more immediate threat to the earl of Lincoln's position as lord of Denbigh had been presented by discontented elements from within the lordship, who resented the considerable demands made on them in terms of manpower and financial resources on account of Lincoln's prominence on the political stage. In 1294 the king called on Reginald de Grey, who was in temporary control of the lordship during Lincoln's absence abroad, to raise a military force from Flintshire and lordships in north-east Wales, including Denbigh.[30] Opposition to this request was expressed in the lordship of Dyffryn Clwyd with a certain Iorwerth ap Cynwrig threatening revolt, and this incident foreshadowed the uprising in this lordship inspired by Madog ap Llywelyn, which broke out that year.[31] A far more severe outbreak occurred in the neighbouring lordship of Denbigh. When Lincoln, one of the commanders destined for the Gascon military expedition, intended to arrive at Denbigh on 11 November, he was encountered by local inhabitants outside the town of Denbigh and driven away.[32] A royal expedition was organised and in December 1294 Edward himself led a force that subdued the Denbigh insurgents. The army was then led by Edward into Snowdonia, but after an initial setback, it withdrew to Denbigh, which had been completely pacified.[33]

Madog ap Llywelyn's steward, Tudur ap Goronwy ap Ednyfed Fychan, his brother, Goronwy Fychan, and his cousin, Gruffudd ap Rhys ab Ednyfed Fychan, witnessed the charter by which Madog, in December 1294, granted lands in Ardudwy, in the shire of Merioneth, and 'Kawer Hepnewid', which has been convincingly identified as being in Llansannan, in Uwch Aled. The recipient of the grant was Bleddyn Fychan, from Uwch Aled, who claimed descent from Hedd Molwynog, and he had been one of the forty-six men from Rhos and Rhufoniog who, on 26 July 1283, had sworn to the earl of Lincoln, as lord of Denbigh, to keep the peace.[34] He seems to have been on good terms with the administration of the lordship, and a local tradition associated him with the establishment of the Forest of Archwedlog in the immediate post-conquest period; 25 per cent of the township of Archwedlog, on the east bank of the river Aled, in the commote of Uwch Aled, had escheated to the lord *racione mortuorum contra pacem* ('on account of deaths against the peace'); plots of land, amounting to 540.5 acres, granted in exchange in various townships, mainly in Uwch Aled, had enabled the administration to acquire the remainder of the township, which was then assembled to form the Forest of Archwedlog, containing 984 acres. A local tradition, recorded in 1650 and stating that 'Blythin Vaughan fallinge out with his tenants in Archwedlog disinherited them & converted the same to a parke or fforest', was accompanied by a reference to a couplet in Welsh proclaiming woe to Archwedlog at the time when Bleddyn Fychan was born.[35]

Edward resumed his military operations in January 1295 and the decision to entrust Lincoln with the defence of Denbigh and the surrounding vale of Clwyd suggests a possible awareness of the possibility of continuing opposition from local inhabitants. However, no evidence is available of any further hostility within the lordship, and fifty-seven prominent individuals (which, significantly, included Bleddyn Fychan) submitted on 29 June 1295. Edward stayed at Denbigh on 13 and 14 July, and by this time the lordship of Denbigh seems to have been completely cowed, as were other areas in Wales, by the success of Edward's military campaign.[36] Whereas the 1294–5 uprising revealed the precarious nature of the earl of Lincoln's hold on the lordship of Denbigh, its failure consolidated his position. This was further strengthened by the solution of the succession problem that had arisen because of the accidental deaths of his two sons, Edmund and John: Edmund being drowned in a well within the Red Tower of Denbigh castle in 1294. Following the drowning incident, Lincoln's inheritance in Cheshire and Lancashire, and also probably the lordship of Denbigh, was settled on Thomas, earl of Lancaster, who had married Alice, Lincoln's daughter.[37]

Tudur ap Goronwy ap Ednyfed Fychan (Tudur Hen), named above as Madog ap Llywelyn's steward, was one of the large number of individuals whose petitions were considered in 1305 at Kennington. He had sworn fealty and performed homage in 1301 to Edward of Caernarvon when he had been installed as Prince of Wales.[38] The latter had ascended the throne as Edward II in 1307, and the loyalty displayed by the earl of Lincoln to his father, Edward I, was not extended to the new monarch. A man of considerable stature in the English realm, Lincoln was one of the many English barons who reacted to the changed conditions in the royal court, and he clearly resented the favoured treatment of Piers Gaveston, who had been created earl of Cornwall in 1307 soon after the accession of Edward II.[39] The extensive powers granted to Gaveston attracted the enmity of the earl of Lincoln, who was fiercely opposed to Gaveston and was the leader of the group that in 1308 secured Gaveston's exile to Ireland.

By late summer 1308, Lincoln had reached an agreement with the king, who then secured the adherence of a number of prominent barons, but not, significantly, Thomas earl of Lancaster, to an agreement that provided for Gaveston's return to England in June 1309 and his re-instatement as earl of Cornwall. However, a further deterioration in relations between the king and barons resulted in the election in the spring of 1310 of the Ordainers, a group of bishops and magnates, with Lincoln significantly one of the first two Ordainers elected on 20 March 1310. Another reflection of his pre-eminence on the political stage was his appointment as Keeper of the Realm on 1 September 1310 during the king's absence.[40] His death on 5 February 1311 was considered to have been a severe blow to the king, and Lincoln has been described as 'by age, experience and wealth the joint leader of the nobility with Lancaster' and as 'the most able and constructive of the barons'.[41]

Following Lincoln's death, Thomas, earl of Lancaster, received the lordship of Denbigh on 1 July 1311, for which he performed homage on 17 July.[42] Lancaster inherited Lincoln's traditional dispute with John de Warenne, earl of Surrey and lord of the neighbouring lordship of Bromfield and Yale, and he also intervened in the middle Welsh March in support of his client, Griffith de la Pole, the son of Gruffudd ap Gwenwynwyn, lord of southern Powys who had assisted Edward I's final campaign against Llywelyn ap Gruffydd. Lancaster was also active within the lordship of Denbigh, where he attracted support for his various political adventures. The list compiled in 1313 of pardoned adherents included the names of Iorwerth ap Llywarch of Lleweni, Iorwerth ap Gruffydd of Abergele, Ieuan ap Goronwy of Talhaearn, William Curteys, Robert Holland and William Holland, who may all be identified as inhabitants of the lordship.[43] The first-named was probably the same person as the 'Yerward de la Chaumbre, king's enemy and rebel, in Denbigh in Wales', named in a fine roll entry dated 20 April 1322 as having been in possession of 'escheated lands held of gift of Thomas of Lancaster'.[44] A contemporary inquisition reveals that these lands were extensive, consisting of 240 acres in Lleweni, with an annual value of £8, a watermill in Berain and Tal-y-bryn, and 750 acres with an annual value of £20 4s. 4d. Also by gift of the earl, he had held the amobrage of Is Aled, at an annual value of £5.[45] The grant of an extensive area of land, together with additional rights, was probably made in return for Iorwerth's support for Lancaster's political ambitions, with the earl determined to secure the adherence of one of the leading individuals within the lordship of Denbigh.

The lordship had been directly influenced by Lancaster's preeminent position in the English realm. In 1322, probably in the second half of February, troops from north Wales, one of whose leaders was Sir Gruffydd Llwyd, great-grandson of Ednyfed Fychan, seneschal of Llywelyn the Great and his son Dafydd from *c.* 1215 until 1246, attacked the lordship of Denbigh and secured control of it for the king.[46] Royal forces defeated those led by Lancaster at Burton on Trent on 10 March, and again at Boroughbridge on 16 March, and soon afterwards, on 22 March 1322, he was beheaded at Pontefract castle in the king's presence.[47] Lancaster's political ambitions clearly had a significant influence on the lands, including the lordship of Denbigh, which he held. He has been described by his biographer as 'a man of great complexity, living under a king whose problems were insoluble', and few positive results arose from his efforts to 'provide answers to some of these problems'.[48]

Following Lancaster's execution, his lands, including the lordship of Denbigh, escheated to the king, and Sir Gruffudd Llwyd, together with Giles de Beauchamp, were responsible for this transaction.[49] On 13 April 1322, the keeper of Denbigh castle was instructed regarding the provision of munitions.[50] The lordship did not remain in royal hands for long and on 9 July 1322 was granted to Hugh de Despenser, the elder, earl of Winchester.[51] An extremely loyal supporter of Edward II, he had been associated with Wales before this time following his marriage to Isabel, the widow of Sir Patrick de Chaworth, lord of Kidwelly. He was confronted within the lordship of Denbigh by a pro-Lancastrian party, whose allegiance to Thomas of Lancaster had been cemented by territorial grants, such as the one to 'Yerward de la Chaumbre'.[52]

The change in possession was accompanied by upheaval within the lordship. On 14 February 1322, a force of infantrymen had been requisitioned from the neighbouring lordships of Bromfield and Yale, and Ruthin, and also in a number of lordships held previously by Lancaster, but, significantly, Denbigh was excluded from this demand.[53] The reason for the omission is implied in a letter close dated 13 April 1322, which, instructing the keeper of Denbigh castle to fortify it, referred to 'the disturbances', with a state of turmoil probably prevailing within the lordship.[54] By the summer, however, the situation had again improved, and on 10

June the lordship was required to contribute a force to the king's army.[55]

The above-mentioned reference in 1322 to 'Yerward de la Chaumbre', whose lands had been confiscated, as 'king's enemy and rebel', reflected the attitude of one of the more prominent Lancastrian supporters within the lordship of Denbigh.[56] His treatment explains the alienation of those local inhabitants who had been favoured by Thomas of Lancaster. Also, their hostility towards Despenser, who was accused of oppression and of withholding certain privileges that they had enjoyed under Lincoln and Lancaster, including a licence to hunt and carry away deer and 'beasts of the woods'.[57] Furthermore, this antagonism towards Despenser was further illustrated by a reference to the concealment of property belonging to him by the lordship's inhabitants,[58] which suggests that the overthrow of the Despensers aroused a minimum amount of resentment in the lordship of Denbigh.

Hugh de Despenser the elder, earl of Winchester, held the lordship of Denbigh solely on the strength of his close association with Edward II, and it was inevitable that his fall would accompany that of his royal master. Having supported Edward II on his flight to Wales in October 1326, he was condemned to death and hanged on 27 October.[59] In view of Roger Mortimer's supremacy at this time, his acquisition of the lordship of Denbigh was a natural move on the marcher chessboard. The custody of Denbigh castle was committed to him on 13 December 1326, and followed by the grant of the lordship of Denbigh on 13 September 1327.[60]

Mortimer's association with Lancaster may well have made his entry into the lordship more acceptable to local inhabitants, with the experience of 'Yerward de la Chaumbre' probably representative of the attitudes of influential members of the local community. 'Yerward', that is Iorwerth ap Llywarch, the loyal adherent of earl Thomas of Lancaster, was restored to his lands following the downfall of Hugh de Despenser, and the grant of the lordship of Denbigh to Roger Mortimer. A letter close dated

10 December 1330 referred to 'Iorward Chaumberleyn ... of the earl's quarrel because the quarrel was adjudged good and just in parliament', and listed his possessions as including the amobrage of Is Aled, mill of Tal-y-bryn and £32 7s. 7d of the annual rents and farms due from tenants in the townships of Berain and Tal-y-bryn.[61] The Survey compiled in 1334 recorded that he was a significant landholder, and that whereas all the free tenants, and possibly all the bondmen of Lleweni, had been granted plots of land in exchange for their hereditary holdings, Iorwerth and his brother Cynwrig were allowed to hold land in the township. Iorwerth had been granted 187 acres in Lleweni in exchange for his original holding as a free clansman in this township, and similarly Cynwrig held here 28 acres and 1 rood, in addition to 30 acres in Ereifiad and 8 acres in Gwytherin.[62] An indication of Cynwrig's eminent social status is the memorial stone inscribed with his name that stands in the church of Ysbyty Ifan.[63]

Edward II had won steadfast adherents, including Sir Gruffydd Llwyd, in the Principality of North Wales, but the extent of his support within the lordship of Denbigh is difficult to assess. Several prominent local families had affiliations in the territory lying to the east of the river Conwy, but a number of other distinctive local factors also seem to have been involved. The king's close relationship with the hated Despensers probably aroused hostile feelings, and their downfall was accompanied by the restoration of Iorwerth ap Llywarch's lands and the grant of the lordship of Denbigh to Roger Mortimer. However, Mortimer's power and predominance in turn attracted enmity and in 1330 he was arrested and executed.[64]

It was in keeping with the recently established tradition in the lordship of Denbigh that the new lord should have played an active part in the deposition of his predecessor. On 18 January 1331, the lordship was therefore granted to William Montagu, a loyal courtier, who has been claimed to have organised and led the plot that resulted in the fall of Mortimer and Queen Isabella.[65] This grant also referred to the quitclaim to Edward II of the possible rights of Alice, daughter of the late earl of Lincoln and widow of Thomas, earl of Lancaster. She was one of the vulnerable widows who had suffered at the hands of the Despensers, even though she had been estranged from her husband for several years.[66]

A reflection on Montagu's steadfast loyalty to the Crown is that the lordship was allowed to recuperate after a tempestuous half-century, with a conscious attempt made to stabilise conditions within it. Lancastrian adherents were favoured and on 21 September 1332, William Curteys, who had been pardoned in 1313 for his support of Lancaster's ambitions, was granted 140 acres in Segrwyd and Ystrad Cynan.[67] On 11 June 1333, after Edward III had embarked on his military expedition to Scotland and sought to raise troops from his kingdom, William Montagu, together with the Justice of north Wales, and a number of marcher lords, including the lords of Bromfield and Yale, Powys, Clun and Oswestry, was ordered to issue a proclamation in his lands to counteract the activities of malefactors.[68] However, this instruction did not refer specifically to his lordship of Denbigh, whose inhabitants probably welcomed this period of respite from turbulence and disorder. It is therefore of interest to observe that, in contrast to the three previous transfers of possession, on 12 February 1344 the lordship was taken into the king's hands following the sudden death from natural causes of its lord, William Montagu, on 30 January 1344, soon after he had participated in a great tournament organised by the king, held at Windsor.[69]

Notes

1   *CPR 1281–92*, p. 216.
2   *CPR 1281–92*, p. 82; P. H. W. Booth, *The Financial Administration of the Lordship and County of Chester 1272–1377* (Manchester, 1981), p. 57.
3   Morris, *Welsh Wars*, p. 178, described the king's actions in making 'such grants during the war in acknowledgement of real military service'.
4   Michael Prestwich, *The Three Edwards, War and State in England, 1272–1377*, 2nd edn (London, 2003), p. 263; *CWR*, 223.
5   *CWR*, 240; D. Pratt, 'The de Warenne lords of Bromfield and Yale 1282–1353', *TDHS*, 62, (2014), 21–8.

6   *CWR*, 241.
7   *CWR*, 243; Gareth Evans and Arnold Hughes (eds), *The History of Ruthin* (Ruthin, 2014), p. 19.
8   Lloyd, 'Who was Gwenllian de Lacy?', 297–8; *supra*, pp. 15, 32.
9   *CWR*, 223, 243, 240, 241.
10 *CPR 1281–92*, p. 82.
11 A. D. Carr, 'Medieval Dinmael', *TDHS*, 13 (1964), 10–13; NLW Peniarth, 236, 116; A. D. Carr, 'Edeirnion', in J. Beverley Smith and Llinos Beverley Smith (eds), *History of Merioneth, volume 2: The Middle Ages* (Cardiff, 2001), pp. 137–51; David Stephenson, *Medieval Powys: Kingdom, Principality and Lordships, 1132–1293* (Woodbridge, 2016), p. 167.
12 Carr, 'Medieval Dinmael', 10–11.
13 *CWR*, 241; J. G. Edwards, 'Note on the Boundaries of Medieval Flintshire', in *Flint Pleas, 1283–1285, Flintshire Historical Society Publications*, 8 (1922), 54: 'the king must have his safeguards – he must have some footing in this unwelcome lordship of Lincoln's ... The feudal flood that has sundered the king's lands can be bridged at need.'
14 David Walker, *Medieval Wales* (Cambridge, 1990), pp. 20–43.
15 David Walker, *The Norman Conquerors* (Swansea, 1977), pp. 20–49; R. R. Davies, *Lordship and Society in the March of Wales, 1282–1400* (Oxford, 1978), pp. 15–62; R. R. Davies, *Conquest, Coexistence and Change, Wales 1063–1415* (Oxford, 1987), pp. 82–107.
16 J. G. Edwards, *The Principality of Wales, 1267–1967: A Study in Constitutional History* (Caernarfon, 1969), pp. 9–20; *infra*, p. 33.
17 *Supra*, pp. 11–12, 21, 34.
18 A. J. Taylor, 'Conway', *in The King's Works in Wales, 1277–1330* (London, 1974), pp. 337–41; and A. J. Taylor, *The Welsh Castles of Edward I* (London, 1986), pp. 46–7 (hereafter, only the 1986 volume will be cited).
19 A. J. Taylor, 'Master James of St George', in *Studies in Castles and Castle-Building* (London, 1985), p. 69; Taylor, *Welsh Castles*, pp. 41–2.
20 John A. Goodall, 'The Baronial Castles of the Welsh Conquest', in Diane M. Williams and John R. Kenyon (eds), *The Impact of the Edwardian Castles of Wales* (Oxford, 2010), p. 158.
21 John R. Kenyon, *The Medieval Castles of Wales* (Cardiff, 2010), p. 42; John Leland, *The Itinerary of Wales of John Leland in or About the Years 1536–1539*, ed. by Lucy Toulmin Smith (1906), p. 98; see Figure 3. See also *supra* for other sixteenth-century references to the castle.
22 TNA, E.101/3/29; Taylor, *Welsh Castles*, p. 36, n. 9, p. 41.
23 TNA, E.101/4/1; Taylor, *Welsh Castles*, pp. 41, 73.
24 Taylor, *Studies in Castles*, p. 69; Taylor , *Welsh Castles*, p. 41; Nicola Coldstream, 'James of St. George', in Williams and Kenyon (eds), *The Impact of the Edwardian Castles of Wales*, pp. 37–45.
25 Taylor, *Studies in Castles*, p. 112.

26 See pp. 35–8 for reference to information presented on construction of Denbigh castle in the surveys compiled in the reign of Henry VIII, and also by Humphrey Lhuyd, as well as the significant contribution made by Wilcok Pigot.
27 George E. Cokayne (comp.), *The Complete Peerage of England*, vol. 7 (Gloucester, 1982), pp. 682–6.
28 *The Complete Peerage of England*, vol. 7, p. 172.
29 W. T. Riley (ed.), *Thomas Walsingham, quondam Monachi S. Albani, Historia Anglicana*, i, *1272–1381* (London, 1863), p. 148.
30 F. Palgrave (ed.), *Parliamentary Writs and Writs of Military Summons*, 2 vols, Record Commission (London, 1822–34).
31 Morris, *Welsh Wars*, pp. 308–9.
32 Nicholas Trivet, *Annales sex regum Angliae ... 1135–1307*, ed. by T. Hog (London, 1945), pp. 333–5; H. Rothwell (ed.), *The Chronicle of Walter of Guisborough*, Camden Society, 3rd series, 89 (London, 1957), p. 251; Morris, *Welsh Wars*, pp. 241–5, 253; R. F. Walker, 'The Welsh War of 1294–5', in E. B. Fryde (ed.), *Book of Prests of the King's Wardrobe for 1294–5, presented to John Goronwy Edwards* (Oxford, 1962), pp. xxvi–xxxi, 222–3; Fryde (ed.), *Book of Prests of the King's Wardrobe*, Appendix C, 'Itinerary of Edward I', pp. 222–3.
33 Morris, *Welsh Wars*, pp. 253–4, 266; Walker, *Medieval Wales*, pp. 154–6.
34 F. Jones, 'Welsh Bonds for Keeping the Peace, 1283 and 1295', *BBCS*, 13 (1950), 142–3; Stephenson, *Political Power*, p. 106; Charles-Edwards, *Early Irish and Welsh Kinship*, p. 240, Table 4.4 for the lineage of Hedd; Cledwyn Fychan, 'Bleddyn Fychan a gwrthryfel Madog ap Llywelyn, 1294–5', *TDHS*, 49 (2000), 15–22; G. R. Smith, 'The Penmachno Letter Patent and the Welsh Uprising of 1294–95', *CMCS*, 58 (Winter 2009), 49–67.
35 *SD*, pp. 203–4; Fychan, 'Bleddyn Fychan', 18: Cardiff City Library MS, 4: 265, f. 165.
36 Jones, 'Welsh Bonds', 143–4.
37 *DWB*, p. 539; *Cal. Chanc. R*, ii, pp. 427, 455; R. Somerville, *The Duchy of Lancaster* (London, 1953), p. 19; Prestwich, *The Three Edwards*, p. 137, commented on the immense significance of this marriage: 'for it made Lancaster by far the richest of the earls.'
38 *Supra*, pp. 33, 38; Glyn Roberts, *Aspects of Welsh History* (Cardiff, 1969), pp. 186–8; Stephenson, *Political Power*, pp. 104, 106.
39 J. R. Maddicott, *Thomas of Lancaster, 1307–1322: A Study in the Reign of Edward II* (Oxford, 1970), pp. 67–73; J. R. S. Phillips, *Edward II* (London, 2010), pp. 126–8; Pierre Chaplais, *Piers Gaveston, Edward II's Adoptive Brother* (Oxford, 1994), pp. 27–34.
40 Maddicott, *Thomas of Lancaster*, pp. 74–114; Phillips, *Edward II*, pp. 146–9, 154–9, 161–2, 169, 173–4; Chaplais, *Piers Gaveston*, pp. 34–89.
41 Maddicott, *Thomas of Lancaster*, pp. 114–15; J. R. S. Phillips, *Aymer de Valence, Earl of Pembroke: Baronial Politics in the Reign of Edward II* (Oxford, 1994), p. 19.
42 *CCR 1307–13*, p. 364.
43 *CPR 1313–17*, p. 21.
44 *C. Fine R. 1319–27*, p. 122.

45 *C. Inq. Misc. 1307–49*, p. 507.
46 J. Goronwy Edwards, 'Sir Gruffydd Llwyd', *EHR*, 30 (1915), 593–4.
47 W. Stubbs (ed.), *Chronicles of the Reigns of Edward I and Edward II*, vol. 2, Rolls Series (London, 1882), pp. 74–6; *CPR 1321–4*, pp. 395, 81; Maddicott, *Thomas of Lancaster*, pp. 309–12.
48 Maddicott, *Thomas of Lancaster*, p. 334. Michael Prestwich commented in *The Three Edwards*, p. 83, that 'the earl was neither temperamentally nor intellectually suited to the part that circumstances compelled him to play'.
49 *C. Fine R. 1319–27*, p. 102.
50 *CCR 1318–23*, p. 437.
51 *C. Charter R. 1300–26*, p. 448.
52 *Supra*, 39–41 (and also references to Iorwerth ap Llywarch on pp. 39, 41–2, 58, 73).
53 *CCR 1318–23*, p. 521.
54 *CCR*, p. 437.
55 *CPR 1321–4*, p. 137.
56 *C. Fine R. 1319–27*, p. 122.
57 *CPR 1324–7*, p. 354.
58 *CPR 1327–30*, p. 554.
59 *The Complete Peerage of England*, vol. 4, pp. 269–70.
60 *The Complete Peerage of England*, vol. 7, pp. 537–9; *C. Fine R, 1319–27*, p. 428; *C. Charter R. 1326–41*, p. 55; Charles Hopkinson and Martin Speight, *The Mortimers: Lords of the March* (Logaston, 2002), p. 95.
61 *CCR 1330–3*, p. 84.
62 *SD*, pp. 57, 62.
63 Colin A. Gresham, *Medieval Stone Carving in North Wales* (Cardiff, 1968), p. 153.
64 E. M. Thompson (ed.), *Chronicon Galfridi le Baker de Swynebroke* (Oxford, 1889), p. 47; Hopkinson and Speight, *The Mortimers*, pp. 104–6.
65 *C. Chart. R. 1326–41*, p. 199; G. A. Holmes, *The Estates of the Higher Nobility in Fourteenth-Century England* (Cambridge, 1957), p. 26, described his career as the 'most conspicuous case in the fourteenth century of a sudden rise to greatness by royal favour and patronage'.
66 *Chronicon Galfridi le Baker*, p. 47; R. Douch, 'The Career, Lands and Family of William Montagu, Earl of Salisbury, 1301–44', *Bulletin of the Institute of Historical Research*, 24/12 (May 1951), 85–6.
67 *CPR 1330–4*, p. 341.
68 *CCR 1333–7*, p. 120.
69 *CPR 1343–5*, p. 200.

4
ADMINISTRATION OF THE LORDSHIP, 1282–1334

The devolution of the lordship of Denbigh, as previously traced, involved several changes in possession. This chapter examines the nature of the administrative machinery thereby created, with an emphasis on the extent of the survival of features derived from the pre-conquest period, and the introduction of new elements as a result of the creation of the lordship. Throughout its history, it formed part of a large complex of lordships in England and Wales held by those members of the baronial families who were successively the lords of Denbigh. On its creation the administration of the lordship was efficiently organised by Henry de Lacy, earl of Lincoln, who was renowned as an able administrator, and the distinctive de Lacy system of accounting was introduced into the lordship. Accounts were rendered by local officials at Michaelmas to the financial centre at Denbigh, which, along with Clitheroe, Pontefract, Bolinbroke, Lincoln and Holborn, was one of the receiverships responsible for the collection of revenue and payment of local maintenance costs. Accounts were then scrutinised by the earl's auditors on a circuit of these receiverships. Changes in possession inevitably resulted in an adjustment of practices, but the basic administrative structure throughout the history of the lordship remained that which was created by the de Lacy officials in the years immediately following the creation of the lordship.[1]

On the establishment of the lordship, the *maerdref* of Dinbych – or Denbigh as it came to be known – was adopted as its administrative centre. The selection of Dinbych was evidently determined by its traditional position as the centre of the commote of Is Aled. The Chancellor's Roll for 1247–50 indicated that Dinbych, though not described as a manor, as were Ystrad and Dinorben, was a royal centre yielding a tallage render. The payment from Dinorben is unknown as the manuscript is defective, but it is surely significant that, whereas the manor of Ystrad contributed a sum of £2, a payment of £6 13s. 4d was rendered by Dinbych.[2]

The central administration of the lordship was located at the castle built at Denbigh in the twenty to thirty-year period immediately following 1282.[3] Detailed information relating to the castle at Denbigh was provided by two sixteenth-century sources. A survey compiled in the latter years of the reign of Henry VIII referred to the castle that had been 'beyld high upon a Rocke of Stone very stately and Bowtifully yn a very swete air', with a 'six square-shape' that 'hath at every square a strong tower'. The castle and accompanying borough were surrounded by 'a strong wall standing high'.[4] Humphrey Llwyd, writing in the late sixteenth century, stated that Henry de Lacy had erected 'a very stoute Castle' and a wall 'of wonderfull thicknesse, made of a very harde kinde of stone, in my opinion the strongest, and best defended thynge in England ... Addyng also therto, a towne walled about'.[5] Also, another sixteenth-century source referred to the involvement of 'Wilcok Pigod', the son of Sir Robin Pigot, as an architect in the reconstruction of Denbigh castle by the earl of Lincoln: 'Pensaer Iarll Lincol'.[6]

Five officials formed part of the central administration of the lordship based at the castle. Of these, the most important, as indicated by their annual salaries, were the steward, receiver and constable. The consistently higher payments to the steward clearly indicate his pre-eminence within the lordship administration, even though generally the authority of the steward in seignorial administration tended to diminish in the thirteenth century.[7] In 1305, the steward, received the highest payment of £13 6s. 8d, the constable was paid £10 and the receiver was awarded a payment of £6 3s. 4d.[8] This award of a higher payment to the constable than the receiver suggests that only ten years after the uprising led by Madog ap Llywelyn, military commitments were more pressing than financial considerations.

The office of steward, occupied in 1297 by John Blackburn[9] and in 1305 by John Midhop,[10] fulfilled functions similar to those of this officer in England, where the steward presided over the judicial aspects of the royal household.[11] His Welsh counterpart, the *distain*, was the predominant judicial and military officer in the thirteenth-century principality. He was also the principal commissariat officer, responsible for supplies, and under the thirteenth-century princes of Gwynedd, the office, which had become a hereditary possession of the Ednyfed Fychan family, was developed so that its holder was also the predominant judicial and military officer in the thirteenth-century principality.[12] Following the creation of the lordship of Denbigh, the steward was the principal judicial officer and, presiding over the various seignorial courts held throughout the lordship, he also fulfilled a general supervisory role in the administration.[13] In the immediate post-conquest period, he drew up accounts for the various manorial centres, together with a deputy who was directly responsible for the manor.

In 1297, John Blackburn, the steward, together with John Salusbury, accounted for Dinorben, and he was also associated, in the account for Denbigh, together with another deputy – or *serviens* – namely, Robert Ormerod.[14] In 1305, John Midhop, as steward, together with Robert de Holland, accounted for Dinorben, and with Juliana, the widow of the recently deceased Richard Simondston, for the manor of Denbigh.[15] These persons who occupied the central offices were often drawn from the leading settler families. John Blackburn, steward in 1297, was probably a member of the same family as Adam Blackburn, who in 1334 held by hereditary right 83 acres for 43s. in the 'Acre' of Lleweni.[16] Also, Thomas Pontefract, receiver in 1297 and 1305, belonged to one of the most prominent settler families in the lordship, with property occupied by members of this family in four of the lordship's five commotes: the Park of Segrwyd in Ceinmeirch; the Acre and Park of Lleweni, township of Alltfaenan and hamlet of 'Bronskip' in Is Aled; the townships of Cilcedig and Hendregyda, hamlet of Maerdref and borough of Abergele in Is Dulas; and township of Penmaen in Uwch Dulas.[17]

The recipient of the second highest salary in 1305 was Marmeduke Clifford, constable of Denbigh castle, and he was responsible for both the military garrison and the castle economy.[18] William Curteys, another member of a prominent settler family, was named as the constable in an undated deed, compiled in the early fourteenth century, while the witnesses included John Salusbury and Thomas Hilton.[19] A later document, dated in 1361, referred to the constable of Denbigh being also the mayor of this town, and specified certain rights attached to this office.[20] Whereas the constable was evidently responsible for similar functions to those of his counterpart in the Principality of North Wales, the duties of the receiver, whose status in the lordship gradually increased as the century progressed, corresponded to those of the Justice and Chamberlain in the Principalities of North and South Wales.[21]

The receiver compiled his account annually, and this both informed the central administration that the lord's rights and lands were yielding maximum income and also allocated responsibility for income and expenditure.[22] On the credit side, after the arrears had been indicated, the anticipated revenue from rents was listed. This consisted of customary renders from the clan lands and payments of rents from individual plots of land that were held at farm: *ad firmam*. Each township, in the five commotes, was accounted for, and a similar order was adopted to that found in the Survey of Denbigh.

Two other officials also associated with the central administration were the escheator and master forester. The 1305 account[23] referred to the escheator, and a number of his accounts have survived from the late fourteenth century. This official assumed responsibility for lands vacated as a result of deaths or escheat, and accounted for them. No evidence survives to define the duties of the master forester, an office occupied throughout this period, and it is therefore difficult to determine the extent of his jurisdiction over the forests of the lordship, which seem to have previously been the property of the Welsh princes. The office was occupied throughout this period, and while the amount of his salary may be gleaned, the relevant sources of income included traditional forest dues such as *pastus ii forestariarum* and sales of wood.[24] This office, again, had been held in the pre-conquest period, and the 1334 Survey recorded that the princes of Gwynedd had been in possession of the woods of Ysgaerwen and Coedrochwyn, in Ceinmeirch, while le Graba, in Is Aled, was described as a '*boscus separabilis Principis*' ('a separate wood of the prince').[25]

There was clearly a considerable degree of survival of pre-conquest features in local government, where the most important unit had traditionally been the commote.[26] Reference has already been made to the administration of the *cantrefi* of Rhos and Rhufoniog in the thirteenth century, and after the creation of the lordship of Denbigh, the five constituent commotes, that is Is Dulas and Uwch Dulas in the *cantref* of Rhos, and Is Aled, Uwch Aled and Ceinmeirch, in the *cantref* of Rhufoniog, together with Dinmael, continued to function as effective units of government. The commote court seems to have been the basic judicial institution, and the continued operation of the commote, after the creation of the lordship, represented the survival of a significant element of the traditional pre-conquest administrative framework.[27]

A limited amount of information relating to the administration of the commote in the post-conquest period appeared in the de Lacy rolls of 1297 and 1305, but further details were provided in the extent[28] and view of account[29] compiled in 1331. Payments made by various commotal officials were listed in the extent, while the view of account, compiled mid-way through the financial year, provided more detailed information concerning the sources of these payments. Various local offices were recorded as having been farmed out, with five officials named in each commote; the raglot (or *rhaglaw*); ringild (or *rhingyll*); sergeant of the peace; raglot a*dvocariae*; and i*udex*. It is difficult to determine the activities of the *iudex*, whose name was normally not provided, but the duties of this official probably corresponded to those of the Welsh y*nad* ('legal official'), and, serving in all five commotes of the lordship in the days of the native princes, as well as in 1334, he may well have been responsible for interpreting Welsh law in the commote court.[30]

The payments of the sergeant of the peace and raglot a*dvocariae* of Is Aled appeared in the account of the ringild of Is Aled, and the association of the officials of these commotes was clearly related to the establishment of an Englishry in this locality.[31] These entries in the accounts reflect the relative value of the commotal offices. In 1331,[32] and in the succeeding period, the highest payment was for the office of raglot, and indicates that he was the pre-eminent official in the commote, as indeed the *rhaglaw* had been in the pre-conquest period.[33] The continued employment of this official after the establishment of the lordship emphasised a conservative aspect of post-conquest policy. No precise definition of the raglot's functions was provided but relevant information is provided from other areas in Wales. The survey of the nearby lordship of Bromfield and Yale, compiled in 1315, stated that the raglot's duties included the levying of rents and execution of summonses and arrests, and the raglot in Flintshire was considered to be 'probably the most powerful Welsh official in the county'.[34] His pre-conquest counterpart in north Ceredigion has been described as 'the lord's principal representative in the commote', and in the period immediately following the conquest the former *rhaglaw* has been considered to have 'survived as the new bailiff'.[35]

The raglot was assisted in his judicial work by the ringild, who, serving as the financial officer of the commote, presented annually at Michaelmas a financial account to the receiver. In some districts in north Wales, this official was in a predominant position, but in the lordship of Denbigh the details of payments to officials emphasised the supremacy of the raglot.[36] Valuable information relating to the officials listed in the 1331 view of account is provided by the 1334 Survey, and it is evident that some of these seem to have been prominent individuals within their community. Gruffudd Fychan, ringild of Uwch Aled in 1331, occupied, in 1334, 29 acres and one rood in the townships of Gwytherin, Talhaearn and Arllwyd; and his counterpart, in 1331, as ringild of Is Dulas, Bleddyn ap Philip, held in 1334 ten plots amounting to 7 acres, half a rood and 16 perches in Abergele, and also, together with his brothers Ieuan and Llywelyn, and nine other clansmen, two-and-a-half of the four *Gafaelion* Gwilym ap Doyok.[37]

Whereas the raglots and ringilds were generally the most important officials in the commote, the sergeants of the peace also played a significant role, and the popularity of this office may be associated with the possibility of extortion involved in its peace-keeping functions.[38] The two other commotal offices generally farmed out were those of raglot *advocariae* and *amobr*. The raglot *advocariae* supervised the affairs of bondmen who entered the lordship from other areas, and the tenure of this office by person with Welsh names suggests that the tenants responsible to him were invariably Welshmen.[39] The history of the *amobr* payment extended back to the pre-conquest period and has been defined as a 'fine for fornication and as a render upon marriage'. Profits from the *amobr* payment were often farmed out in this lordship with a specific official, the *amobrager*, responsible for its collection.[40] Another official of the commote was the woodward, responsible to the forementioned master forester.[41] The woodward of Is Dulas in 1331, Tudur ap Gronw, held in 1334 together with Gronw ap Hywel, 29 acres at a rent of 16s. 8¾d, and, together with Gruffudd ap Hywe,l a watermill valued at £1 2s. – both possessions located in the hamlet of 'Bodeluennan'.[42]

Whereas the continued activity of these commotal officers represented the survival of administrative procedures dating back to the period before the creation of the lordship of Denbigh, officials introduced after 1282 included the bailiffs of the newly created boroughs of Denbigh and Abergele,[43] and the bailiff for the Englishry: the *ballivus Anglicorum*; who was responsible for the administration of the Englishry of the lordship. His accounts referred to profits from the courts of the Englishry, for which he was responsible. All the English tenants in the commotes of Ceinmeirch and Is Aled might be summoned to this court, which was described as the court held for English persons – *curia tenens inter Anglicos*. Another name used to denote this official was *ballivus itinerans inter Anglicos* ('the itinerant bailiff among the English persons').[44]

Another innovation in the local administration resulted from the establishment of six parks in the lordship: at Kilford and Postin, in Ceinmeirch; and Garsnodiog, Galghull, Castle Park and Moel-y-wig in Is Aled. The latter three, situated near to the castle of Denbigh, were enclosed by a fence and ditch, with Galghull comprising 62 acres, Castlepark 264 acres and the largest one being the 442-acre Moel-y-wig.[45] Each park was individually managed by a parker, who was responsible for maintenance costs within the park, disposing of the proceeds of the parks, and also for handing over actual profits to the receiver. This office again, without exception, was held by persons with an English background.

Notes

1 J. F. Baldwin, 'The Household Administration of Henry de Lacy and Thomas Lancaster', *EHR*, 42 (1927), 182.

2 TNA E 352/43. The text of this roll has been published in Roderick, 'The Four Cantreds', 255–6.

3 A. J. Taylor, 'The King's Works in Wales 1277–1330', in H. M. Colvin, *The History of the King's Works, volume 1: The Middle Ages* (London, 1963), pp. 333–4; and A. J. Taylor, *The Welsh Castles of Edward I* (London, 1986), pp. 46–7. Taylor pointed out the connection between 'the king's works, properly so called, and similar works carried out by feudatories from the resources of their lordship in the furtherance of royal policy'; see also Chapter 3, n. 21.

4   TNA, LR 2/242, see also the plan of Denbigh included in John Speed, *The Theatre of the Empire of Great Britain* (1610), which has been reproduced as Appendix 7.
5   Humphrey Llwyd, *The Breviary of Britayne … written in Latin and lately published by Thomas Twyne, Gentleman* (1573), f. 66v; Humphrey Llwyd, '*The Breviary of Britain*' *with selections from 'The History of Cambria*', ed. by Philip Schwyzer (London, 2011), p. 114; see also the discussion on the borough of Denbigh in Chapter 7.
6   Peter C. Bartrum (ed.), *Welsh Genealogies, AD 1400–1500*, IX, O-Sandde (Aberystwyth, 1983), p. 1447.
7   N. Denholm-Young, *Seignorial Administration in England* (London, 1937), pp. 68–9, stated that, generally, the authority of the steward, in seignorial administration, tended to diminish in the thirteenth century.
8   TNA DL 29/1/1; DL 29/1/2.
9   TNA DL 29/1/1.
10 TNA DL 29/1/2.
11 T. F. Tout, *Chapters in the Administrative History of Medieval England*, vol. 2 (Manchester, 1920–3), p. 33. A wide-ranging discussion on the dispensation of justice in the Welsh March is provided in R. R. Davies, *Lordship and Society in the March of Wales 1284–1400* (Oxford, 1978), pp. 149–75.
12 Stephenson, *Political Power*, p. 11, described the distain as 'the principal servant of the thirteenth-century princes'; also pp. 11–20. For further information on the duties of this official is provided by Glyn Roberts, 'Wyrion Eden, The Anglesey Descendants of Ednyfed Fychan', in *Aspects of Welsh History* (Cardiff, 1969), pp. 179–84.
13 The predominance of the steward in the lordship contrasted to the position in the Principality of Wales where the important central officers were the justiciar and chamberlain; for north Wales, see Lewis, *Medieval Boroughs*, p. 147; and Waters, *Edwardian Settlement*, pp. 33–4, 89–90; and for south Wales, see Ralph A. Griffiths, *The Principality of Wales in the Later Middle Ages: The Structure and Personnel of Government, volume 1: South Wales 1277–1536* (Cardiff, 1972, 2018), pp. 19–45, 91–192.
14 TNA DL 29/1/1.
15 TNA DL 29/1/2.
16 *SD*, p. 65.
17 *SD*, pp. 13, 64, 65, 86, 88, 226, 232, 235, 252, 23, 254, 317.
18 TNA DL 29/1; 29/2.
19 NLW, Aston Hall, 5260.
20 Register of the Black Prince, 405, n.34.
21 See note 13 above.
22 R. H. Hilton, *Ministers' Accounts of the Warwickshire Estates of the Duke of Clarence* (Oxford, 1952), p. xii.
23 TNA DL 29/1/2. The escheator made his first appearance in the Principality of North Wales in 1306 (Waters, *Edwardian Settlement*, pp. 43–4) and in the Principality of South Wales in 1323 (Griffiths, *Principality of Wales*, p. 55).

24 Rees, *South Wales and the March*, p. 112, stated that 'The whole of the business affairs of the forest was in the hands of the forester'.
25 *SD*, pp. 87–8.
26 Lloyd, *History of Wales*, vol. 2, p. 221 when discussing the commote and *cantref*, stated that 'in the laws it is the commote which appears as the living and active body', while J. G. Edwards, 'The Normans and the Welsh March', p. 169, emphasised that the commote represented not only land but also lordship.
27 *Infra*, pp. 51–3.
28 TNA E 142/3.
29 TNA SC 6/1182/1.
30 *CWR*, p. 196: Ifor ap Tegwared of Tegeingl (Englefield) who gave evidence at Rhuddlan in 1281, was described as being called in Welsh 'Eynat' and in Latin 'iudex'; *SD*, pp. 48, 152, 209, 270, 314; T. Jones Pierce, 'The Age of the Princes', in *Medieval Welsh Society*, ed. by J. Beverley Smith (Cardiff, 1972), pp. 34–5; T. Jones Pierce, 'Bardsey: A study in monastic origins', *Ibid.*, p. 379, n. 34, 382–3, 405; Stephenson, *Political Power*, p. 78; R. R. Davies, 'The administration of law in medieval Wales, the role of the *ynad cwmwd* (*iudex patrie*), in T. M. Charles-Edwards, Morfydd E. Owen and D. B. Walters (eds), *Lawyers and Laymen: Studies in the History of Law presented to Professor Dafydd Jenkins on his seventy-fifth birthday* (Cardiff, 1986), p. 263.
31 *Infra*, pp. 58, 74, 78–9, 83–92, 97.
32 TNA SC 6/1182/1.
33 Jones Pierce, *Medieval Welsh Society*, pp. 32, 39, 356.
34 N. Neilson, 'Officers and Agents', Introduction, *Survey of Denbigh*, pp. lxxv–lxxvii. In discussing the raglot's duties, Miss Neilson used the evidence of a document relating to the lordship of Bromfield and Yale, and printed in the Introduction to the *Record of Caernarvon*, R. Ellis (ed.), *Registrum vulgariter nuncupatum, 'The record of Caernarvon'*, Record Commission (London, 1838), p. xi; Arthur Jones (ed.), *Flintshire Ministers Accounts 1301–29*, Flintshire Historical Society Record Series, vol. 3 (1913), p. xxxv.
35 Griffiths, *The Principality of Wales*, pp. 59–60.
36 A. N. Palmer and E. Owen, *A History of Ancient Tenures of Land in North Wales and the Marches* (Printed Privately, 1910), p. 194; TNA SC 6/1182/1.
37 TNA SC 6/1182/1; *SD*, pp. 191, 193, 207, 245–6, 257.
38 *Flintshire Ministers Accounts*, pp. xlvi–xlvii.
39 See *Flintshire Ministers Accounts*, pp. xxxii–xxxiii for reference to tendency for Welshmen to serve as *raglot advocariae* in Flintshire.
40 *Flintshire Ministers Accounts*, pp. xviii–xx; Rees, *South Wales and the March*, pp. 236–7. For an account of the activities of this official in the Principality, see Stephenson, *Political Power*, p. 78.
41 *Infra*, pp. 50–1.
42 TNA SC 6/1182/1; *SD*, p. 259.
43 *Infra*, p. 53.
44 *Infra*, pp. 53–4, 213–14.
45 *SD*, p. 51.

5

SOCIETY AND ECONOMY 1282–1334: SEIGNEURIAL REVENUE, ESCHEAT AND EXCHANGE

The 1334 Survey again represents an extremely important source providing information on the society and economy of this area in the period 1282–1334, as was also the case for the preceding period.[1] This supplements the data provided in a series of financial documents, with the earliest one, the 1297 account concerned mainly with activities at the manorial centres.[2] The counterpart for 1305 included the accounts of the escheator and receiver, but unfortunately in this account entries for the commotes of Is Aled, Uwch Aled and Is Dulas were blurred and difficulties were thereby experienced in reading certain sections.[3] Therefore, apart from the *Summa Totalis Recepta* – that is, the total charge – only the evidence for Ceinmeirch and Uwch Dulas has been used for comparison with later data. The Montague rental compiled in 1330[4] differed only slightly from the 1334 Survey, and a view of account, drawn up in 1331, represented a half-yearly summary of the condition of the economy of the lordship.[5] Another valuable source is the *History of the Gwydir Family*,[6] written soon after 1580 by Sir John Wynn whose home, Gwydir, was located in the Conwy valley in the immediate neighbourhood of the western areas of the lordship of Denbigh. Its references to the lordship, together with the information contained in the accounts listed above, have been set against the wealth of information contained in the comprehensive 1334 Survey.

Hugh Buckley, the extentor responsible for the Survey of Denbigh, assiduously listed every possible source of revenue, and the total revenue, specified at the end of the entries for each commote, was followed by a statement of possible increments, provided that other sources were developed. Therefore, the possible revenue derived from each commote, with the potential increment provided in brackets, ranged from Is Aled at £394 17s. 6¼d (+ £34 11s. 9½d)[7] to Uwch Aled at £139 11s. 9½d (+ £20 14s. 1d),[8] with payments of £244 4s. 7¾d (+ £23 12s. 11¼d); £199 3s. 2d (+ £17 8s. 11d); and £150 2s. 10½d (+ £11 19s. 3d) respectively recorded for Ceinmeirch,[9] Is Dulas[10] and Uwch Dulas.[11] Also, nearly every herbage entry recorded both the current and potential revenue, and therefore the statement in the entry for Garthserwyd, that a herbage rent of 1s. 8d was rendered annually, was accompanied by the comment that this could possibly be increased to 10s. 5½d.[12] The provision of this information reflected the administration's determination to extract as much revenue as possible, and this policy, which had evidently been adopted when the lordship was established, followed the pattern established in the other lands held by the earl of Lincoln.[13]

A significant distinction may be observed between the policy adopted in the lordship of Denbigh and that of other constituent parts of the Lincoln possessions. This was the adoption on the lands in Wales of a social policy, with the creation within the lordship of an 'Englishry', that is, a zone of English settlement and influence.[14] The adoption of this policy may be explained by political motives, with the administrative centre and its neighbourhood being colonised by English settlers whose loyalty could be guaranteed. The earl of Lincoln was enabled by this inexpensive method to reward his troops, and also prominent members of the local Welsh community, such as Iorwerth ap Llywarch, were granted lands as a reward for rendering services to their lord.[15] This social policy ran counter to the purely economic aim of exploitation, and the interaction of these apparently contradictory motives may be illustrated by an examination of the economy and society of the lordship in this period.

The seigneurial revenue seems to have fallen in the period 1305-31, and difficulties also appear to have been experienced by the four manors of the lordship. Information has already been provided on the early history of the two manors of Dinorben Fawr and Ystrad Owain, whose history extended back to the period before the creation of the lordship of Denbigh.[16] Following the conquest, an increase may be observed in the revenue for which accounts were rendered for the manor of Dinorben Fawr. In 1297, it was expected that £10 15s. 4d would be collected, while expenses amounted to £11 0s. 7d., whereas by 1305 manorial receipts were charged at £80 1s. 8d, while the total anticipated revenue was as high as £95 11s. 6¾d. This represented a remarkable increase of nearly nine times the amount expected in 1297.

While one should be aware that the 1305 amount might have been exaggerated by the reference to arrears of £15 9s. 10¾d and a debit balance of £19 18s. 4¾d, it is evident that the period 1297–1305 had witnessed a considerable increase in the scope of manorial activities at Dinorben Fawr, with substantial revenues accruing from the sale of wheat and oats.[17] It is true that the 1331 account referred to Dinorben Fawr and Ystrad Owain not being farmed as the goods of the manor had been sold: *eo quod fructum dictorum manerii vendebantur*,[18] but a similar statement was not included in the 1334 Survey, which revealed that a certain amount of demesne farming continued to be practised at Dinorben Fawr that year, with the manor being valued at £24 10s. 7¾d.[19]

Arable land here was described as being cultivated in three seasons, with both the meadow and pasture recorded as being held in demesne. The detailed survey of the manor in 1334 recorded that 201 local acres (255 statute acres) of demesne arable land had been converted into three seasons, comprising 67 acres and 15 perches in the first season, 64 acres, 1 rood and 30 perches in the second season and 69.5 acres and 31 perches in the third season. The reference to the revenue derived from individual plots of land, together with the extentor's concentration on the value of arable, meadow and pasture land, signifies that by 1334 Dinorben Fawr was considered to be primarily a rent-contributing unit, rather than as a centre for demesne agriculture. This impression is also confirmed by references to the partly dilapidated condition of the manor. Whereas one grange was considered to be satisfactory ('competens'), the other one was described as completely destroyed apart from a large wood ('*penitus vastata preter grossum maeremium*'). An attached house was considered to be frail ('debilis') and the associated dovecot as being ruined ('ruinosum'). These descriptions clearly suggest that in 1334, the manor of Dinorben Fawr, although still functioning, was in a state of decline.[20]

By 1334, the bondmen of the townships of Meifod, Cegidog and Dinorben Fechan who had previously undertaken various duties at the *maerdref* of Dinorben, paid a cash rent instead of the traditional ploughing and harrowing duties. The evidence of the survey suggests that as the forty-four bondmen possessed between them only nine ploughs they would have to practice co-aration.[21] Also, the bond tenants of nearby Talgarth, who had previously undertaken the services of half a plough team, seem to have left the township which by 1334 was vacant for lack of tenants, with the pasture subsequently grazed by the sheep of the manor of Dinorben Fawr.[22] A development of drainage work may well explain the contrast between the 120 acres of arable demesne specified in 1311 and the far higher amount recorded in 1334, with an extension from the more desirable brown earths below the limestone ridge northwards, on to more imperfectly drained brown soils.[23] The lack of balance between oats and wheat in the 1305 account indicated an imperfect rotation that year and the later extension of arable lands may well have been responsible for the three-season organisation recorded in 1334.[24]

With regard to Ystrad Owain, the other pre-conquest manor, the de Lacy accounts are less informative. The 1305 account referred to the farm of 268 acres for £8 18s. 8d, and payments of 4¾d for the services of freemen and 6s. 9d for the labour of fifty-four bondmen on the demesne of Ystrad.[25] By 1331, no account was provided for the farm of the manor because, as in Dinorben, its goods had been sold. A sum of 3s. 6d was rendered for the various works – *diversis operibus* – of two bondmen, and this represents a significant comment on the decline of demesne agrarian activities at Ystrad Owain.[26] In 1334, following the accounts for the capital messuage, arable land, demesne meadow, rented land and court profits, it was recorded that the total value of the manor amounted to £11 19s. 9½d. This entry, in contrast to that for Dinorben Fawr, contained a reference to a home farm, and capital messsuage containing two granges, a cow house, sheep fold and manor court, which was valued at 10s. 4d.[27] A comparison of the evidence of the 1305 and 1331 accounts and the 1334 Survey suggest that there was also a certain degree of deterioration in Ystrad Owain.

The 1331 account differentiated between, on the one hand, Dinorben Fawr and Ystrad Owain, and, on the other hand, the two recently established manors of Denbigh and Kilford. Whereas Dinorben Fawr and Ystrad Owain seem to have been in a state of decline, the cultivation of the demesne in the other two manors had evidently ceased. These two locations, established in the post-conquest period, seem to have been unable to weather the difficulties that had also adversely affected the two older centres. The manorial revenue expected to be collected in Denbigh, between 1297 and 1305, fell from £67 4s. 6d to £54 3s. 0d ¾d, while expenses fell from £78 7s. 11d to £58 5s. 8¾d.[28] In 1331, the manor was farmed for £5 6s. 8d, while in 1334 it was valued at £ 6 7s. ½d., which represented an increase of £1 0s. 4½d.[29] A similar trend may also be observed in the other new manor that was established at Kilford from lands that escheated in the townships of Cilffwrn, Llwyn and Ystrad Cynon. The 1334 Survey stated explicitly that the manor was established in the post-conquest period,[30] and although not mentioned in the 1297 account, it could be contended that it may possibly have been founded before this date, especially as there was no reference in this account to the manor of Ystrad Owain, a pre-conquest foundation. In fact, the 1305 account suggests that at this time the manor of Kilford was well-established and in fact may well have been the most highly developed of the lordship's four manorial centres. Manorial receipts expected to be collected amounted to £152 0s. 3½d and expenses to £121 4s. 7½d, and a strong impression is conveyed that the manor of Kilford had been created in the immediate post-conquest period, rather than in the period 1297–1305.[31]

By 1331, however, Kilford, following a similar trend to Denbigh; it was farmed out,[32] while the 1334 Survey valued the manor at £48 12s. 2½d. Its total acreage of 886 acres consisted of 239 acres of arable land, 240 acres of meadow, 248 acres of pasture and 159 acres of rented demesne land, while the messuage here again contained two granges and a cow house, in addition to a bakery, dovecote and room for the bailiff. This entry for Kilford is characterised by the frequent use of the adjective 'debilis' ('barren') in the references to the dovecot and upland pasture (*ffridd*) and suggest the dilapidated condition of the manor, which is also reflected by the reference to the 'alnetis' ('alder tree') often found in cultivated land allowed to run to waste.[33] There was also a noticeable absence of any reference to repair work, and it is probable that variants of the three-field system were in operation at Kilford and at Dinorben Fawr.[34]

In addition to the four manorial centres mentioned in the survey, the 1297 account referred to a *manerium* at Wigfair. However, the 1305 account did not mention Wigfair as a manor, and it is probable that by this date the intention to maintain a second manor in Is Dulas had been abandoned.[35] It is therefore significant that the entry for Wigfair in the 1334 Survey, with its detailed list of clan and farmed-land tenures, contained no reference to a manor,[36] and this omission is a significant comment on the evident failure of the attempted development suggested by the 1297 account. The probable abandonment of a manorial enterprise at Wigfair by 1334 suggests that this may possibly be explained by the increases in the entry for Dinorben Fawr.

The fluctuating fortunes of the four manors illustrate a degree of financial difficulties in the lordship, and the accompanying strain imposed on the inhabitants of the lordship was compounded by the policy of total commutation of dues with a considerable acceleration of the process set in motion in the pre-conquest period. The areas least affected before 1282 were now subjected to the greatest degree of change, but these regional variations, although informative with regard to the varying impact of the post-conquest policy, should not blind us to the tremendous general impact of total commutation on the inhabitants of all five commotes. Moreover, whereas previously the level of commutation had been higher among free than bond units, the impact of widespread post-conquest commutation was greater on the bond kindred groupings. Commutation had been exerted to a considerable degree among certain freemen, whereas *twnc* and *treth*, and the continuation of this privilege in the post-conquest period emphasised a degree of continuity in the social life of the area, and also the possible assistance provided by these clans to the newly established regime.[37]

While *treth* has been claimed to have constituted a secondary stage of commutation for free kindreds, *ardreth* seems to have represented a similar process for bond groupings. The new administration seems to have sought to extend the scope of a commutation device that it had inherited when the lordship was established.[38] The entry for Nant dinhengroen, in the commote of Is Dulas, referred to the free Gafael Cad' ap Tegwared being held by the lord because of the failure to render *ardreth* since the time of the earl of Lincoln – '*pro diffyk Ardreth a tempore Comitis Lyncolnie*' – and also part of the half *gafael* that had belonged to Dafydd ap Tegwared that had been transferred to the lord for the same reason – '*pro defectu … amobr a tempore Comitis Lincolnie*' ('for the failure to pay *amobr* since the time of the earl of Lincoln').[39] A more intriguing situation may be observed in Penporchell, where the free tenants of Gafael Ithon paid 10d for *twnc* and 2s. for *ardreth*. The other free unit of Penporchell was the half Gafael Rhys Grŷg, whose services, rendered at Alltfaenan, revealed an initial commutation of 12.9 per cent. An air of unreality, however, surrounds the position of Gafael Ithon, and here *ardreth* might possibly stand for a post-conquest grant to a favoured family, and thereby represent another means by which the administration sought to implement and develop those 'extra-tribal' elements that had emerged in this area before 1282.[40]

Whereas the policies of the post-conquest administration towards commutation reflected its intention to fully exploit the available financial resources, it also pursued a social policy whereby a zone of English settlement and influence was established in the lordship. In addition to the clearing of wastelands, land was acquired by means of the operation of escheat and the resettlement of local inhabitants. Territory formerly occupied by kindred groupings was divided into individual plots of land and offered to immigrant English families on favourable terms. The political motivation for this policy ensured that the administrative centre of the lordship would be inhabited by settlers whose allegiance to the new regime could be guaranteed, and the process of escheat that accompanied the conquest facilitated the creation of a cohesive English colony.

There were frequent references in the 1334 Survey to the operation of escheat, but an analysis of the escheat entries represents a difficult task. In most townships escheat is stated to have occurred partly because of rebellion and partly on account of an inability to render services. Eleven-and-a-half of the twenty-two-and-a-half townships in the township of Segrwyd escheated partly because of deaths resulting from actions against the peace and partly because of a failure to render services – *partim racione mortuorum contra pacem et partem pro defectu serviciorum*.[41] Of these, only a minority of entries specified the actual cause of escheat. Various entries in Ceinmeirch referring to land escheating on account of deaths against the peace reveal that there was a considerable upheaval in this commote in the period leading up to and following the foundation of the lordship. Royal armies passed through territory that would later form the lordship during the campaigns of 1277 and 1282–3.[42] Inhabitants of the lordship also participated in the revolt of 1294, and again a royal army marched through the lordship.⁴³ Whereas the extent of escheat fluctuated in the five commotes, with a high ratio of 64.9 per cent recorded in Rhiw, in Uwch Dulas,⁴⁴ the ratio was generally higher in the two commotes of Ceinmeirch and Is Aled than in the other three: this suggests that administrative control and an accompanying social re-organisation had been exerted more thoroughly in these two commotes, which were located in the immediate vicinity of the castle of Denbigh, the administrative centre of the lordship.

A consistent feature was the higher level of escheat among bond units in those mixed townships that contained both free and bond clan groupings. In Galltfaenan, where 75.8 per cent of the bond units and only 13.3 per cent of the free units had escheated, a similar trend may be observed in the townships of Ereifiad (75.4 per cent of the bond units, and 41.7 per cent of the free units); Berain (82.1 per cent of the bond units and 25 per cent of the free units); Wigfair (60 per cent of the bond units and 35.2 per cent of the free units); and Nant dinhengroen (70.8 per cent of the bond units and 21.2 per cent of the free units).⁴⁵ The post-conquest administration, seeking to promote a social re-organisation within the lordship, exerted far greater pressure on bond than free kindred groupings, and the latter were often induced to move to other townships following the grant of lands in exchange for their hereditary holdings. There was also a comparatively high level of escheat among certain leading free groups in the lordship, and the following two examples indicate the divided loyalties of leading kindreds in this period. In Brynffanugl, 50 per cent of the holdings of members of the 'Wyrion Eden' clan, who seem to have co-operated with the post-conquest administration, escheated to the lord.⁴⁶ Similarly, 41.7 per cent of Ystrad Cynon, held exclusively by another prominent grouping, that of Cynon ap Llywarch, escheated as a result of tenants who had died because of activities against the peace – '*racione tenencium qui obierunt contra pacem*'.⁴⁷

Fluctuations in the level of escheat also throw light on policies designed to radically modify the social and tenurial framework of the lordship. In this respect, the comparatively low escheat percentage of 24.8 per cent in the township of Dinbych ('*Denbigh*') is of particular interest, with the probable explanation being the central location of this bond township, which became the focal point of the lordship.[48] The low ratio probably refers to the lands of those who opposed the royal army in 1282 and that afterwards the township was largely undisturbed by internal upheaval. An examination of the escheat figures for other townships in the neighbourhood of Denbigh reveals a considerable degree of fluctuation. Ystrad Cynon had an escheat ratio of 41.7 per cent, its hamlet Bodeiliog one of 30.1 per cent and that of Llwyn, in the commote of Ceinmeirch, was as low as 25 per cent.[49] This evidence seems to suggest that it was these townships, near to the castle of Denbigh, the ancient *maerdrefi* of Ystrad Owain and Dinbych, and the recently established manor at Kilford, that experienced the initial stages of the social re-organisation that was introduced into the lordship after 1282. Greater difficulty was evidently encountered in the application of this policy in neighbouring townships, which also came to be incorporated in the Englishry: the escheat ratio of Lleweni stood at 75.9 per cent, Ereifiad at 60.2 per cent and Gwenynog Wyntus at 85.4 per cent.[50] It is therefore surely significant that the level of escheat was generally low in the immediate vicinity of Denbigh on account of the comparative ease of maintaining order here, and also in comparatively remote Uwch Dulas, which the administration possibly found more difficult to subdue. Contradictory factors may therefore have been responsible for identical patterns of escheat ratios.

One of the reasons for the escheat of land was involvement in rebellion, which resulted in deaths against the peace: *mortuorum contra pacem*. Participation in hostile military action could have occurred during the campaigns of 1277, 1282–3 or 1294–5, and the frequency of *contra pacem* entries reflects the dislocation caused in this area by military hostilities. While it is impossible to determine the precise date when the land escheated for this reason, a tentative attempt may be made to relate the incidence of escheat to the routes of the royal armies in this area. The 1282 route from Denbigh to Dolwyddelan passed near to the townships of Deunant and Caledan, and the escheat figures for these townships, at 18.8 per cent and 5 per cent,[51] respectively, are among the lowest for the commote of Uwch Aled. These low percentages may reflect a lack of opposition in the townships through which the royal armies passed and even possibly a successful bid by the invaders to gain local support. On the other hand, the escheat percentages for the bond townships of Ceinmeirch suggest that proximity to the path of the royal army occasioned a high level of escheat. Purely economic forces were also responsible for the escheat of land, but yet it is surely significant that the highest figures of 62.1 per cent and 62 per cent prevailed in Postyn and Llewesog,[52] which were the two townships nearest in location to the route of the 1294 army. The upheaval in these two townships suggest that the royal army may well have encountered considerable opposition from local inhabitants resentful of policies adopted by the new regime. However, absence of concrete evidence prevents these possibilities from being advanced in stronger terms than as speculations.

One is on firmer ground when discussing the re-settlement of local families that accompanied the escheat of land. While escheat could be applied only when tenants had committed an offence or had failed to render their dues, the administration employed another method – namely, re-settlement – to circumvent these restrictions. Local inhabitants were often granted lands in other townships *in lieu* of their original holdings. References to this policy of land exchange are less extensive than those of escheat, and are concentrated mainly in the commote of Is Aled, but with several examples in Ceinmeirch and Uwch Aled.

Sgeibion, in the commote of Ceiknmeirch, was divided in 1334 into ninety-eight plots comprising six 'tyddyns', one 'placea' and 677 acres held by thirty-four Welsh and forty-four English tenants.

One half of this township had escheated to the lord because of deaths against the peace – *ratione mortuorum contra pacem* – with the other half passing into the lord's hands as a result of granting to Dafydd ap Gruffudd ap Caradog 167.5 acres in exchange in the townships of Mathebrwd and Trebwll, in the commote of Uwch Dulas.[53] Further information on this transaction was provided by Sir John Wynn in his *History of the Gwydir Family*, whose account of relevant activities in the area that later formed the lordship of Denbigh has been outlined previously.[54] The descendants of the forementioned Gruffudd ap Rhodri were stated to have been 'large possessors in Denbighland called Rhos and Rhufoniog, near and about Denbigh castle, in the chiefest and best part of the same', while Rhodri's great grandson, Gruffudd ap Caradog, was named by Wynn as the lord of 'Ystrad, Ysgeibion and of other great possessions in Rhos and `Rhufoniog'. Wynn then stated that, following the creation of the lordship of Denbigh in 1282, Henry de Lacy, earl of Lincoln:

> minding to make a princely seat of the castle of Denbigh, perforce compelled the children of the said Dafydd ap Gruffudd to exchange their possessions about Denbigh castle (which were great) with him for other land of less value in the said lordship in the furthest part from him.[55]

Escheated lands, in this case, were granted in a distant commote, yet a similar motive underlay the administration's policy of granting escheat lands to displaced Welsh tenants in order that entire townships, where there had already been an element of escheat, were not divided anew into individual plots of land. The fact that these two instances represented the only examples of land being granted in exchange in Ceinmeirch may possibly be explained by the presence in this commote of large bond townships, and it is therefore significant that they were found in townships occupied by free kindred groupings.

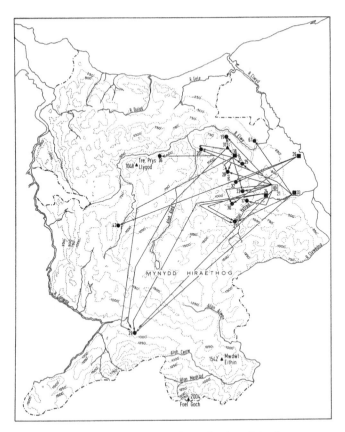

Figure 4: The dispersal of the Welsh population at the time of the Conquest

The policy of granting land, in exchange, was applied mainly in the commote of Is Aled, with the administration succeeding here in exerting complete control over the townships of Denbigh, Lleweni, Ystrad Cynon, Gwenynog Cynon and Berain. In Denbigh, the total level of escheat was only 24.8 per cent, and the crucial factor here was re-settlement. Bond and free clansmen were granted lands in the neighbouring townships of Ereifiad, Bodeiliog, Penporchell, Tywysog and Taldrach, and also the more distant townships of Bodysgawen and Prŷs.[56] On the whole, it is difficult to trace the fortunes of the dispossessed persons, for the new holdings were usually contained in a compound entry, as in Ereifiad, where it was stated that 645 acres were granted in exchange to the tenants of Denbigh, Lleweni, Ystrad Cynon and Berain.[57] However, some individuals also received plots of land in the townships where they had been recently settled and a study of the individual entries reveals the position of some of the dispossessed individuals. Dafydd ap Bleddyn Saer, who had held at Denbigh a third of half a *gafael* in '*tir prid*', was granted in Bodysgawen 6 acres of the land of Ednyfed ap Einion – '*de terra Eden ap Eign*' – at an annual rent of 4s.[58]

In the other townships that passed completely into the lord's hands, the level of escheat was higher than in Denbigh. In Ystrad Cynon escheat amounted to 41.7 per cent of the total acquisition, while in Lleweni and Berain the extent of escheat was as high as 75.9 per cent and 80 per cent, respectively.[59] Details of the escheat process in Gwenynog Cynon were not provided in the survey, which stated that the entire township was acquired by the lord partly on account of deaths against the peace and partly by way of exchange: '*integre devenit in manu domini partim racione mortuorum contra pacem et partim per viam excambii*'.[60] For these four townships re-settlement was enforced mainly in the neighbouringp townships. The dispossessed freemen of Lleweni were granted lands in Ereifiad, Llechryd, Twysog and Taldrach in the same commote, and the only references to grants in another commote were those of lands in the townships of Deunant and Gwytherin in Uwch Aled, which will be further discussed.[61] In only one instance was the position of the Lleweni bond population outlined, with the reference to the grant to four bondmen of lands in Ereifiad in exchange for their tenure of a half of Gafael Philip Southern.[62] The other dispossessed bondmen were generally described as having been granted lands in other townships – *in aliis vills* – and a study of the *survey* suggests that these localities may possibly have included Prŷs, Barrog and Wigfair, which were all located at a considerable distance from Lleweni.[63]

The freemen of Ystrad Cynon were re-settled fairly locally at Nantglyn Cynon, Ereifiad, Llechryd and Penporchell; and further afield in Prŷs, Carwedfynydd. Dincadfel, Barrog and Wigfair.[64] A similar dualism was also evident in the re-settlement of the tenants of Berain and Gwenynog Cynon. Tenants of Berain were induced to settle at nearby Ereifiad and Llechryd; and in more distant Prŷs and Carwedfynydd; and those of Gwenynog Cynon similarly at Nantglyn Cynon and Prŷs.[65] The treatment of the clansmen of Gwenynog Cynon is of particular interest in emphasising certain integral features of the policy of social re-organisation. The inducement to settle in Prŷs represented part of the re-settlement policy of the post-conquest administration, and a determined effort was made to develop this remote township by the introduction of dispossessed clansmen. Moreover, the granting of land in Nantglyn Cynon to the clansmen of Gwenynog Cynon suggests that the administration was fully aware of the traditional link between these two townships, which had a common founder, Cynon ap Llywarch. It is therefore surely significant that the escheated lands of Nantglyn Cynon were granted to the clansmen of Ystrad Cynon and Gwenynog Cynon as this served to consolidate the holdings of the kindred within the township of Nantglyn Cynon and minimise the impact of territorial re-organisation on its members.[66]

The commote of Uwch Aled was influenced to a considerable degree by developments in Is Aled. Of the 153 acres of escheated lands in Deunant, 8 acres were granted to a certain Ieuan ap Llywarch who was described as a free tenant of Lleweni, in exchange for his holding there.[67] Similarly, dispossessed clansmen from Lleweni were granted 61 acres, in exchange in Gwytherin, out of a total escheat of 1,204 acres.[68] Also, clansmen from Lleweni and Ystrad Cynon received, in exchange, 124.5 acres and 1 rood of the total Barrog escheat of 561 acres.[69] There was also an element of re-organisation within this commote, and this was particularly evident in the township of Archwedlog – 25 per cent of this township escheated to the lord because of deaths against the peace *ratione mortiuorum contra pacem*, and the remainder was acquired by the grant, in exchange, of land amounting to

566 acres in various townships of Uwch Aled (namely, Beidiog, Pennantaled, Deunant, Grugor and Talhaearn), with a further 5 acres previously held in this township but in 1334 occupied by Iorwerth ap Llywelyn in the township of Brynlluarth in Ceinmeirch. The escheated portions were then assembled to form the Forest of Archwedlog, which contained 984 acres. Of this land, 480 acres were granted to twenty-four burgesses of Denbigh and ten Englishmen held by a stock and land lease: the development of Archwedlog, largely through the granting of land in exchange, represented a conscious policy of Anglicisation in the commote of Uwch Aled.[70]

The impact of social changes introduced after 1282 in the two commotes of Is Dulas and Uwch Dulas, in the *cantref* of Rhos, was relatively slight, with the limited examples of land-exchanges associated with re-settlement in other commotes. The process of land exchange in Is Dulas was confined to the township of Wigfair, significantly located on the border of the commote of Is Aled, which experienced the greatest degree of upheaval. In Wigfair, 176 acres of the total escheated land of 1,638 acres were granted, in exchange, to dispossessed tenants of Lleweni and Ystrad Cynon, in Is Aled.[71] The commote of Uwch Dulas, furthest removed from the administrative centre at Denbigh, was the one least influenced by the social and economic policies of the post-conquest administration. Reference has already been made to the escheat of land in the township of Sgeibion, in Ceinmeirch, whereby Dafydd ap Gruffudd, who had formerly held one-half of Sgeibion, was granted lands on privileged terms in Trebwll and Mathebrwd, in Uwch Dulas. There was no reference to this grant in the Trebwll entry, but it is stated in the entry for Mathebrwd that Dafydd Chwith and his brothers Maredudd and Hywel held five-sixths of Gwely Gronw ap Ithel in exchange for their inheritance in Sgeibion '*quitas de Twng et Treth ex concessione Comitis Lyncolnie*' ('quit of Twnc and Treth by grant of the earl of Lincoln').[72]

Also, the entry for Esgor Ebrill, again in Uwch Dulas, recorded that while four brothers held land in this township belonging to

Gwely Bleddyn ap Gwilym, another escheated portion in this township was held by Dafydd Chwith ap Dafydd ap Maredudd and his brother Hywel, in fee and quit of *twnc* and *treth* by gift of Henry de Lacy in exchange for their half portion of the township of Sgeibion that they had inherited.[73] Further information on this transaction is provided in Sir John Wynn's account of the history of the Gwydir family. Reference has already been made to the tradition that a forefather, Gruffudd ap Rhodri, the second son of Owain Gwynedd, the twelfth-century ruler of Gwynedd, had settled near Denbigh. However, his descendants, Dafydd Chwith, Maredudd and Hywel, the sons of Dafydd ap Gruffudd, had been forced by Henry de Lacy to exchange their extensive lands 'about Denbigh castle [which were great] with him for other land of less value ... in the furthest part from him'. The lands granted in exchange were defined as 'the township of Esgair Ebrill in Eglwysbach and half of Mathebrwd in Llanrwst', in the commote of Uwch Dulas.[74]

Resentment at his family's treatment as a result of an exchange policy involving movement to a remote region in the commote of Uwch Dulas may well have been responsible for Dafydd Chwith's involvement in the attack and murder of Henry Shaldeford, a burgess of Caernarfon, on 14 February 1345.[75] Another example of the feelings of antagonism caused by the forcible exchange of landed property was the complaint lodged by members of the Cynon ap Llywarch clan against the transaction that provided for a grant of land in Dincadfel in exchange for holdings in Lleweni taken from them by the Earl of Lincoln – *ablata ab eis per Comitem Lincolnie*.[76]

Despite its apparent care in certain instances to conciliate local opinion, the administration, by means of escheat and exchange grants, succeeded in securing possession of extensive tracts of land. In some townships, clansmen were allowed to retain their original holdings. It is certainly true that one person, Iorwerth ap Llywarch, was allowed to retain lands in Lleweni, where he was also granted a specific plot of land amounting to 187 acres.[77]

On the other hand, total control was exerted over a number of townships, including Denbigh, Lleweni and Ystrad Cynon, with the administration then able to develop them according to its own wishes. There were evidently five centres of English settlement in the lordship; the vicinity of Denbigh itself; the townships of Berain, Tal-y-bryn and Bodysgawen in the north-west of Is Aled; the township of Archwedlog in Uwch Aled; and two areas in the commote of Ceinmeirch.[78]

Surrounding these English zones there were parallel centres of Welsh influence that had been formed largely by the concentration of displaced tenants. Certain townships in Is Aled constituted what amounted to reception centres for dispossessed clansman. Therefore, on the periphery of the Anglicised area centred on Denbigh, Welsh settlement was encouraged in Nantglyn Cynon and Llechryd, and also to a lesser extent in Nantglyn 'Sanctorum', Penporchell, Twysog and Taldrach.[79] In addition to these main centres, some displaced tenants also received lands in Ereifiad and the hamlet of Bodeiliog; however, the latter two units cannot be placed in the same category as the other 'intaking' townships as they contained a considerable degree of English settlement with a balance thereby drawn between English and Welsh tenants.

Notes

1. *SD*.
2. TNA DL 29/1/1.
3. TNA DL 29/1/2.
4. Hatfield House Library, Cecil Papers, p. 287.
5. TNA SC 6/1182/1.
6. *History Gwydir*.
7. *SD*, p. 154.
8. *SD*, p. 210.
9. *SD*, p. 50.
10. *SD*, p. 271.

11 *SD*, p. 316.
12 *SD*, p. 41.
13 G. Tupling, *The Economic History of Rossindale* (Manchester, 1927), pp. 17 *et seq*.
14 For assessments of the extent of English settlement in the lordship of Denbigh, see T. P. Ellis, 'The English Element in the Perfeddwlad', *Y Cymmrodor*, 35 (1925); D. Huw Owen, 'The Englishry of Denbigh: An English Colony in Medieval Wales', *THSC* (1974–5), 57–76; R. R. Davies, 'Race Relations in Post-Conquest Wales: Confrontation and Compromise', *THSC* (1974–5), 32–56; and R. R. Davies, *The Age of Conquest: Wales ,1063–1415* (Oxford, 2000); also, for relevant developments in the neighbouring lordship of Ruthin, see Diane M. Korngiebel, 'English Colonial Ethnic Discrimination in the Lordship of Dyffryn Clwyd: Segregation and Integration, 1282–c.1340', *WHR*, 23/2 (December 2006), 1–24; Matthew Frank Stevens, *Urban Assimilation In Post-Conquest Wales: Ethnicity, Gender and Economy in Ruthin, 1282–1348* (Cardiff, 2010).
15 *Supra*, pp. 41–2.
16 *Supra*, pp. 22–3.
17 TNA SC 6/1182/1; DL 29/1/2.
18 TNA SC 6/1182/1.
19 *SD*, p. 232.
20 *SD*, pp. 230–3; A. R. H. Baker and R. A. Butlin, *Studies of Field Systems in the British Isles* (London, 1973), pp. 465–7.
21 *SD*, pp. 222–9, 270; Baker and Butlin, *Studies of Field Systems*, pp. 466–7.
22 *SD*, p. 229.
23 *SD*, pp. 222–9; D. F. Ball, *Memoirs of the Soil Survey of Great Britain: The Soils and Land Use of the District around Rhyl and Denbigh* (London, 1960), pp. 33–4, 55–7; Baker and Butlin, *Studies of Field Systems*, p. 468.
24 Baker and Butlin, *Studies of Field Systems*, p. 468.
25 TNA, DL 29/1/2.
26 TNA, SC 6/1182/1.
27 *SD*, pp. 2–3.
28 TNA, DL 29/1/1, DL 29/1/2.
29 TNA, SC 6/1182/1, *SD*, p. 52.
30 *SD*, pp. 1–2.
31 TNA DL 29/1/1; DL 1/2.
32 TNA SC 6/1182/1.
33 *SD*, pp. 3–7.
34 J. A. Todd, 'Agriculture', in *SD*, pp. lviii–xlix.
35 TNA, DL 29/1/1; DL 29/1/2.
36 *SD*, pp. 210–20.
37 *Supra*, pp. 26–8.
38 D. Huw Owen, 'Treth and Ardreth: Some Aspects of Commutation in North Wales in the Thirteenth Century', *BBCS*, 25/4 (May 1974), 446.
39 *SD*, p. 241.
40 *SD*, p. 140.
41 *SD*, pp. 7–9.

42 *Supra*, pp. 14–16.
43 *Supra*, pp. 36–7.
44 *SD*, pp. 310–12.
45 *SD*, pp. 85–6, 107–9, 129–31, 210–16, 239–42.
46 *SD*, p. 261.
47 *SD*, pp. 80–3.
48 *SD*, pp. 53–6.
49 *SD*, pp. 80–3, 116, 36.
50 *SD*, pp. 57–62, 107–9, 88–9.
51 *SD*, pp. 157–61, 199–201.
52 *SD*, pp. 195–7, 37–9.
53 *SD*, pp. 27–33, 278.
54 *Supra*, pp. 72–4.
55 *History Gwydir*, pp. 4, 5, 6, 88, 89.
56 *SD*, pp. 53–5, 109, 145; see also Figure 4.
57 *SD*, p. 109.
58 *SD*, pp. 53, 121.
59 *SD*, pp. 57–62, 83, 130–1.
60 *SD*, p. 90.
61 *SD*, pp. 57–58, 161, 190, see also *infra*.
62 *SD*, p. 59.
63 *SD*, pp. 103, 180, 216.
64 *SD*, pp. 93, 109, 118, 142, 103, 126, 129, 180, 181, 216.
65 *SD*, pp. 92–3, 103.
66 *SD*, pp. 92–3.
67 *SD*, p. 161.
68 *SD*, p. 190.
69 *SD*, p. 180.
70 *SD*, pp. 202–5, 40, 165. Also, the 1305 account (TNA DL 29/1/2) referred to the grant, in exchange, of 5 acres located in the township of Brynlluarth in Ceinmeirch.
71 *SD*, p. 216.
72 *SD*, pp. 27–8, 277–8.
73 *SD*, pp. 284–5, 27–8.
74 *History Gwydir*, pp. 13, 16, 32, 99.
75 *Supra*, pp. 115–17.
76 *SD*, p. 129.
77 *SD*, pp. 57, 62.
78 See Figure 1.
79 *SD*, pp. 109–17.

6

SOCIETY AND ECONOMY: AN ENGLISH COLONY, PREDOMINANT MEMBERS OF SETTLER FAMILIES

The deliberate policy of establishing distinctive zones of influence, as noted in the previous chapter, suggests that an attempt was made to conform to the broad pattern that prevailed in the older marcher lordships that were divided into Englishries and Welshries. An Englishry, containing centres of English settlement with a nucleus in the Vale of Clwyd, had been established in the lordship of Denbigh by 1334, and incorporated those features, including a castle, manors and boroughs, which characterised the 'typical Englishry' of a marcher lordship. Surrounding this Englishry was an area that was essentially Welsh in character and may conveniently be described as a Welshry.[1]

The existence and operation of Welshry and Englishry are reflected in the activities of their respective officials: the ringild and the bailiff of the English – *ballivus Anglicorum* – whose accounts, presented separately throughout the period under consideration, throw light on the responsibilities of the two officials.[2] These indicate that the distinction between Welshry and Englishry in the lordship of Denbigh differed markedly from that which prevailed in the older marcher lordships. In the latter, the determining factors were predominantly geographical and economic with the Welshry: an upland unit whose inhabitants were subject to communal demands for tribute, and the Englishry located in fertile lowlands where rents and services were paid for individually held plots of land.[3] While it is true that the core of the Englishry in the lordship of Denbigh was located in the fertile Vale of Clwyd, there was no clear-cut economic differentiation between the two units.

Figure 5: The Englishry: townships subject to the *Ballivus Anglicorum*

The widespread commutation of services and the acceleration in all areas of individualist tendencies in land tenure resulted in the distinction between Welshry and Englishry being based not so much on economic grounds as on national identity. This division of the economic organisation of the commotes of Ceinmeirch and Is Aled was also reflected in their financial records. Therefore, in 1360 the escheator referred to the profits of the *terre Wallicorum* ('the land of the Welsh persons'), and in 1363 the forest court of Is Aled was divided into two sections: one for *Wallenses* ('the Welsh') and the other for *Anglici* ('the English').[4]

Although the individual plots of land were generally held by Englishmen, especially in the commotes of Ceinmeirch and

Is Aled, there were a number of Welsh tenants in these two commotes. An appreciable proportion of Welsh tenants holding individual plots of land may also be observed in the other three commotes. Some of the displaced tenants succeeded in obtaining possession of these plots in the townships in which they had been resettled. This was true of both free and bond tenants. Dafydd ap Bleddyn Saer, a bondman, who had held a third of Gafael Gwaspadrig in Denbigh, was granted land in exchange in Bodysgawen, amounting to 6 acres, for a payment of 4s.[5] Cadwgan ab Einion ap Ithel, who had been dispossessed of his one-third share of Gafael Ithel Foelwyn, in Denbigh, in 1334 held 10.5 acres, in two plots of farm-land, in Prŷs, at an annual rent of 5s. 3d.[6] Likewise, by 1334 a Berain bondman, Iorwerth Llwyd ap Iorwerth Fychan, occupied 7 acres, in two plots, in Prŷs where he had been re-settled.[7] This opportunity of acquiring individual plots of land was also open to displaced freemen. Therefore, Iorwerth ap Gronw ap Adda, a freeman dispossessed of his hereditary lands in Berain, was granted 4.5 acres and 1 rood, at 2s. 4¾d, in addition to a share of parts of two *gafaelion* in Carwedfynydd.[8]

Individual plots of land were also occupied by members of the more prominent Welsh families. In view of trends that prevailed in the pre-conquest period, one may conclude that individualist tendencies had revealed themselves among some enterprising persons at an early date. Thomas, earl of Lancaster and second lord of Denbigh, was able to secure support from within the lordship for his political ambitions. The extensive lands granted to Iorwerth ap Llywarch, a prominent supporter of the earl, has already been discussed.[9] Another enterprising Welsh landholder, Cynwrig Routh held 7.5 acres in Nantglyn Cynon, 3 acres in an adjoining hamlet, a water mill and a licence to build a fulling mill. Also, three plots of 5 acres and two-thirds of 1 acre in Nantglyn 'Sanctorum' of which one and half acres were described as *assartis bosci* ('cleared wood'). The inclusion of these grants of assarted land in Nantglyn 'Sanctorum', and land that had formerly belonged to other tenants – namely, Ithel Foel in Nantglyn Cynon, and Madog Ddu in Nantglyn 'Sanctorum' – suggests that they were of recent origin. Cynwrig Routh therefore appears to be a favoured protégé in the period preceding the compilation of the Survey.[10]

It is also significant that Cynwrig Routh held another 18 acres of land in Nantglyn Cynon as the result of an exchange of land with Hugh Pigot, who received Cynwrig's hereditary lands in Gwenynog Cynon.[11] This township was associated with the township of Ystrad Cynon which had formerly been entirely occupied by the clan of Cynon ap Llywarch – *in manibus progeniei Cynon ap Llywarch*. A member of one of the four *gafaelion* of Cynon ap Llywarch's clan that occupied Ystrad Cynon was a certain Cynwrig ap Routh ap Ieuan. It is possible that Cynwrig Routh, the enterprising tenant who formerly held land in Gwenynog Cynon, was the same person as Cynwrig ap Routh ap Ieuan, a prominent member of the clan of Cynon ap Llywarch. Certain individuals sought to break out from the tribal 'nexus' in order to obtain an individual estate. The case of Cynwrig Routh provides us with a classic example of an individual furthering his own interests by enterprising actions that were evidently supported by the administration.[12]

The favoured treatment of individuals such as Iorwerth ap Llywarch and Cynwrig Routh prevents us from stating categorically that the policy of exchange was imposed from above by an alien administration on an unwilling and oppressed native society. The post-conquest land settlement had evidently benefitted some enterprising members of the local community, and there were evidently opportunities for being involved in administrative service, especially at commotal level, with the descendants of Cynwrig Routh regularly serving as local officials.[13] Another indication of the co-operation of members of the local community was their involvement as occupants of plots of land. Those members of clan groupings named in the 1334 Survey were generally males but an exception to this trend was the reference in the entry for the Segrwyd township to the descendants of 'Wen Goch', which may possibly include female persons. This clan grouping comprising free persons held one-half of the hamlet of Cathus of which one-eighth, consisting of 43.5 acres, 1 rood and 18 perches, was the property of the lord.[14]

Also, whereas most of the Welsh tenants named in the 1334 Survey were males, some female tenants, holding individual plots of land, were also recorded. Those female tenants with Welsh names occupying individual plots of land in the commote of Ceinmeirch included Gwenllian, the wife of Ednyfed, who held 1.5 acres in the township of Segrwyd; Cecilia, the wife of Iorwerth Meddyg ('Doctor') who occupied 1.5 acres in Postin; and Agnes Gruffudd who held 3.5 acres and 1 rood in Llewesog.[15] In Sgeibion, a larger plot of 13 acres and 1.5 roods was held by Lleucu, the wife of 'Githe' ap Michelin; and also 1 acre was occupied by Angharad, the daughter of Heilyn whilst Efa, the wife of Ithel ap 'Missehel', was listed as the former occupant of 1 acre.[16]

In the commote of Is Aled, two females – 'Erthelot', the wife of 'Teg', and Efa, the wife of Iorwerth Goch – occupied, respectively, 4 acres and two parts of 1 acre in the township of Nantglyn 'Sanctorum'.[17] The tenure in Ereifiad of three plots of assarted land amounting to 1 acre, half a rood and 16 perches by 'Erthelot', the wife of Goronwy; 1 acre and 1 rood by Gwladus, the wife of Iorwerth Llwyd, and 2.5 acres by Lleucu, the wife ('wreik' ('gwraig')) of a certain Einion; was accompanied by the occupation of two plots: one of half an acre by Angharad the wife of Ithel Pannwr, and the other of 1 acre occupied by Lleucu, the daughter ('vergh') of a certain Ph'.[18] Also, Gweret', the wife of Goronwy, held 3 acres in Bodysgawen, and a plot of 2 acres, half a rood and 16 perches of assarted land in the township of Twysog occupied by 'Everich' the wife of Ieuan ap Meilir.[19]

When one turns to Uwch Aled, their Welsh Christian names prompt one to include in this section Gwenllian Steyn, who held 6.5 acres in Melai and who was named as the previous owner of another 2 acres in Barrog.[20] Also Angharad, the wife of Wiliam Darnel, who held 1 acre of land in Talhaearn.[21] Similarly, in the commote of Is Dulas, Gwenllian, the daughter and heiress of Robert de Borebache, held 1.5 burgages in Abergele. In addition, she occupied in Hendregyda 3.5 acres and 1 rood, and six plots amounting to 4.5 acres, 1 rood and 10 perches, together with another 3.5 acres and 1 rood held jointly with Agnes de Stretton, who also held, with Roger de Birches, a burgage in the borough of Abergele.[22] There seems to be no doubt concerning the Welsh identity of the other female landholders in this commote. Lleucu, who was the wife of Cynddelw ap Cynwrig, held in Wigfair three plots, amounting to 4.5 acres and half a rood. Again, in this township, Ceferys, the wife of Madog, occupied 1 acre; Tangwystl, the wife of Einion, held 5 acres of land previously the property of Cynwrig ap Meilir; and Gwladus, the daughter of Ednewyn held half an acre in the associated hamlet of Bodrochwyn.[23]

Gwenllian, the wife of Ieuan ap Meurig, together with Cynwrig ap Elidir, occupied in Hendregyda 5 acres of the land of Heilyn ap Meurig; and Nest, the wife of Einion Goch Cynwrig, held six plots in 2 acres, 1.5 roods and 13.5 perches. Also, Gwenllian Goch was in possession in this township of 16 parcels, 8 acres, 1 rood and 5 perches, and, together with Dionisius de Wath' and Iorwerth ap Cynwrig, another 2 acres.[24] In Dinhengroen, 13 acres were occupied by Dyddgu, the wife of Iorwerth, and another 1 acre by Efa, the wife of Cynwrig.[25] Gwladus, the wife of Ithel, occupied 3.5 roods in *Cegidog*, and in this township 6.5 acres were held by Lleucu, the wife of Dafydd, who also held 2.5 acres and half a rood in neighbouring Dinorben Fychan.[26] Two other persons named Lleucu were named as landholders in the commote of Uwch Dulas. Lleucu 'ferch' ('the daughter of') Llywarch held one burgage at will in the borough of Llanrwst, and Lleucu the wife of Adda Goch occupied 21 acres in Twynnan: her presumed son Goronwy ap Adda also held here five plots of land amounting to a total of 12 acres, and the occupant of another 3 acres was named as Adda Fychan.[27]

The involvement of numerous females as tenants represented an indication of the support rendered to the new administration by some individuals and families. However, one may also detect, in the post-conquest period, an underlying sentiment of hostility among other sections of the Welsh population, and this was illustrated in the rebellion of 1294 and the attack on Henry de Shaldeford in 1345.[28] The resentment of many inhabitants had undoubtedly been fanned by the tenurial arrangements introduced after 1282, and an examination of the various tenures recorded in the 1334 Survey clearly reveals an element of discrimination in favour of the English settlers. J. R. H. Weaver, in his chapter 'English Tenurial Arrangements', published in the volume *Survey of the Honour of Denbigh, 1334*, stated that 'the most honourably-placed tenants were doubtless the holders by the service of castle-guard'.[29] At Lleweni, all eleven English tenants were responsible for performing castle-guard for forty days during wartime, and these tenants included members of the predominant Swynemore and Pontefract families. Also, William and John Swynemore held 92.5 acres and 1 rood in Cilcedig, and the heirs of Thomas Pontefract 80 acres in Alltfaenan by this service.[30] Other indefinite hereditary tenures included those referred to as being held *in feodo* and *hereditarie*. William Swynemore held 160 acres in fee at Lleweni, and the listed items for Llaethfan included six entries for lands held *in feodo*: two other entries in the latter township specified lands occupied *hereditarie* by Ithel the Parson and the heir of Richard Holland.[31] Also, *per relevium* may be considered to be a hereditary tenure, and the numerous entries included the tenure of 80 acres by Henry Totenhale in Lleweni.[32]

Other tenures, however, were limited to a definite period. Ten English tenants at Archwedlog each held for term of life, 31 acres of land, one bull and twenty-four cows, and a total annual payment of £36 13s. 4d was rendered for the farmed vaccary (dairy farm).[33] Significantly, these various tenures were generally confined to the English settlers, while the less favourable and less secure *ad voluntatem* ('at will') tenure was more commonly held by Welshmen, and also, in some instances, by less prominent English landholders such as Adam Annesone who held a plot of land amounting to 1.5 acres, 1 rood and 11 perches beneath the wood of Pendinas in Dinorben Fawr.[31] Also, Richard Whitacre's tenure in three plots of 15 acres and 1 rood in Berain included 6 acres held at will after they had been surrendered to the lord because of an unspecified problem ('*pro debilitate*').[35] Examples of tenancies-at-will held by Welshmen in Uwch Dulas were Gronw ap Llywarch ap Hywel's occupation, at-will, of 22.5 acres and 1 rood at Dinerth, in Llwytgoed; and Einion ap Ieuan tenure of two plots at Tŷ-brith, of which one, again held at-will, amounted to 9.5 acres of old land ('*veteris terre*').[36] As will be shown in Chapter 7, more favourable tenurial conditions prevailed in the boroughs of Abergele and Denbigh than in the urban settlement of Llanrwst, which had been established in the pre-conquest period.[37]

Moreover, following the foundation of the lordship, a deliberate policy had clearly been adopted to displace native inhabitants and attract immigrant English families. Several of the leading settler families were concentrated in the vicinity of the borough of Denbigh in 1334, and the core of the Englishry was occupied by a number of English settler families who played an important role in the administration of the lordship in the later Middle Ages. Other families succeeded in extending their estates to other centres of English settlement in the lordship, such as Archwedlog, the Anglicised zone in the commote of Uwch Aled,[38] but their base often lay in the central Denbigh area. One may therefore confidently assert that the social re-organisation in the immediate area of the caput of the lordship succeeded in attracting settlers to the Englishry thereby established. It was from this base that further extensions were made into other commotes, as seems to have been the case with the Pontefract family, whose total estate was mainly concentrated near Denbigh but included a number of scattered holdings in Is Dulas. It is also significant that none of the larger landholders, who have been named in this section, held land in Uwch Dulas, and there was an evident reluctance among the settler community to hold land in what was regarded as a comparatively remote locality. Here, where the impact of re-organisation was least pronounced, the individual rented lands were generally occupied by Welshmen and members of the less prominent English families.

Tracing the origins of the settler families presents problems, even though some have attracted extensive speculation. Insufficient evidence is available to support the claim that the Pigot family, which in 1334 held a total of 309 acres and 13 perches, was descended from Hugh Bigod, the younger son of Roger Bigod, earl of Norfolk, and reputed to have accompanied Henry II on his expedition to Wales.[39] Also, the suggestion that the Salusburies of Lleweni traced their descent from Adam of Salzburg, grandson of Eberhard, duke of Bavaria, who accompanied William I to England, may be completely discarded.[40] It is more probable that this family came to Denbigh from either Lancashire or Herefordshire, with the personal names of these settlers providing the main guide to their origins: a district known as 'Salusbury' or 'Salebiri' has been identified in Herefordshire, where Henry de Lacy held extensive estates, while de Lacy's lands in Lancashire included the manor of Salusbury.[41] It has been suggested that the Swynemore and Rosse families came from Herefordshire, and the 1334 Survey refers to a William of Hereford holding a plot of 2 acres, 1.5 roods and 7 perches in Polflat lands in Lleweni.[42] Other families, including the Hetons,[43] as well as the Cliderowes, Ramsbothoms, Rossindales and Symondestones, may also be traced to a Lancastrian origin, and the Doncaster and Pontefract families to a Yorkshire background.

When one considers the leading settler families in terms of their landed property the more significant ones were represented predominantly by male individuals in the 1334 Survey. These included members of the Hulton family, the largest landholding family in the lordship occupying a total of 648.5 acres, 1 rood and 17.5 perches. An earlier reference to a member of this family was the grant in fee farm, in *c.* 1300, by the earl of Lincoln to Robert Hulton, of land amounting to 75 acres and 1 rood in Lleweni for a rent of 46s. 9d per annum. The names of the family representatives in 1334 present some problems, with two individuals named as Robert Hulton senior, and Robert Hulton junior, together with another 'Robert' listed as a landholder. Another family member was 'Richard', who was also described in two entries as 'the son of Robert': the persons named as Richard or Robert Hulton occupied in Is Aled a total of 298 acres and 17.5 perches, with the largest units being the 116 acres, 1 rood and 7.5 perches held by Robert Hulton senior in the Acre of Lleweni for a rent of £4 1s. 6¼d. The mills of Lleweni and Henllan were held for a payment of £7 10s. by Robert Hulton junior, who was also, with Richard Hulton, the tenant of 25.5 acres in the Park of Lleweni.[44]

Other landholding members of this family were Hugh, who held 81 acres, John who occupied 45 acres, and Thomas the occupant of 154 acres and 1 rood: the total holdings of these three thereby amounting to 280 acres and 1 rood.[45] The greater part of the territory held by this family was located in the commote of Is Aled, apart from the 82 acres in Archwedlog, in Uwch Aled, leased by Robert and Thomas Hulton, with another 51 acres occupied here by Robert Hulton and 31 acres by his kinsman Thomas Hulton.[46] Five acres were occupied by Hugh Hulton in Wigfair, in Is Dulas; and also four plots in Ceinmeirch by members of this family: 37.5 acres and 39.5 acres held, respectively, by Thomas and Robert senior in the Park of Segrwyd, 2 acres in Garth-y-moch occupied by Robert Hulton and 13 acres in Oakwood held jointly by Robert Hulton and Roger Wharton.[47]

The next family in terms of landholding prominence was the Pontefract grouping, with the name possibly suggesting a connection with the Yorkshire area, which was also associated with the de Lacy family.[48] Two entries noted John Pontefract's tenure of 12 acres in the Park of Segrwyd, with one of these referring to the bovate amounting to 10 acres held in relation to his burgage in Denbigh.[49] As with the Hulton property, most of the lands were held in the commote of Is Aled with the plots of 3.5 acres held by Hugh and John, the sons of Robert Pontefract, and 140 acres in Lleweni at Foxholes and 'Brennskip' occupied by Robert Pontefract, together with Richard Everdene. A further entry for 'Bronnskip' referred to the occupation here by these two individuals of 105 acres and 1 rood near to the 'Ward' of the castle of Denbigh; and the same tenure characterised the occupation by the heirs of Thomas Pontefract of 80 acres in Alltfaenan. Also, John, the son of Thomas, occupied a plot of 10 acres in the Park of Lleweni.[50]

When one turns to the commote of Is Dulas, John Pontefract held 7.5 acres in Cegidog, seven plots in Hendregyda amounting to 19.5 acres, half a rood, and 5 perches, and, together with Robert Castleford, a plot of 6 acres named as Lle Tŷ Madog in the hamlet of Maerdref in the manor of Dinorben Fawr. Also, 3 burgages and two plots, and additional plots amounting to a total of 115.5 acres, 1.5 roods and 16 perches were held by him in the borough of Abergele. Another burgage at Abergele was held by Robert, the son of Robert Pontefract, who was also named, in an exceptional example, together with two Welshmen, as the occupant of clan land in the township of Penmaen recorded together with the township of Llysfaen at the conclusion of the Survey of Denbigh.[51] On the basis of ignoring the lower assessment recorded above of the land held at 'Brennskip', that is 105 acres and 1 rood, the total amount of land held by members of the Pontefract family amounted to 394.5 acres, 1 rood and 1 perch.

A family occupying only slightly less property than the Pontefract one was the Swynemore family, with John and William Swynemore the tenants of a total of 362.5 acres, 1.5 roods and 13 perches. John held a total of 172.5 acres, 1.5 roods and 3 perches, comprising in the commote of Ceinmeirch 90.5 acres, 1 rood and 23 perches in Postin, Sgeibion, 'Lughern' and Cilcedig, and another 24 acres held jointly with John the son of John Pygot in Llewesog. Also, in Is Aled, a bovate in Lleweni and another bovate held jointly with John, the son of William Egelyne in Ystrad Cynon; both bovates comprising 10 acres; 60 acres in Cilcedig and 2 acres held jointly with his brother William in Ystrad Cynon.[52]

William occupied 300 acres in these two commotes, comprising 112 acres in Ceinmeirch, that is one-eighth of the township of Llwyn, defined as 67 acres and 1 rood, and 44.5 acres and 1 rood in Cilcedig; and also, in Is Aled, 188 acres in the township of Lleweni and the associated territory of Polfllat.[53]

Another family represented only by males in 1334 was the Heton family, which was in possession of only a small estate that year. The total estate of 20 acres comprised two plots of 3 acres occupied respectively by William Heton in Prys, in Is Aled and by John in Grugor, in Uwch Aled. Property in these two commotes were also occupied by Richard Heton: 2.5 acres in Archwedlog and 11.5 acres in Chwilbren.[54] As previously noted, members of the Heton family had been attracted to the Denbigh area on account of the earl of Lincoln's landed estates in Lancashire, including the Honour of Clitheroe (a reference will appear below regarding its expansion by the early nineteenth century).[55]

A notable feature of these four families was that all the named representatives were males. In contrast, the Pigot estate of 309 acres and 13 perches contained one entry whereby Alice Pigot held, with her husband Thomas, 10 acres in the Acre of Denbigh. Thomas also held here a plot of 4.5 acres and 1 rood, as well as two plots of 14.5 acres, and 5 acres in Gwenynog Cynon. Other property occupied in Is Aled by Hugh and William Pigot amounted to 60 acres and 1 rood.[56] In the commote of Ceinmeirch, the territory held by John Pigot amounted to 162.5 acres and 13 perches in the townships of Sgeibion and Llewesog, and hamlet of Brynbagle, and in Llewesog another plot of 24 acres was shared between John Pigot and John Swynemore. Also, Thomas occupied 40 acres in Archwedlog, the Anglicised zone in Uwch Aled.[57] On the basis of sharing equally the 24-acre plot in Llewesog, one would assess the total amount of the Pigot estate to be 309 acres and 13 perches.

Another estate that contained female tenants was that of the Plesyngton family, which, in 1334, occupied 198.5 acres and 13 perches, with two females Cecilia and Matilda recorded as landholders in the 1334 Survey. In Ceinmeirch, Cecilia Plesyngton held 3 acres, 1 rood and 8 perches of meadow, and together with William de Londsdale, one plot and 2 acres in Bachymbyd; while in Is Aled, Matilda occupied 11 acres and half of a rood of the land of Goronwy Bondus in the hamlet of Bodeiliog.[58] Other property held by members of this family included, in Ceinmeirch, the occupation in Sgeibion by Elias of two plots comprising 6 acres and 1 rood, and by William and Henry respectively of 12 acres and 5 acres; while Richard, Henry, John, Robert, William and Elias Plesyngton were all tenants in Bachymbyd, occupying here a total of 82 acres, 1 rood and 5 perches.[59] Lands held by this family in Is Aled comprised 26.5 acres and 1 rood held by Robert Plesyngton in Berain, and the latter's tenure of 20.5 acres and half a rood in the Acre of Lleweni: another entry for this locality referred to a plot of land, amounting to 30 acres and 1 rood, held by Robert de Hulton, formerly occupied by John Plesyngton but later the subject of a legal claim by Robert Plesyngton.[60]

Agnes Wilberley was another female tenant who, in Ereifiad, held with her husband John three plots, which together amounted to 27.5 acres and half a rood.[61] John also occupied 9 nine acres arranged in three plots, and the entry for Dinbych ('Denbigh') referred to the exchange in Ereifiad of his tenure of Gafael Osbern. Also, in Ceinmeirch, John, together with two Welshmen, held at farm the water mill of Segrwyd for an annual rent, payable in two terms, of £9. His son Henry held in Ereifiad a plot of assarted land amounting to 1 acre, half a rood and 8 perches, and he, or possibly another person called Henry, was the tenant here of two plots amounting to 6 acres.[62] Three other members of this family – Richard, Robert and William – held plots of land amounting to 58 acres, half a rood and 13 perches in Ceinmeirch and Is Aled; in the Parks of Segrwyd and Lleweni, and the townships of Gwenynog Cynon, Gwenynog Wyntus, Ereifiad, le Graba wood, Forlond and Polflat.[63] Therefore, a total property of 102 acres and 1 perch was held by members of the Wilberley family in addition to their share in the watermill of Segrwyd.

Marjorie and Joan, the daughters of Henry Duckworth, were members of another prominent settler family, which held a total of 89.5 acres, 1.5 roods and 18 perches in the lordship. The two sisters held 5 acres in the Park of Segrwyd. Another landholder in the Park was William Duckworth, who occupied a plot of 28 acres. He also held in the commote of Ceinmeirch 14 acres in Cernenyfed, and in Is Aled 26 acres in Garsnodiog, the plot of land and wood within the township of Lleweni. Henry was also named in relation to a plot of land in the manor of Denbigh, measuring 16.5 acres, 1.5 roods and 18 perches.[64] The Ramsbothom family, which may possibly have had its origin in the Manchester area in Lancashire, was recorded as occupying 78 acres, half a rood and 26 perches in the commote of Ceinmeirch. Margery Ramsbothom held 11.5 acres and 9 perches in Cernenyfed, and William also held here three plots amounting to 28.5 acres, half a rood and 17 perches. In a section following the entries for Segrwyd, Elias Ramsbothom was recorded as a tenant who occupied 38 acres. In addition, William, together with Simon Whitacre, occupied in Cernenyfed 22.5 acres, 1 rood and 16 perches.[65]

Another family that, as with the Heton family previously discussed, possessed a comparatively limited amount of territory in 1334, but in a later period was in possession of a substantial estate was the Salusbury family. An earlier reference to a member of this family was the one to John Salusbury, who was one of the witnesses to a grant of 5 acres in Lleweni, *c*. 1300. In 1334, Alicia, wife of Thomas Salusbury, held a bovate comprising 10 acres in Lleweni. Also, in the Acre of Lleweni, 4 acres were occupied by Henry the son of Adam, and another plot of 15.5 acres and 1 rood was held by John Salusbury.[66]

In addition to the female occupants of territory already noted, several other examples were provided in the 1334 Survey of female landholders. In Ceinmeirch, they included, in the Park of Segrwyd, Matilda, a widow who occupied 6.5 acres, Emma del Mos, the tenant of 4 acres and 1 rood, and Agnes Welford, the tenant of 4 acres in this township and also 6 acres in Llech. The tenants of Sgeibion included Amisia, Agnes and Anabilla, the daughters of Robert Eccleston, who held 9 acres and 21 perches; and Katerina Spilleponne who occupied 1 acre and 1 rood. Also, Alicia, the daughter of Alan Forde, was named as the former tenant of 18 acres held by Henry Bolde in Bachymbyd. Margareta, the daughter of John Kilford, was the tenant of another large plot, comprising 18 acres and 10 perches in Llewesog, and Agnes, the daughter of Richard Billyng was named as the former occupant of 18 acres held there in 1334 by John Pigot.[67]

Other plots of land in Ceinmeirch were associated with territories also held by family members in the commote of Is Aled. Adam, the son of Isolde, who had been recorded as the tenant of 10 acres in the Park of Segrwyd, held 5 acres in the Park of Lleweni and, with his wife Matilda, occupied here in two parcels of 6.5 acres and 1 rood. Marjorie and Alicia, both of whom were described as the wife of William Mody, respectively held 12 acres in two plots in Sgeibion, and 4 acres in Garthsnodiog in the township of Lleweni, in Is Aled. In addition to holding in Ceinmeirch 4 acres in Segrwyd and 10 acres in the Park of Segrwyd, Juliana and Sibillla Hallum occupied a plot containing 1.5 acres in Is Aled in the 'Acre' of Lleweni, and in the associated territories of Garthsnodiog, 20 acres of land and wood, and Polflat 2 acres, 1 rood and 13.5 perches. Also in this commote, Margery Hallum occupied a plot together with 8 acres in Tal-y-bryn.[68]

Those occupying plots of land exclusively in one township in Is Aled included Matilda Bonk, the occupant in Forlond of 3 roods, and Alice Sonderlond, the wife of William, who held a 10-acre bovate in Lleweni. Also in this township, Elena Paunton held 40 acres with her husband Richard. Margery Bercarius occupied with her husband Robert 3.5 acres and 10 perches in the associated 'Acre' of Lleweni, and Robert also held here another 1 acre and 1 rood. In addition, Agnes Halghton was the occupant with her husband Thomas of 3 acres, Margery Heend was the tenant of 2 acres with her husband Nicholas; Joanna Symondston with her husband Henry held 5 acres; and Alicia Verdon occupied one plot that was called 'Garthmeily'. An exceptional example of two apparent sisters occupying land was the tenure in this township of 6.5 acres and half a rood by Margerie and Alicia, the daughters of William Henglewood.[69]

Another plot together with half a rood were occupied by Cecilia Rybchester in the 'New borough' of Lleweni, and three plots, together with 35 perches, were held here by Isabella Hendebury, who was also a tenant of three roods in the Park of Lleweni. A further entry for the Park referred to 26 acres occupied by Alan de Craven, and another 10 acres held in relation to his burgage within the walls of Denbigh that had been granted to him by Elene, the wife of Alfred Ely. Cecilia Rochdale was the tenant of a small plot of 1 rood in Gwenynog Cynon. Alicia, the wife of William Cruce occupied in Ereifiad two plots of 10 acres and 17 acres, formerly held by her husband but that had been forfeited by him. Margery Brodfoot, the tenant of 10 acres in Bodysgawen, also occupied 6 acres and 7 perches in Tal-y-bryn, where Matilda, the daughter of Richard Golden, the tenant of 1 acre and 1 rood in Berain held 9 acres. Also in Tal-y-bryn, where Agnes and her husband John Whiteacre held 4 acres, John also was the sole tenant of another 10 acres in this township.[70]

With regard to the other commotes in the lordship, only a very limited number of entries provided information on female occupants of plots of land. Reference has already been made to the property held in the commote of Is Dulas by Agnes Stretton, in the township of Hendregyda and the borough of Abergele.[71] In the commote of Uwch Dulas, a certain Elena, the daughter of Hugh, held 1 burgage in the borough of Llanrwst.[72] The scarcity of relevant data in these commotes emphasises again the extent of the colonisation process and its concentration in the commotes of Ceinmeirch and Is Aled located in close proximity to the castle of Denbigh. Also, several instances of spasmodic outbursts of violence, as in 1294, 1345 and during the first decade of the fifteenth century, illustrate an underlying sentiment of resentment against the nature and objectives of the tenurial arrangements introduced in this area following the Edwardian conquest.[73]

Notes

1 See Figure 5, 'The Englishry: townships subject to the *Ballivus Anglicorum*'; Rees, *South Wales and the March*, pp. 30–1, pointed out that, in the southern march, the division of the lordship into Englishry and Welshry, 'though nominally based on racial grounds, had a more significant economic origin'.
2 *Supra*, pp. 51–4.
3 J. Beverley Smith, 'The Lordship of Senghennydd', in T. B. Pugh (ed.), *Glamorgan County History, volume 3: The Middle Ages* (Cardiff, 1971), pp. 312–18; Davies, *Lordship and Society in the March of Wales*, pp. 302–91.
4 TNA SC 6/1182/4; 1182/6.
5 *SD*, pp. 53, 121.
6 *SD*, pp. 55, 105.
7 *SD*, pp. 105, 130.
8 *SD*, pp. 130, 125–7.
9 *Supra*, pp. 41–2.
10 *SD*, pp. 92–5.
11 *SD*, pp. 93, 90.
12 *SD*, pp. 80–1, 92–5.
13 *Supra*, p. 80, *Infra*, p. 179.
14 *SD*, p. 9.
15 *SD*, pp. 9, 27, 35.
16 *SD*, pp. 29, 32, 31.
17 *SD*, p. 95.
18 *SD*, pp. 110–13, 115.
19 *SD*, pp. 121, 143.
20 *SD*, pp. 175, 180.
21 *SD*, p. 194.
22 *SD*, pp. 252, 236.
23 *SD*, pp. 218–20.
24 *SD*, pp. 235, 236, 238.
25 *SD*, p. 243.
26 *SD*, pp. 226, 227, 229.
27 *SD*, pp. 281, 297.
28 *Supra*, pp. 115–17.
29 J. R. H. Weaver, 'English Tenurial Arrangements', *SD*, p. cix.
30 *SD*, pp. 64–5, 43, 86.
31 *SD*, pp. 64, 321.
32 *SD*, p. 65.
33 *SD*, pp. 204–5.
34 *SD*, p. 231.
35 *SD*, p. 132.
36 *SD*, pp. 305, 273.
37 *Supra*, pp. 27–8, 104–7, 109–10.
38 *SD*, pp. 202–5.

39 Williams, *Ancient and Modern Denbigh*, pp. 189 *et seq.*
40 W. A. Evans, 'The Salusburies of Lleweni', *TDHS*, 5 (1955), for reference to the information provided to the author by J. E. Lloyd, who described the statement on the mural monument in Eglwyswen church (Whitchurch) that this family were descended from the royal house of Bavaria as 'one of the greatest fabrication of the truth to be found on any monument in Wales'.
41 J. Gwenogvryn Evans (ed.), *Oll synnwyr pen Kembero ygyd* (copied by William Salesbury from a collection by Gruffudd Hiraethog) (Bangor, 1902), pp. xxv–xxviiii; W. J. Smith (ed.), *Calendar of Salusbury Correspondence 1553–circa 1700* (Cardiff, 1954), pp. 2–4; Iwan Rhys Edgar, 'William Salesbury: Cipolwg ar y dyn, ei feddwl a'i ddylanwad', *Llên Cymru*, 33 (2010), 61–79.
42 Smith, *Calendar of Salusbury Correspondence*, pp. 3–4; *SD*, p. 79.
43 Edmund R. Heaton, *The Heatons of Deane: The Varying Fortunes of a Lancashire Family Over 850 Years* (Aberystwyth, 2000), pp. 27–8, 184–6.
44 *SD*, pp. 62, 66, 68, 72, 73, 76, 78, 144; NLW, Aston Hall, 5261.
45 *SD*, pp. 56, 63, 67, 68, 73, 84, 87.
46 *SD*, p. 204.
47 *SD*, pp. 216, 14, 15, 18.
48 Baldwin, 'Household Administration', 182.
49 *SD*, p. 13.
50 *SD*, pp. 64, 65, 77, 86, 88.
51 *SD*, pp. 226, 232, 235, 252, 253, 254, 317.
52 *SD*, pp. 27, 30, 38, 42, 43, 63, 65, 83, 84.
53 *SD*, pp. 37, 43, 64, 71, 82, 84.
54 *SD*, pp. 106, 163, 165, 204.
55 *Supra*, p. 88; Heaton, *The Heatons of Deane*, pp. 186–7.
56 *SD*, pp. 56, 90, 93, 133, 204.
57 *SD*, pp. 21, 29, 30, 38, 42.
58 *SD*, pp. 5, 36, 116, 117.
59 *SD*, pp. 28, 31, 35, 36.
60 *SD*, pp. 66, 70, 133.
61 *SD*, p. 110.
62 *SD*, pp. 110, 39, 54.
63 *SD*, pp. 15, 64, 77, 80, 88, 89, 90, 112.
64 *SD*, pp. 14, 15, 23, 78, 52.
65 *SD*, pp. 23, 22, 24, 10.
66 *Supra*, p. 71; NLW, Aston Hall, 5260; *SD*, pp. 63, 66, 69.
67 *SD*, pp. 13, 15, 42, 30, 31, 33, 37, 38.
68 *SD*, pp. 12, 76; 28, 78; 9, 14, 56, 78, 79, 137.
69 *SD*, pp. 63, 64, 65, 68, 71, 70.
70 *SD*, pp. 74, 75, 77, 91, 113, 123, 138, 135.
71 *Supra*, p. 82; *SD*, pp. 236, 252.
72 *SD*, p. 281.
73 *Supra*, pp. 36–7, 115–17.

7

THE BOROUGHS OF THE LORDSHIP, 1282–1334

The 1334 Survey referred to four localities in the lordship – namely, Denbigh,[1] Abergele, Llanrwst and Pennant Erethlyn – that contained burgages, and another one, significantly named the 'New borough' of Lleweni, which was divided into *placeae*.[2] Of these five locations, the foundation charter of only one – Denbigh – has survived,[3] while another document, an *inquisition post mortem* dated 21 February 1311, referred to urban settlements at Abergele and Denbigh.[4] Reference has already been made to the strong possibility that Llanrwst was a pre-conquest Welsh urban centre,[5] while entries in various ministers' accounts, from the mid fourteenth-century onwards, confirm the designation of Abergele, Denbigh and Llanrwst as boroughs. On the other hand, the absence of such references to Pennant Erethlyn and Lleweni prompts one to question Vinogradoff's definition of Pennant Erethlyn as a borough and the 'New borough' of Lleweni as 'possibly the germ of a fifth'.[6]

With regard to Denbigh, a combination of military, strategic and commercial factors governed the selection of the site, located on the summit of a hill, for the construction of the castle,[7] and also the foundation of the associated borough. Following the military successes that resulted in the creation of the lordship of Denbigh, the administrators of the lordship soon exerted total control over the bond township of *Dinbych* ('Denbigh'). This was subjected to a process of radical change, with Henry de Lacy, earl of Lincoln, the first lord of Denbigh, evidently aware of the potential economic advantages of establishing a borough in close proximity to his military stronghold.[8]

One of the methods employed to achieve this objective, as in other localities of the lordship, was the process of escheat, which could be applied when tenants had committed an offence or had failed to pay their dues.[9] As previously noted, 24.8 per cent of the bond tenements of Denbigh were subject to escheat. Representing a surprisingly low percentage in view of the greater incidence of escheat among bond as compared to free properties in the lordship, this probably reflects the ease with which the administration was able to exert control over this township, located at the centre of the recently established lordship.[10] A more conclusive method by which the lord achieved absolute authority in *Dinbych* was the re-settlement of the original inhabitants in other townships. The dispossessed bondmen of Denbigh were granted lands in neighbouring Bodeiliog, Bodysgawen, Ereifiad, Penporchell, Tywysog and Taldrach, and in the more distant township of Prys.[11]

The early history of the borough of Denbigh, from 1282 until 1305, enables one to identify those factors that characterised its development during the later Middle Ages. Two basic objectives — economic and sociopolitical — were reflected in the various charters granted to the burgesses, with the lordship administrators seeking to foster an institution that represented a lucrative source of financial and political support. However, the borough occasionally suffered from its close association with the administration, and the inhabitants of the surrounding rural areas evidently resented the privileged status of this favoured urban community.

The economic considerations influencing the decision to establish a borough at Denbigh reflected the contemporary encouragement of the growth of urban centres, and an appreciation of the financial possibilities inherent in the venture. The borough would not only represent a direct source of revenue for the lord but as a commercial centre would also stimulate the economy of the surrounding area. As has been discussed, the establishment of the lordship of Denbigh was an integral part of the sociopolitical policy forged by the administration of the lordship which now experienced a drastic re-organisation. The extensive immigration of English families that led to the creation of an English colony, or Englishry, within the lordship, resulted in the largest of the five main Anglicised zones being centred on the castle and borough of Denbigh. By 1334 this locality both contained the predominant settler families and also represented a base from which some of these families were able to extend their landed possessions to other areas of the lordship.[12] The physical association of the borough with the castle, the military and administrative centre of the lordship, underlined the crucial role played by the newly established borough in the process of economic and social reconstruction.

The adoption of this policy, however, was beset with difficulties, and this is reflected by the conferment of two foundation charters on the borough of Denbigh by Henry de Lacy, earl of Lincoln. The circumstances underlying the two grants emphasise the problems confronting the lordship administrators seeking to establish a borough at Denbigh. The undated charter housed for many years at Denbigh among the corporation muniments was previously assumed to be the original foundation grant. This charter, which listed a total of forty-five burgages held by thirty-nine burgesses, together with the conditions under which they held their lands, was clearly modelled (as were many other Welsh borough charters) on that of Hereford (and ultimately on the Breteuil model).[13] However, another charter, granted by Henry de Lacy and dated 1 October 1285, and now preserved among the Duchy of Lancaster records, recorded the existence of sixty-three burgesses, with each one holding one burgage and contributing a sum of 1d at Christmas as his *housegable* due.[14]

An examination of the diplomatic formulae and wording of the two charters reveals many similarities, but there were also significant differences, and these, together with the marked contrast between the names of the burgesses, suggest that the original charter was the one dated in 1285, with each burgage granted '*en nostre vyle de Dynebegh*' ('in our town of Denbigh'), and also '*un curtilage de hors la vyle*' ('a curtilage outside the town'). The burgesses in 1285 were empowered 'to have and to hold, to them and to their heirs, and to their assigns' the designated property in the new town.[15] On the other hand, according to the undated charter, each burgess received a burgage 'dedenz les murs ('within the walls'), a curtilage 'dehors les murs' ('outside the walls'), together with a bovate in a specified township and a statement referring to a requirement to 'have and to hold, to them and to their heirs and to their English assigns'.

The reduction in the number of burgages as recorded in the two documents, and the contrast between the two lists of burgesses, suggest that in the period immediately following its creation, the borough experienced a complete transformation. This new development was forced on the lordship administrators by the events of 1294, when local inhabitants supported the uprising led by Madog ap Llywelyn. Also, the more comprehensive nature of the burgage holding; the reference to walls, the construction of which was set in motion in 1282 but that was impeded by the 1294 uprising; and, possibly most significant of all, the inclusion of the epithet 'English', indicate that the undated charter was of a later date than the 1285 charter and had probably been issued after the 1294 rebellion.[16]

Difficulties are involved in the identification of several of the burgesses named in the original charter.[17] In some cases, the relevant occupation was provided after the personal name and three of the burgesses – John, Richard and Reynold – were described as masons. Prominent members of the earl's administration also appeared among the recipients of burgages, and these included William le Vavasur and William Stopham, who had served respectively as steward and marshal in 1283, and John de la Chambre, the earl's chamberlain.[18] Members of the Adlington, Doncaster, Mostyn, Pye and Shoresworth families were granted burgages according to both the 1285 and undated charter, and the specific names of two individuals – John Alington and Richard Shoresworth – also appeared on both occasions.[19] The Doncaster, Mostyn, Pye and

Shoresworth families were again represented in the 1334 Survey,[20] while members of the Clayton, Hereford, Hoghton, Plesington, Preston, Russell, Shenington, Steynbourne, Sutton and Totenhale families held both burgages in 1285 and plots of land in 1334.[21] When comparing burgage-holders in 1285 and those named in the undated charter it is clear that it is the latter that contains the names of those who may be readily identified as the more prominent landholders in the lordship. Information is provided below of the extensive estates held in 1334 by members of the Hilton, Pontefract and Swynemore families.[22]

An early fifteenth-century transcript of the 1285 charter has also been preserved among the archives of the Duchy of Lancaster in one of the Great Cowcher volumes.[23] Comparison with the 1285 charter reveals numerous errors caused by defective transcription, but the relationship of this transcription to an associated group of documents relating to Denbigh in the Great Cowcher volume provides valuable information on both the nascent borough of Denbigh and the chronology of the undated charter. This collection contains a copy of a bond, dated 29 June 1295, issued by substantial freeholders in the lordship, which illustrates the disruptive effects of the 1294 rebellion.[24] Other transcripts recorded grants by Henry de Lacy in 1286 of 88 acres in Galltfaenan to a cook, Richard Estanc, and in 1296 to another cook, 'William', of 50 acres of land in Llewesog held formerly by Thomas Seynpol.[25] On the same day, William was granted one burgage and a bovate of land in Denbigh and the tenurial conditions were to correspond to those of other burgesses in Denbigh.[26] The second grant did not refer to the former occupant but as Thomas Seynpol also appeared as a burgess in the 1285 charter it is probable that his burgage would henceforth be occupied by William, the cook. Two other burgesses listed in 1285, William le Vavasor and William Stopham, witnessed these two grants and as they had served as senior administrators of the lordship in 1283, their participation in the 1296 transactions indicates that there had not been a complete breakdown in the administration of the lordship.

This suggests a considerable degree of dislocation that was further illustrated by a petition submitted by William Hereford and his wife Mary and described in an inquisition *post mortem* of 1331.[27] Mary was the daughter and heiress of Richard Hereford – a certain William Hereford was granted a burgage in the 1285 charter – and according to the petition Richard had held within the lordship, by gift of Henry de Lacy, an estate comprising a messuage and 180 acres in Wigfair. Also, a burgage and curtilage at Denbigh held for an annual payment of 1d, *housegable* with the other lands occupied by services that included the provision at wartime of two armed horsemen for service at Denbigh castle for four days or one armed horseman for eight days. Richard's copy of the charter confirming his possessions had been burned during the last war in north Wales called 'the war of Madoc'. Accused of certain trespasses William was deprived of his estate and his lands in Wigfair were granted to certain freemen in exchange for their holdings in Ystrad Cynon.[28] His displacement, and that of Thomas Seynpol, together with the impression that other burgesses were forced to leave the new town, emphasised the extent to which the newly created borough of Denbigh had evidently suffered from the ravages of the uprising.

Following the pacification of the lordship another group of individuals may well have been encouraged to settle in the borough. Several of these burgesses were named on a long list dated 6 September 1310, and included in the foremestioned Great Cowcher volume of individuals who rendered a sum of £800 to their lord, Henry de Lacy, in return for various concessions and privileges.[29] A comparison of the 1285 charter and 1310 list reveals that the Mostyn, Plesyngton and Shoresworth families were represented in both documents, with William de Plesyngton appearing among the *Anglici* of the commote of Ceinmeirch and John Mostyn, Ralph Shoresworth and John Wyberlye on the corresponding list for the commote of Ceinmeirch. However, there was a far greater similarity between the 1310 list and the undated charter, with Richard Duckworth, Thomas Hilton, Ralph and Thomas Peake, Thomas Pontefract, Adam Swynemore and Henry Wyce named as burgesses of Denbigh who also rendered sums of money in return for concessions in these two commotes. Moreover, the witness list to the 1310 document bears a striking resemblance to that of the undated charter. Six of the nine witnesses in 1310 – John Grey, William Nony, Thomas Fishbourne, William the parson of Denbigh, Robert Byncestre and William Caldicot – witnessed the undated charter while another two – Thomas Pontefract and Adam Swynemore – were named both as contributors in the 1310 list and as burgesses in the undated charter. Thomas Pontefract and Adam Swynemore also served as jurors in the 1311 inquisition following the death of Henry de Lacy and on this occasion were accompanied by Gruffudd ap Rhys, who may probably be identified as Sir Gruffudd Llwyd, a leading member of the Welsh official class in the reigns of Edward I and Edward II.[30] He also witnessed the undated charter and this evidence would suggest that this charter preserved at Denbigh was compiled in the latter years of Henry de Lacy's life and probably towards the end of the first decade of the fourteenth century.

A significant contrast between the two charters was the specific reference in the undated charter to town walls, with the progress on their construction reflecting a full awareness of the need to ensure the defence of the borough. The financial account compiled in 1305 distinguished between burgages held within and outside the walls, with the *housegable* levied on fifty-two burgages within the walls amounting to 4s. 4d and to the 183 burgages outside the walls to 15s. 3d.[31] It also recorded that income was also derived from the farm of two ovens (£2 13s. 4d), one mill (£3 6s. 8d) and court profits that yielded £3 10s. 0d, with a sum of £20 6s. 2d paid by the borough officials to the central receiver of the lordship. The increase in the number of burgages, together with the accompanying evidence, suggest that the undated charter, compiled between 1295 and 1305, represented a second and more successful attempt to establish a borough at the centre of the lordship.³² The first foundation charter had required that each one of the sixty-three burgesses should contribute a sum of 1d at Christmas as his *housegable* due, thereby yielding a total payment of 5s. 3d.³³ By the time of the second foundation charter, granted in the period 1295–1305, the total rent demanded of the thirty-nine burgesses had increased to £4 9s. 11d, and with four exceptions, a payment of 1d for *housegable* was again stipulated. Some of the burgesses also occupied lands outside the confines of the borough. This second charter provided for the grant of thirty-four bovates to thirty of the thirty-nine burgesses. Most of these bovates – twenty-five in Lleweni, six in Ystrad Cynon and one in Kilford – were located in townships that were situated in close proximity to the borough; only two, one each in Berain and Wigfair, were located at some distance from Denbigh, and a rent of 3s. 4d was levied on each bovate. The tenure of these bovates – that is, plots of land normally comprising 10 acres and sited beyond the confines of the borough – ensured from the outset a close relationship between the borough and a number of the surrounding townships.³⁴

The connection between a burgage and bovate was specified in some instances in the 1334 Survey. Bovates occupied by John Hilton, Adam Mostyn and John Swynemore indicate that these families, which were among the most prominent landholders in the lordship, were represented in the borough of Denbigh in 1334.³⁵ Members of the Duckworth family, again named in the 1334 Survey, also featured in the second foundation charter.³⁶ Burgesses introduced after the second foundation charter, and whose presence was again indicated by bovate-entries in the survey, included Alan Cravene, Thomas Faber, Richard Ferrmery and Adam Mody.³⁷ The survey also specified the connection between burgages and bovates in the Forest of Archwedlog, in Uwch Aled; 972.5 acres had been granted here by a charter awarded by William de Montagu, earl of Salisbury and fifth lord of Denbigh to twenty-four burgesses of Denbigh with 480 acres held in twenty-four bovates, with each bovate comprising 20 acres.[38]

The favourable tenurial concessions in the foundation charters had been supplemented by a variety of agrarian and domestic privileges, with the various rights granted to burgesses including *housebote* and heybote in Coed Lleweni, and specified rights of pasture, baking and mill-grinding. Additional commercial privileges granted to the burgesses of Denbigh by a central administration seeking to promote the borough's economic interests included the right to hold an annual fair, which was held by 1311, with tolls levied on trading activities. The burgesses were exempt from these tolls, as indeed they were freed from various tolls levied in other towns. In August 1290, a royal charter had released the burgesses from paying various dues in Wales and in six of the border shires: these privileges were extended in 1332 throughout the whole kingdom. The specified dues included tolls; stallage, defined as a rent for setting up a market stall; murage, a toll for the construction or repair of town walls; and pannage, the practice of releasing pigs in the forest.[39]

With regard to the offices held by the burgesses, they periodically served as the constable, who was responsible for both the military garrison and the castle's economy. The steward and receiver were the two other prominent officials who operated at the castle, the administrative centre of the lordship, and members of burgess families again periodically held these offices. In 1297, John Blackburn served as steward, the principal judicial and administrative official, and Thomas Pontefract as receiver, the main financial officer, and members of these families – Anable Blackburn and Thomas, the son of Thomas Pontefract – were also named as burgesses in the second foundation charter.[40] The other officials based at the castle included the escheator, who assumed possession of lands vacated as a result of death or forfeiture, and the master forester.

The close relationship between the borough and castle both stimulated and hindered the development of the urban community at Denbigh. The series of grants providing enhanced privileges effectively contributed towards the increasing stature of Denbigh as a commercial and administrative centre. However, the borough simultaneously suffered on account of its identification with the central administration of the lordship. The lords of Denbigh were, throughout this period and without exception, prominent figures on the English political stage, and considerable demands were made on the lordship in terms of both military and financial resources.[41] The reluctance of local inhabitants to fulfil military service abroad was the immediate cause of the 1294 rebellion, which terminated the first attempt to establish a borough at Denbigh.[42]

The success of the second creation of the borough was illustrated by the growth of this urban centre. Attention has already been drawn to the distinction between the 'old' and the 'new' towns in the second undated charter, probably compiled between 1295 and 1305, and again in the 1305 account, which referred to the fifty-two burgages held within the walls and the 183 burgages held outside the walls of the borough.[43] The 1334 Survey provided some information on the extent of the borough and the *burgus*, or area within the walls, was assessed at 9.5 acres and the *villa mercatoria*, or locality outside the walls, at 57 acres, 1 rood and 8 perches.[44] Further information on the borough's administrative machinery appears in Chapter 15.[45]

With regard to the other two boroughs recorded in the lordship – Abergele and Llanrwst – a striking contrast emerges between them. Abergele resembled Denbigh in being a centre of English influence, with the 1334 Survey recording that of the twenty-two burgesses who held twenty-nine burgages and one oven here for an annual rent of 20s. 1d, twenty were Englishmen and only two Welshmen.[46] On the other hand, Llanrwst, with its predominantly Welsh population, had probably been established as a pre-conquest urban centre, and, in 1334, seventeen burgage entries yielding 57s. from twenty-one burgages were occupied by nine burgesses, of whom six were clearly Welshmen and three

Englishmen.[47] A contrast between the two groups was also evident in the tenurial arrangements that applied in them. In Abergele, as in Denbigh, burgages were normally held for the payment of 1d each, while at Llanrwst burgage rents varied from 1s. to 4s.[48] In view of the different backgrounds of the burgage occupants in the three boroughs, it is evident that different policies were adopted towards them by the lordship administration. In Denbigh and Abergele burgage rents seem to have been kept deliberately at a low level as an inducement to attract English settlers to these newly established urban centres. On the other hand, in Llanrwst, with its predominantly Welsh population, the policy adopted by the administration seems to have been characterised by an element of financial exploitation.

The impression that Llanrwst had been established in the pre-conquest period, and had existed for a period longer than the half-century following the conquest, is reinforced by the composition in 1334 of this borough, which, consisting of twenty-one burgages held for a total annual payment of 57s., comprised a number of compound entries. Four separate entries recorded that Maredudd ap Dafydd held six burgages for an annual rent of 13s. 4d, and two other entries referred to Robert fil' Einion ap Trehearn's tenure of four burgages for a payment of 9s.[49] Despite the essential Welshness of Llanrwst's character, and its high burgage rents, there was a small but significant element of alien settlement here in 1334. Richard Steynebourne held two burgages *pro relevio* for an annual payment of 5s., Elena, *filia* Hugonis, one burgage, similarly for 6s. 8d, and William Curteys two burgages, again *pro relevio*, for 3s. A distinction may be drawn here between the Welsh and English burgesses, in that whereas the Welsh burgesses of Llanrwst held their burgages at will, the three Englishmen were allowed to occupy theirs by the privileged and more secure relief tenure. An attempt therefore seems to have been made to attract English families to settle in Llanrwst, and this seems to have represented a post-conquest adaptation of an earlier development. By 1334, however, Llanrwst seemed to be in a state of decline with the entry in the survey referring to a vacant burgage, *burgagia in decasu* and also an oven that was *in decasu*.[50]

The condition of Llanrwst in 1334, together with the evidence of aggregation of property with nine burgesses holding twenty-one burgages, was in marked contrast to the position in Abergele, which was certainly a post-conquest foundation created from the escheated lands of a township that had originally been held by free clans.[51] The 1311 inquisition had recorded that in Abergele twenty-four burgesses rendered annually 5s. 3d for the twenty-four burgages held by them. The burgesses held tenements outside the borough for a payment of £8, and they paid a sum of 30s. as the rent of assize of a mill. The tolls of the borough, valued at 30s. per annum, were let out at farm, and a fair worth 28s. 4½d per annum was held within the borough. Also, the earl of Lincoln had held the *advowson* of the church of Cedigog, which yielded annually ten marks, and the tenants claimed that court pleas and perquisites were worth 60s. per annum.[52] By 1334 the borough consisted of twenty-nine burgages and one oven held by twenty-two individuals for a rent of 20s. 1d, together with eight *placeae* and one-third *aule placitorum* held by eight tenants for 16s. 10d.[53] Therefore, Abergele had been extended considerably in the period 1311–34 despite a fall in the number of burgesses, and these statistics clearly indicate that Abergele, like Denbigh, was a young town and in an initial stage of growth.

As yet, the borough of Abergele had not been established long enough for some families to secure a predominant position, but despite this, it is possible to detect the emergence of a growing process of burgage-aggregation. In 1334, Thomas Bron is stated to have held 4.5 burgages for 4½d, and Robert Castleford three burgages for 3d and one *placea* for 6d. Henry Talbot occupied two burgages for 2d, and two *placeae* for 9d, while Iorwerth ap Gruffudd held 2.5 burgages for 2½d. The strong position of the Pontefract family was illustrated by John Pontefract's tenure of three burgages for 3d, and also two *placeae* for 3s. 6d, and Robert fil' Robert Pontefract's holding of one burgage for 1d. Moreover, a notable feature of these burgage tenures at Abergele was the low rents demanded for them, with the average burgage rent levied at 1d each – this was identical to the position at Denbigh whose burgesses similarly rendered sums of 1d at Christmas.[54] This was in marked contrast to that experienced at Llanrwst, where rents varied from 2s. to 3s. 6d,[55] and it is therefore probable that burgage rents at Denbigh and Abergele, with their considerable proportion of English tenants, had been kept at a deliberately low level for the purpose of attracting immigrant families to settle there.

Efforts also seem to have been made to initiate urban developments at two other localities in the lordship of Denbigh. The evidence of various ministers' accounts, surviving from the fourteenth century, confirmed the definition of Denbigh, Abergele and Llanrwst as boroughs, but the absence of relevant accounts in the entries for Lleweni and Pennant Erethlyn prompt one to question Vinogradoff's designation of Pennant Erethlyn as an urban centre and the New borough of Lleweni as an incipient borough on the bases of the existence of burgages at Pennant Erethlyn and *placeae* in the 'New borough' of Lleweni.[56] It is certainly true that the entry for Pennant Erethlyn in the 1331 view of account stated that a rent of 7s. 6d was paid for six burgages and two *placeae*.[57] Also, the minister's account of 1363 referred to the payment of £14 0s. 2½d for the farm of six burgages, 33 acres, half a rood and 23 perches, together with the payment of a rent of 9s. 10¾d for the farm of sixteen *placeae*, 1 acre, 1.5 roods and 8 perches in the New borough of Lleweni.[58]

A possible explanation for the complex situation in these two localities may be provided by an awareness of developments in the period leading up to 1334, when the survey referred to the escheat, at the time of the conquest, of 884 acres and 20 acres in the township of Pennant Erethlyn, which had previously been completely occupied by free clansmen. This property comprised six burgages, held by four Welsh tenants rendering 14s. 4d, and another twenty-four holdings, amounting to 643 acres, 1.5 roods, again held by Welsh tenants for which a sum of £7 5s. 6d was paid. The reference to burgages undoubtedly led Vinogradoff to consider Pennant Erethlyn to be one of the lordship's urban centres. Two burgages, and another 18 acres in the succeeding 'Acre' section, were described as having been formerly occupied by Richard Whalley.[59] This suggests that there had been an element of alien settlement at Pennant Erethlyn, which by 1334 was completely Welsh in character. Therefore, in view of the probable presence, in the pre-conquest period, of a Welsh borough, namely Llanrwst, in the commote of Uwch Dulas, it is possible that Pennant Erethlyn represented an attempt, by the post-conquest administration, to establish here an English borough, on the same pattern as Abergele and Denbigh, which would eventually rival and usurp the position of Llanrwst.

A similar failure to foster initial urban developments may also be related with regard to the 'New borough' of Lleweni, but in this case, however, it probably resulted from the conscious policy of the administration. This hamlet, significantly styled the 'New borough', and containing sixteen *placeae*, together with 1.5 acres and 6 perches, prompted Vinogradoff to describe the unit as 'possibly the germ of a fifth (borough)'.[60] In contrast to burgage rents, which were generally fixed at an uniform amount, the rents of the *placeae*, representing individual holdings of different sizes, and not constituting integral features of a borough as did burgages, varied considerably. Therefore, numerous examples of *placeae* are to be found in the 1334 Survey, with eighteen *placeae* to be found in the *Firme acrarum* entries of seven different townships. However, the 'New borough' is distinguished from these other townships in that the *placeae* were gathered together in a compact unit, while the significant designation of the 'New borough' represents another indication of possible urban developments in this hamlet. This opinion is confirmed by the evidence of later financial accounts which again indicate the consolidation of *placeae* in the 'New borough'.

This constituted a hamlet of the township of Lleweni, which, in the pre-conquest period, had been overwhelmingly bond in character. Unfortunately, no evidence is presented relating to the hamlet at this time, and the English term 'New borough' suggests that urban developments were initiated after 1282, with the *placeae* created in this hamlet in the immediate post-conquest period. It is noteworthy that there was a considerable amount of land-aggregation here. Seven individuals, all English settlers, held sixteen *placeae*, 1.5 acres and 16 perches for a total annual payment of £19 9s. ½d, with William Romworth holding, in two plots, three *placeae* and 10 perches at an annual rent of 3s. 4½d, and Elias Steel, again in two plots, two and a half *placeae* and 1 rood at 4s. 5½d.[61]

Also in the 'New borough', there was no uniform rent for the *placeae*, which varied from the 13s. 0½d paid by Cecilia Rybchester for one *placea* and half a rood, to the 2s. 1½d rendered by William Stonefield for two *placeae* and half a rood.[62] These references to land aggregation and varying rents suggest the existence of the 'New borough' for some time, and the question arises as to why these developments were stunted and did not develop as did those at the boroughs of Denbigh and Abergele. A possible explanation may possibly be provided by its location, as Lleweni might well have provided a threat to the borough that had been established at Denbigh. It is therefore probable that the lord, who would naturally be concerned to safeguard the commercial interests of the burgesses of Denbigh, and who represented a central focus for his administration, would be careful to prevent the development to full burghal status of this nearby locality.

The distinction in the attitude adopted towards the 'New borough' of Lleweni and Llanrwst, the pre-conquest urban centre, on the one hand, and the two post-conquest boroughs of Denbigh and Abergele, on the other hand, reflected the administration's policy towards urban developments within the lordship. The growth of Denbigh and Abergele represented the success of this policy, while the decline of the 'New borough' of Lleweni may clearly be attributed to the growth of Denbigh. The inability to establish Pennant Erethlyn as an Anglicising agency in the economy of Uwch Dulas illustrated the administration's failure to impose its will in what was possibly regarded as a comparatively remote locality.

Notes

1. Further information on Denbigh in the Middle Ages is available in my chapter 'Denbigh', in Ralph A Griffiths (ed.), *Boroughs of Mediaeval Wales* (Cardiff, 1978), pp. 164–87.
2. *SD*, pp. 52, 252–3, 280–2, 288, 74.
3. TNA DL,42/1, ff. 30v, 3 1r and 31v: I appreciated being informed of this reference by the late Professor, Sir R. R. Davies; for a transcript of the second charter see Williams, *Records of Denbigh*, pp. 119–24, and a translation in Williams, *Ancient and Modern Denbigh*, pp. 302–9.
4. TNA, *Cal. Inq. P.M.*, 158: for full a transcript and translation, see Williams, *Records of Denbigh*, pp. 99–108.
5. *Supra*, pp. 27–8.
6. P. Vinogradoff, 'Kindreds and Villages', in *SD*, p. xv.
7. *Supra*, pp. 34–5, 40, 48.
8. The commercial and military advantages of borough creation were emphasised by E. A. Lewis, *The Mediaeval Boroughs of Snowdonia* (London, 1912), and in the various contributions to Ralph A. Griffiths (ed.), *Boroughs of Mediaeval Wales* (Cardiff, 1978), and Helen Fulton (ed.), *Urban Culture in Medieval Wales* (Cardiff, 2012).
9. For fuller discussion on escheat and exchange, see above, pp. 64–74.
10. *SD*, pp. 53–5.
11. *SD*, pp. 109, 145.
12. See above, pp. **; M. W. Beresford, *New Towns of the Middle Ages: Town Plantation in England, Wales and Gascony* (Gloucester, 1967), pp. 55–97; M. M. Postan, *Medieval Trade and Finance* (Cambridge, 1973), p. 131; *Boroughs of Snowdonia*, pp. 29–30, and p. 273 for a description of the fortified boroughs of Wales as 'the vantage ground for the pleasure and profit of the Marcher lords'; Ellis, 'The English Element in the Perfeddwlad', 187–99; Davies, 'Race Relations', 32–56; Owen, 'Englishry of Denbigh', 57–76; Davies, *Lordship and Society*, R. R. Davies, *Conquest, Coexistence and Change: Wales 1063–1415* (Oxford, 1987), pp. 408–11, 415–30.
13. For a transcript, see Williams, *Records of Denbigh*, pp. 119–24, and a translation in Williams, *Ancient and Modern Denbigh*, pp. 302–9.
14. TNA DL 27/33.
15. TNA DL 27/33.
16. See n. 13 above.

17 TNA DL 27/33.
18 TNA DL 42/1, f. 28r. John de la Chambre was also granted an estate of 160 acres in the township of Lleweni; see *Arch. Camb.*, 6th series, 12 (1912) for a transcript of this deed. The document is not dated but the witnesses included William de Vavasor.
19 Henri le Clerk was identified as a burgess in the two charters but this may well refer to his occupation. John de Chirche was granted a burgage in 1285 but Robert de Chirche, according to the undated charter, was the occupant of a bovate in Lleweni.
20 *SD*, pp. 252, 6, 10, 14, 22, 44, 73, 79, 84, 90, 113, 133, 10, 16, 67.
21 TNA DL 27/33; *SD*, pp. 90, 79, 13, 76, 84, 163, 28, 31, 34, 35, 36, 66, 70, 116, 117, 133, 69, 14, 78, 79, 254, 139, 281, 282, 283, 30, 34, 35, 36, 65, 66.
22 *Supra*, pp. 83, 85–8, 101; *Infra*, pp. 151–2, 233.
23 TNA DL 42/1, ff. 30v, 31r, v.
24 TNA, ff. 29v, 30r; DL 25/2064; F. Jones, 'Welsh Bonds for Keeping the Peace, 1283 and 1295', *BBCS*, 13 (1950), 143–4.
25 TNA DL 42/1, ff. 33r, v; DL, 36/2, no. 248.
26 TNA DL 42/1, ff. 33v.
27 *Cal. Inq. Misc. 137–49*, p. 240.
28 Owen, *Englishry of Denbigh*, pp. 68–72; Davies, *Lordship and Society*, pp. 344, 347–8, for other examples of displacement of the native population in the lordships of Bromfield and Yale, Dyffryn Clwyd, Kidwelly and Coety.
29 TNA DL 42/1, ff. 28v. 29 r and v.
30 Williams, *Records of Denbigh*, pp. 99–108; J. G. Edwards, 'Sir Gruffydd Llwyd', *EHR*, 30 (1915), referred to his possession of family lands within the lordship of Denbigh.
31 TNA DL 29/1/2.
32 Three witnesses to this charter also appeared as witnesses to a grant of land by Henry de Lacy to Cadwgan Ddu, dated 3 September 1300 (NLW, Wigfair Deeds and Documents, 5). The remaining seven witnesses of the charter, together with William the parson of Denbigh, also witnessed a grant of lands made by Henry de Lacy to Robert de Hilton, *c*. 1300 (NLW., Aston Hall Deeds and Documents, 5261).
33 TNA DL 42/1, ff. 30v, 31r and 31v.
34 Williams, *Records of Denbigh*, pp. 119–24, and a translation in Williams, *Ancient and Modern Denbigh*, pp. 302–9.
35 *SD*, pp. 10, 14, 15, 18, 63, 66, 68, 72, 73, 76, 78, 84, 87, 139, 144, 204, 216, 6, 10, 14, 22, 44, 73, 79, 84, 90, 133, 138, 27, 30, 37, 38, 42, 43, 63, 64, 65, 71, 80, 83, 84.
36 *SD*, pp. 14, 15, 23, 52, 63, 78.
37 *SD*, pp. 77, 235, 255, 63, 131, 83, 14, 78, 79.
38 *SD*, pp. 204–5.
39 *CPR 1281–92*, p. 383; *CPR 1330–4*, p. 362; Williams, *Ancient and Modern Denbigh*, pp. 119–24.

40 TNA DL 29/1/1; Williams, *Records of Denbigh*, pp. 119–24, and a translation in Williams, *Ancient and Modern Denbigh*, pp. 302–9.
41 *Supra*, pp. 31–46 for information on the first five lords of Denbigh, who were all prominent figures on the English political stage.
42 *Supra*, pp. 36–7.
43 Williams, *Records of Denbigh*, pp. 119–24, and a translation in Williams, *Ancient and Modern Denbigh*, pp. 302–9; TNA DL 29/1/2.
44 *SD*, p. 56.
45 *Infra*, pp. 213–16, 224.
46 *SD*, pp. 252–3.
47 *SD*, pp. 280–2.
48 *SD*, pp. 252–3, 280–2.
49 *SD*, pp. 280–2.
50 *SD*, pp. 281–2.
51 *SD*, pp. 280–2, 252–3.
52 Williams, *Records of Denbigh*, p. 107.
53 *SD*, 252–3.
54 *Supra*, pp. 97, 102, 105.
55 *SD*, 280–2.
56 Vinogradoff, 'Kindreds and Villages', pp. xv, cxvi–cxvii.
57 TNA SC 6/1182/1.
58 TNA SC 6/1182/6.
59 *SD*, p. 288.
60 *SD*, p. 74; Vinogradoff, 'Kindreds and Villages', pp. xv–xvi.
61 *SD*, p. 74.
62 *SD*, p. 74.

8
POLITICAL CONTROL, 1344–1382

In the period between 1344 and 1382 the lords of Denbigh found it necessary to face and seek to surmount difficulties that had presented themselves earlier, and that arose from their relations with the principality of Wales, marcher lords and the inhabitants of the lordship. The problem with their relationship with the principality of Wales arose on the sudden death, on 30 January 1344, of William Montagu, whose close relationship with the king was reflected by the decision to observe a period of court mourning following Montagu's death.[1] On 12 February 1344, Hugh Berwick was commissioned to receive into the king's hands the castle and town of Denbigh, which 'pertain to him by reason of the *nonage* of the heir'.[2] This was certainly the correct and traditional practice on the death of a marcher lord.[3] There is therefore considerable interest in the declaration made on 8 April, within two months of Montagu's death, at an *inquisition post mortem* held by Richard Stafford and Hugh Berwick, that the lordship of Denbigh, valued at £1,000 per annum, was held by the Prince of Wales 'because the king gave the principality of Wales to the said prince, and the said castle, town and lordship from all time were, and of right are members of the principality of north Wales, whoever might be prince of Wales'.[4]

This declaration evidently referred to the king's grant to the prince, on 12 May 1343, of the Crown possessions in Wales, with specific references on the following day to a number of lordships in north-east Wales: Denbigh, Bromfield and Yale, Chirk, Oswestry, Clun and Ruthin/Dyffryn Clwyd.[5] As a direct consequence of this inquisition, Berwick was forbidden from dealing further with the lordship of Denbigh, which was associated with the principality of Wales until October 1353.[6] This statement provided a reminder of the traditional relationship between the territory to the east and west of the river Conwy, with the designation Gwynedd-is-Conwy for the eastern area a reminder of its incorporation in 1267 in Llywelyn ap Gruffydd's principality of Wales.[7] An identical policy was adopted with regard to Bromfield and Yale, another lordship created in 1282. In 1347, following the death without heirs of John Warenne, earl of Surrey, the prince ordered that *seisin* should be made of his lands 'which the earl of Surrey held of us in chief as of our principality'.[8] It should be emphasised that these lands were not formally incorporated in the principality but rather that the prince was responsible for their custody until their lords came of age.[9]

The prince's officials seem to have been anxious to retain custody of the lordship of Denbigh, and this may well explain the delay in granting the lordship to Montagu, and also the difficulties later experienced by Roger Mortimer in safeguarding his possession of the lordship. The marcher lords, for their part, endeavoured to ensure that they should hold their lordships as tenants in chief of the Crown. Therefore, on 24 October 1353, William Montagu, together with Richard, earl of Arundel and lord of Bromfield and Yale, performed homage to the king for the said baronies 'as immediately subject to the crown', but yet it is significant that this feudal acknowledgement was performed in the presence and with the consent of Edward, Prince of Wales.[10] Their position was regulated by statute in 1354 when it was declared that the marcher lords were responsible to the English king 'as they and their ancestors have been all times past' and not to the Prince of Wales.[11] However, despite this enactment, the Prince of Wales again assumed responsibility for the lordship of Denbigh in 1360, but the haste with which he assumed custody of the lordship possibly illustrated an awareness of the weakness of his legal title.[12]

The earlier association of the lordship with the principality in 1344, following the death of William Montagu, earl of Salisbury, who had been granted the lordship after the fall of Roger Mortimer, first earl of March,[13] had an immediate, albeit indirect impact on the lordship. The new energy unleashed in the administration of lands to the west of the river Conwy seems to have caused an incident that occurred on 14 February 1345, when eighty men attacked and murdered Henry Shaldeford on the road from Denbigh to Caernarfon. The attackers were led by Hywel ap Gronw, a cleric and member of the influential *Wyrion Eden* clan, while the victim, a burgess at Caernarfon, had been recently appointed one of the Prince's attorneys in north Wales.[14] The incident instantly provoked a spate of letters sent to the prince's council from the burgesses of Caernarfon,[15] Conwy,[16] Rhuddlan,[17] and Denbigh[18]; and from two royal officials – John Pirye, Chamberlain of north Wales[19] and Richard Stafford, prince's steward[20] – and an un-named person, who was probably a third official, namely John Swynemore, Stafford's deputy and member of an influential family in the lordship of Denbigh.[21] These letters provide information on the political climate within the lordship, and the burgesses of Denbigh declared that 'the Welsh have never since the conquest been so disposed as they are now to rise against their liege lord'.[22] Also, Richard Stafford attributed the restlessness of the Welsh population to 'the maintenance of Hywel ap Gronw',[23] while the Caernarfon burgesses referred to 'the assent and compassing of the leading Welshmen of the country'.[24]

The disaffection of the *uchelwyr* was further illustrated by the list of seventy-four Welshmen attainted at this time of conspiracy.[25] A study of the list suggests that several prominent individuals from the lordship of Denbigh were involved in the murder, even though the evidence only provided the name of the specific township from which the conspirator was drawn. Gronw Ddu ab Einion of Wigfair was probably the same person as the Gronw ab Einion ab Madog, who, according to the 1334 Survey, occupied in Wigfair, together with three others, the free *Gafael Iorwerth ap Cynddelw*.[26]

The other insurgents are not so easily identified,[27] but two individuals, with distinctive names – Rhirid Goch and Dafydd Chwith – may be recognised with some certainty. The Survey recorded that a Rhirid Goch held 7 acres, in two plots, for a rent of 1s. 9d in Llaethfaen.[28] Dafydd Chwith seems to have been a more prominent figure, and was the member of a leading landowning family in the pre-conquest period, as indicated by the clan's possession in 1334 of one-half of the township of Sgeibion, in the commote of Ceinmeirch. The 1334 Survey also recorded that Dafydd Chwith ap Dafydd and his two brothers Maredudd and Hywel, held the escheated one-half and one-eighth of *Gwely Bleddyn ap Gwilym* at Esgorebrill, in the commote of Uwch Dulas, in fee by a special tenure, free of *twnc* and *treth*, granted by the earl of Lincoln, in exchange for a half of the township of Sgeibion, which had formed their inheritance. In addition, Dafydd Chwith ap Dafydd occupied at will in Mathebrwd, also in the commote of Uwch Dulas, escheated lands formerly belonging to Madog Ddu ap Cynwrig, and containing one-sixteenth of the township, measuring 115 acres and 35 perches, for an annual rent of 10s.[29]

Despite Dafydd Chwith's apparent readiness to collaborate with the new regime, this prominent freeman ('*uchelwr*') was prepared in 1345, as were others of the same class, to jeopardise his prominent position.[30] It has been suggested that the conspiratorial *uchelwyr* were motivated by self-interest, and John Pirye referred to the Welsh officials as being afraid of Shaldeford 'because he has more knowledge than any other men of those who have disinherited my lord'.[31] In addition, Richard Stafford emphasised that Shaldeford was murdered because of his possession of evidence against members of the *uchelwyr*.[32] A long-standing feud seems to have prevailed between the Shaldeford family and the *Wyrion Ednyfed* clan, and this may explain the participation of Hywel and Gronw ap Tudur in the 1345 plot. In addition, although the *uchelwyr* in the principality had resented the rapacious English officials who had operated during the period of Mortimer's supremacy, they soon capitalised on the lax administrative supervision.[33] On realising that the principality, which he had received in 1343, was not producing the anticipated revenue, the Prince of Wales set out to overhaul his weakening administration.[34] It was probably the determination of the Prince's leading administrators to closely supervise local officials that forced the hand of *uchelwyr* such as Dafydd Chwith.

Although predominantly concerned with safeguarding their own positions, the *uchelwyr* were able to exploit the popular anti-English sentiment still prevalent in north Wales. The fear felt by alien burgesses was expressed by those of Caernarfon against the damage and destruction caused by a hostile Welsh population, and many English officials and burgesses are reported to have been slain.[35] The burgesses of Rhuddlan referred to disturbances caused by Welsh inhabitants and presented the murder of Shaldeford as the climax of an extended series of outrages, rather than as an isolated incident.[36] An atmosphere of suspicion and hostility evidently prevailed in the lordship of Denbigh, with the burgesses of Denbigh stating that 'the Prince's English tenants in these parts hardly dare to go out of the towns' or proceed with their daily occupations 'for fear of being slain and plundered'. They also claimed that 'the Welsh have never, since the conquest, been so disposed as they are now, to rise against their liege lord to conquer the land from him'. When one considers this statement in the light of the violent uprising of 1294, an indication is provided of the extent of racial hostility within the lordship.[37]

The 1345 insurgents included several clerics, and the election in that year of a bishop to the diocese of St Asaph involved the Church even further in the prevailing dissension. Although the king had pressed the claims of John de Lincoln, an Englishman, the canons of St Asaph insisted on the election of a Welsh-speaking Welshman. Their pleas were upheld by the Pope, and the canons, withstanding pressure from the prince's council, chose Gruffydd Trefor, one of their group. A further problem arose when he refused to serve, but in 1346 his nephew, John Trefor, was nominated by the Pope. This development, which has been considered to have recognised the 'claims of nationality', was a further illustration of the upsurge of pro-Welsh sentiment in the lordship of Denbigh.[38]

The custody of the lordship by the prince's officials was only intended to operate during the minority of William Montagu, born on 20 June 1328 and heir to the earldom of Salisbury.[39] While Montagu had been described in August 1346 as 'farmer of the lordship', and although he had received livery of his inheritance in July 1349, he was not granted the lordship of Denbigh until 24 October 1353.[40] This delay suggests that there may well have been opposition to Montagu's possession of the lordship of Denbigh, and that this might have stemmed from the counter-claims of Roger Mortimer, the second earl of March and the Prince of Wales, even though the latter had witnessed the grant to Montagu. The latter document therefore referred to 'the barony of Denbigh in north Wales, which the earl holds of the king in chief, as immediately subject to the king of England, the said prince consenting to this'. The Prince's later reluctance to allow Roger Mortimer to secure the undisputed succession of his heir Edmund to the lordship implies that he may have been partly responsible for the delay to Montagu's possession of the lordship.

On the other hand, Roger Mortimer's counter-claim for the lordship of Denbigh was undoubtedly influenced by his probable resentment of Montagu's tenure of the lordship, which was the direct result of the active participation of Montagu's father in the downfall and death of Mortimer's grandfather, the first earl of March. Therefore, the acquisition by a Montagu of Denbigh, a family prize secured from the Mortimer cupboard, would naturally arouse the resentment of Roger Mortimer, especially as other lands in the Welsh March had been restored to him in the period 1341-6. Moreover, Montagu's father, the first earl of Salisbury, had been granted in 1336 the marriage of the Mortimer heir, and as a result his daughter Philippa had married Roger Mortimer. This marriage to the daughter of one of his father's murderers may well have been a further humiliation for a proud Mortimer, and in the mid-fourteenth century, the two brothers-in-law, motivated possibly by family discontent as well as a long-established feud, struggled strenuously for a prize whose value, both materially and symbolically, was an attractive one for both parties.[41]

On 20 January 1355, Edward III reversed his earlier grant of the lordship of Denbigh to William Montagu, the second earl of Salisbury, and the king, 'of his certain knowledge, and after mature deliberation with his council, granted to Roger, earl of March, the said castle … by name of the Castle of Denbigh'.[42] This was consistent with his previous decision in 1354 to restore to Roger the title of 'earl of March' and family lands in the Welsh march.[43] While the king was undoubtedly aware of the potential threat presented by an over-powerful Mortimer family, a member of which had been responsible for the death of his father and had subsequently ruled the realm, he may also have been conscious of the need to curb the growing power of the Montagu family. Sybil, eldest daughter of William Montagu, the first earl of Salisbury, was married to Edmund Fitzalan, earl of Arundel, and lord of Bromfield and Yale; while the husband of Agnes, his fourth daughter, was John, the son and heir apparent of Roger de Grey, the first lord of Ruthin. A possible extension of influence to the southern Welsh march explains the marriage of the third daughter Elizabeth to Hugh, lord Despenser, and reference has already been made to the marriage of the second daughter Philippa to Roger Mortimer.[44]

While undoubtedly aware of the possible threat of strengthening a family whose record of loyalty to the Crown was suspect, this also might well prove to be the lesser of two evils in that Denbigh was isolated from the main grouping of Mortimer estates in the middle March. Although in receipt of the lordship on 20 January 1355, Roger Mortimer seems to have been aware of the precarious nature of his tenure, and on 26 September 1335 he was licensed to enfeoff the lordship to three individuals – Richard de la Bere, Ralph Spigurnel and John

Gour – which they could then re-grant to him, with remainder to his heirs.[45] By means of this fairly common contemporary legal device, Mortimer sought to safeguard the succession of his heir to an undivided estate.[46] This licence was re-issued on 18 August 1359 and the delay of four years suggests that certain difficulties remained before the completion of this transaction.[47] This is also implied in the reference in the letter patent, dated on 12 August 1373, that 'Mortimer died before they had made for him and Philippa estate',[48] as the terms of the 1355 licence could well have been executed by the time of Mortimer's sudden death on 26 February 1360. This prevented the realisation of an attempt to safeguard the possession of the lordship of Denbigh, which was not recovered by the Mortimer family until 1373, and resulted in a period of uncertainty with an official document declaring on 23 May 1360 that 'it had been shown on the prince's behalf that the lordship of Denbigh is part of the principality'.[49] The historical background to this claim relating to the attachment of the lordship to the principality of Wales was then outlined, with reference made to the prince taking possession of the lordship following the death of William Montagu, the first earl of Salisbury, in 1344; and then the second earl of Salisbury, in 1353, performing homage for the lordship to the prince of Wales. A possible uncertainty as to the legality of his actions is implied by the prince's determination to conclude the transaction as speedily as possible, as reflected by the statement on 9 May 1360 'that 'the prince does not wish the matter to be delayed, but rather be hastened day and night until it be completed'.[50]

The element of haste that characterised the attachment of the lordship to the Principality in 1360 was accompanied by the adoption of an intensive programme of re-organisation, as noted below.[51] This antagonised many of the lordship's inhabitants and in 1361 a petition of grievances was presented to the prince's council by 'the commonalty of two-thirds of the lordship'. Four main grievances were presented with each one objecting to the abuse of authority by officials. Reference was made to the rapacity of officials who prevented disputing parties from making mutual agreements because of their desire to obtain amercements. They also offended local inhabitants by demanding tolls from the sale of livestock and imposing the penalty of *croys* for a failure to attend township general assemblies, which, it was claimed were summoned far too frequently. The resentment caused by the actions of local officials was reflected by the statement that the bailiffs 'act out of malice and for their own advantage'. The petitioners, who consisted of representatives of both the native Welsh and the settler community, demanded that disputes be settled 'by the law of those parts', and they also emphasised the general illegality of the actions of the local officials that were 'against any kind of law'.[52]

The prince's officials responded immediately to the petition, and Delves and Brunham, at the head of the lordship's administration, were ordered 'to examine diligently the petition' and to 'treat with the petitioners'.[53] This response again reflected the determination of the Black Prince's Council to improve the administration of the lordship of Denbigh, and to take resolute action against local officials, whose activities had been responsible for the petition. Moreover, the presentation of the petition resulted in a grant of privileges to inhabitants of the lordship, as indicated in a complaint sent to the prince's auditors by Thomas Holland, farmer of the toll of Llanrwst.[54]

During this period, the administration also experienced various threats presented from outside the lordship, especially a possible French invasion led by the exiled Owain ap Thomas ap Rhodri, known as Owain Lawgoch.[55] Closely associated with Owain was Ieuan Wyn, who was probably Ieuan ap Rhys ap Roppert, an experienced professional soldier, member of the influential *Wyrion Eden* family group, and leader of the Welsh company in France following the assassination of Owain Lawgoch by John Lamb in July 1378.[56] An inquisition held at Flint on 20 December 1372 named a certain Ieuan as traitor to the king and serving in the company of Owain Lawgoch, and also referred to Ieuan's brother

Madog, as being in the French service at this time and again in the 1390s.[57] Their father, Rhys ap Roppert, was stated to have been aware of Ieuan's activities, and had sent him a sum of 500 marks over a six-year period to assist him and Owain Lawgoch. Rhys was evidently an influential figure: a direct descendant of Ednyfed Fychan, he had farmed the raglotry of the commote of Dinmael in 1360 and in 1365–6, and had been sergeant of the lordship of Denbigh in 1374–5, in addition to occupying the important offices of sheriff and escheator of Flintshire.[58] A further inquisition on 25 September 1374 referred to Rhys and Ieuan as adherents of Owain Lawgoch and traitors and enemies of the king of England and prince of Wales. Also, on several occasions in 1371, 1372 and 1373 Rhys had sent gold and silver by Madog to be sent on to Ieuan to assist him in the service of the king of France.[59]

A climate of disturbance and unrest clearly prevailed in the Welsh march at this time. The lordship of Denbigh, together with other units in the Welsh march, had been required on 10 February 1367 to provide a number of armed men to defend the realm in the event of a possible attack by the king's enemies.[60] Further instructions requesting marcher lords to fortify their castles for the same reason were again issued on 24 December 1369 and 15 March 1377.[61] A letter close dated 13 March 1380, referring to inhabitants of marcher lordships committing crimes in English border shires, revealed the government's dissatisfaction with the extent of crime in the marcher lordships 'where the king's ministers have no jurisdiction', and also of increasing hostility on the Welsh border.[62]

There is a certain lack of clarity with regard to the possession of the lordship of Denbigh at this time. On 10 February 1361, Isabella, daughter of Edward III and Philippa of Hainault, had been granted wardship of two-thirds of the lands formerly belonging to Roger Mortimer,[63] and on 15 November 1364 Isabella leased to Philippa, Roger Mortimer's widow, the Mortimer lands in the middle march.[64] Philippa was thereby in full possession of the Mortimer estate, which on 6 January 1373 was bequeathed to her son, Edmund Mortimer.[65] It is probable that Denbigh was included in these transactions but its status was complicated by the deaths of both Philippa and Edmund Mortimer within a few days of each other, Edmund on 27 December 1381 and his mother on 5 January 1382.[66] This resulted in a certain amount of disparity in the references to Denbigh in 1382 with the lordship described in some sources as having escheated to the Crown 'as among other lands late of Edmund Mortimer'[67] and 'by reason of the death of Philippa, late the wife of Roger Mortimer'.[68]

Notes

1 *Cal. Inq. P.M.*, viii, Edward III, 532, pp. 386–390; W. Mark Ormrod, *Edward III* (New Haven CT, 2011), p. 134, referred to William Montagu as 'the man who undoubtedly enjoyed closest familiarity with the king'.
2 *CPR 1343–5*, p. 200.
3 D. L. Evans, 'Some Notes on the History of the Principality in the Time of the Black Prince, 1343–76', *THSC*, (1925–6), 89: 'one of the essential qualities of a marcher lord was that he held in chief of the king'.
4 *Cal. Inq. P.M.*, viii, Edward III, 532, p. 388.
5 *C. Charter R. 1341–1417*, pp. 14–15.
6 *CCR 1343–6*, p. 306.
7 *Supra*, p. 14.
8 Evans, 'Some Notes on the History of the Principality', 91.
9 The administration of the two territories was kept separate: in 1345 Richard Stafford was described as chamberlain of the Principality but as steward of Denbigh (TNA, SC 6 1214/3).
10 *CCR 1349–54*, p. 562.
11 I. Bowen (ed.), *The Statutes of Wales* (London, 1908), p. 30.
12 *Supra*, p. 120.
13 *Supra*, p. 113.
14 A full discussion of this incident is provided in Glyn Roberts, *Aspects of Welsh History* (Cardiff, 1969), pp. 179–214.
15 *CAC*, 231, no. liv, 41.
16 *CAC*, 234–5, no. liv, 46
17 *CAC*, 231–2, no. liv, 42.
18 *CAC*, 230–1 liv, 40.
19 *CAC*, 232–3, no. liv, 43.
20 *CAC*, 233, no. liv, 44.
21 *CAC*, 233, no. liv, 45.
22 *CAC*, 230, no. liv, 40.

23 *CAC*, 233, no. liv, 44.
24 *CAC*, 231, no. liv, 41.
25 *CAC*, 227–8, no. liv, 37; 228–9, no. liv, 38.
26 *SD*, p. 212.
27 A similar problem, arising from the nature of Welsh patronymics, is presented in the identification of Welsh office holders.
28 *SD*, p. 296.
29 *SD*, pp. 27–8, 277–8, 284–5.
30 See Roberts, *Aspects of Welsh History*, pp. 193–7, for a discussion on the motives and involvement of Hywel and Tudur ap Goronwy, members of the Ednyfed Fychan family, and prominently involved in the 1345 incident.
31 *CAC*, 232, no. liv, 43.
32 *CAC*, 233, no. liv. 44.
33 Waters, *Edwardian Settlement*, pp. 69–86.
34 *C. Charter R. 1341–1417*, p. 14.
35 *CAC*, 231, no. 41.
36 *CAC*, 231–2, no. liv, 42.
37 *CAC*, 230, no. liv. 40.
38 Glanmor Williams, *The Welsh Church from Conquest to Reformation* (Cardiff, 1962), pp. 124–6.
39 Cokayne, *The Complete Peerage of England*, vol. 11, p. 388.
40 *BPR*, i, 9; *CCR 1346–9*, 109; *CCR 1349–53*, 562.
41 Hopkinson and Speight, *The Mortimers*, pp. 108, 110, 143.
42 *CPR 1354–8*, p. 159.
43 H. G. Richardson and G. O. Sayles (eds), *Rotuli Parliamentorum Angliae hactenus inedita*, Camden Society, 3rd series li (London, 1935), n. 255, p. 267.; Hopkinson and Speight, *The Mortimers*, pp. 110, 143.
44 Cokayne, *The Complete Peerage of England*, vol. 11, p. 388; Hopkinson and Speight, *The Mortimers*, pp. 145–6.
45 *CPR 1354–58*, p. 327.
46 Holmes, *Estates of the Higher* Nobility, p. 46: 'If this conveyance had been completed, the most valuable of the Mortimer lordships would have been kept out of reach of the escheator.'
47 *CPR 1358–61*, p. 267.
48 *CPR 1370–4*, 353.
49 *CPR 1360–4*, 32–3.
50 *BPR*, iii, 381.
51 *Infra*, pp. 176–8.
52 *BPR*, iii, 410; Sara Elin Roberts, 'Legal practice in fifteenth-century Brycheiniog', *SC*, 35 (2001), 307–25, for a discussion of legal procedure involving 'dadl croes' relating to a territorial claim in the fifteenth century lordship of Brecknock.
53 *BPR*, iii, 410.
54 *BPR*, iii, 486.

55 J. H. Davies, 'Owain Lawgoch', *Trans. Cymm* (1899–1900); A. D. Carr, *Owen of Wales: The End of the House of Gwynedd* (Cardiff, 1991), p. 3, for a table showing Rhys's position in the genealogy of the Gwynedd ruling dynasty.
56 Carr, *Owen of Wales*, pp. 21–3, 27, 58–60.
57 TNA Chester, 25/24 m. 81 a; Carr, *Owen of Wales*, pp. 42–4.
58 A. D. Carr, 'Rhys ap Roppert', *TDHS*, 25 (1976), 155–8, 263–6, 168.
59 TNA, Chester, 25/24 m. 10 b; Carr, *Owen of Wales*, pp. 42–5.
60 *CCR 1364–7*, p. 371.
61 *CCR 1369–74*, p. 61; *CCR 1374–7*, p. 487.
62 *CCR 1377–81*, p. 365.
63 *CPR 1358–61*, p. 577
64 *CPR 1364–7*, p. 37.
65 *CCR 1369–74*, p. 418.
66 Cokayne, *The Complete Peerage of England*, vol. 8, pp. 448, 445.
67 *CPR 1381–5*, pp. 90, 92, 100, 261, 268.
68 *CPR 1371–5*, p. 65.

9
POLITICAL CONTROL, 1382–1425

The Crown was nominally responsible for various lands in England and Wales during the period leading up to the grant, on 25 February 1394, of the lordship of Denbigh to Roger Mortimer, fourth earl of March, whose virtues were extolled by Iolo Goch.[1] In these years, professional administrators supervised the vast Mortimer estate and Walter Brugge, the receiver-general in the 1380s, journeyed with Thomas Hildeburgh, the auditor, from Usk to Denbigh in 1386.[2] A Welshman, Philip ap Morgan – a member of a gentry family in south-east Wales, who had served his local lords, members of the Mortimer family, as steward of Usk in 1385, and Clifford and Glasbury in 1388 – was appointed steward of the lordship of Denbigh in 1394.[3]

Within three years, possession of the lordship was claimed by John Montagu, who became earl of Salisbury on his father's death in 1397. A loyal adherent of Richard II, one of his first acts as earl was to stake a claim for the lordship of Denbigh, which had been granted in 1331 to his forefather following the downfall of the first earl of March.[4] It has been suggested that Richard II was suspicious of the motives of Roger Mortimer, his heir-presumptive, who, based in Ireland, was summoned to Shrewsbury early in 1398 for the express purpose of taking an oath of loyalty to Richard and to the proceedings of the 1397–8 parliament.[5] In the complex political narrative of the period 1397–8, the lordship of Denbigh seems to have been an instrument whereby Richard II was able to exert pressure on his rival Roger Mortimer.

The latter's death in Ireland on 20 July 1398 resulted in the lordship again escheating to the Crown.[6] A dower was provided for his widow, Eleanor, daughter and co-heir of Thomas de Holland, earl of Kent, but the lordship of Denbigh was not included in the lands specified in this transaction, and by 1402 the whole lordship was in the king's hands.[7] Earlier in 1399, when Richard II was in Ireland, Henry Bolingbroke, eldest son of John of Gaunt, launched his successful bid to seize the throne of England.[8] Richard responded by despatching from Ireland the earl of Salisbury with a contingent of troops and instructions to raise an army in north Wales.[9]

Salisbury's connection with Denbigh suggests that troops may have been recruited from the lordship, but no evidence is available to support this possibility. A large force seems to have been assembled but the army soon disbanded following the rumour, possibly believed by Salisbury, that Richard had died. Richard's later attempt to revive this army never materialised, and on 30 September 1399 he was supplanted by Henry Bolinbroke (of Lancaster), who reigned as Henry IV until his death in 1413.[10] Soon after his accession, on 6 November 1399, Henry IV granted custody of the lordship to Henry Percy, 'Hotspur', son of the earl of Northumberland, a transaction that was confirmed on 14 December 1401.[11] Despite the fact that Percy was married to Elizabeth, the daughter of Edmund and Philippa Mortimer, and was thereby the fourth earl's brother-in-law, there is no reason for believing that he pressed Edmund's claims in 1398. On the contrary, the earl of Northumberland and his son, who were dissatisfied with Richard's favoured treatment of Ralph Neville, earl of Westmorland, their rival northern magnate, seem to have been solely concerned with their own dynastic interests. Their support of Henry Bolingbroke enabled them to secure influence in north Wales, an area from which they had previously been excluded. However, by 1403 they had lost their enthusiasm for Henry's cause: a change of attitude largely caused by the impact on them, and on their Welsh estates, of the Glyn Dŵr uprising, and this represented one of the many ways whereby the rebellion influenced the course of English politics in the early fifteenth century.[12]

Following his proclamation as Prince of Wales at Glyndyfrdwy on 16 September 1400, Owain Glyn Dŵr led a band of followers on attacks on numerous towns in north-east Wales including Denbigh and Ruthin.[13] Contemporary court rolls for Ruthin reveal that the insurgents involved in the initial attacks numbered 280, of whom a substantial proportion, amounting to at least eighty, came from the lordship of Denbigh. This group was listed separately on the roll, with 'Denbigh' inserted in the margin alongside the names. The origins of the other insurgents were not similarly specified, although place-names attached to some personal names indicate that several came from Edeirnion, Penllyn and Glyndyfrdwy. Some of these were associated with the lordship of Denbigh, including Dafydd ab Einion of Twysog and Dafydd ap Conyn of Dinmael.[14]

The main group from the lordship of Denbigh appeared at the end of the court roll. Numerous Welsh personal names may not be identified with certainty, and the home townships of only two are recorded; namely; Ieuan Offeiriad of Cerrig y Drudion and Cynwrig Garthmeilyr.[15] An inability to identify, among contemporary office-holders and lease-holders in the lordship, those involved in the attack on Ruthin suggests that these may well have been persons of low social status, and it would seem that at this early stage participants in the local administration remained aloof from the rebellion.

The succeeding period was characterised by sporadic actions, but on 1 April 1401 Rhys and Gwilym ap Tudur, two powerful individuals in north-west Wales, succeeded in capturing Conwy castle.[16] Henry Percy, justiciar of North Wales, Cheshire and Flintshire in addition to being keeper of Denbigh castle, marched from Denbigh in June 1401 and routed Welsh forces at Cader Idris.[17] He appointed Sir William Swinburne, a faithful follower from Northumberland, as steward of Denbigh, and William Lloyd, of Foxhall, near Denbigh, as his personal squire and deputy steward of Denbigh. The reference to Lloyd, a significant local figure, having served as rhingild of Uwch Aled in 1397 and 1398, and escheator in 1397 and 1402, indicates the active involvement of some of the prominent individuals in the lordship.[18] In June 1402, a force of archers and esquires was sent from Cheshire to Denbigh, and repair work undertaken at Denbigh included the cleaning of ditches, the erection of barriers to defend the town and the hiring of carpenters and masons to repair the Westgate, Towngate and town walls.[19]

The series of parliamentary acts, enacted in 1401 and 1402 and designed to penalise Welshmen, included the provision for the garrisons of castles and town walls in Wales to be manned until the restoration of peace not only by Englishmen but even by strangers to the area.[20] However, in 1402 Denbigh castle was garrisoned by representatives of several prominent local settler families, including members of the Dolben, Peake, Pigot, Salusbury and Swynemore families. Their recruitment illustrates both the trust placed in these families and also the absence, as yet, of a serious upheaval in the lordship.[21]

On the whole the lordship of Denbigh was spared the ferocious attacks launched on Ruthin, and in May 1402 William Curteys, constable of Denbigh, was ordered by Henry Percy to render assistance to those defending Ruthin castle.[22] In September, Henry IV led from Shrewsbury his army, which caused considerable damage in Llanrwst.[23] The royal administration seems to have shown a decreasing confidence in Henry Percy's ability to crush the rebellion, and also an awareness of the growing possibility of an alliance being forged between Owain Glyn Dŵr and Percy, who was becoming increasingly dissatisfied with Henry IV's Welsh policy. A contemporary chronicler related that late in 1401 Percy had tried to arrange a settlement between himself and Glyn Dŵr, but his efforts were foiled by bellicose members of the king's council.[24] Finally, incensed by the delay in the king's efforts to ransom Edmund Mortimer, Percy's brother-in-law, in contrast to the speed with which Reginald de Gray had been ransomed,

Henry Percy came to terms with Glyn Dŵr in 1403.[25] The intermediary in the negotiations between Percy and Glyn Dŵr was William Lloyd, the son of Robert Lloyd of Foxhall, who travelled to Berwick to confer with Percy, and soon afterwards Glyn Dŵr, Percy and Edmund Mortimer, who had married Catherine, Glyn Dŵr's daughter, agreed to form a coalition to oppose Henry IV. Percy's forces, however, which included men from the counties of Chester and Flint and the lordship of Denbigh, were defeated by Henry IV's army at Shrewsbury on 21 July 1403, and he, together with his envoy, William Lloyd, were killed in battle.[26]

Following the death of Henry Percy, custody of the lordship of Denbigh was granted to Henry, Prince of Wales. This involved a renewal of the association with the other royal lands in north Wales, forming the Principality of North Wales, as had occurred following the death of Roger Mortimer in 1398, with Henry Percy, at that time, in addition to being keeper of the lordship of Denbigh, occupying the offices of Justice of North Wales and of Chester. However, there would now be a change in the policy of the administration that would henceforth be responsible to a person who, unlike his predecessor, would be determined to eliminate the threat presented by Glyn Dŵr, and make skilful use of Welsh castles and English sea-power as crucial military assets.[27]

The strength of Glyn Dŵr's influence within the lordship survived the defeat at Shrewsbury. It was probably at this time that certain individuals, who may be identified as members of native and settler families, and who were motivated by personal as well as patriotic motives, supported the rebellion; the alignment of these individuals of property and position reflected a change in the character of the revolt. Another consequence of the latter development was that the lordship would no longer avoid the destructive raids of the Welsh leader. The evidence of material destruction, recorded in the 1437 rental of the lordship, probably reflected events in the lordship in the period after the 1403 grant. No information was presented on the borough of Denbigh, which had been attacked by rebels in 1400, but this rental recorded that the fulling mill of Berain, the old mill of the Clwyd, in the 'Acre' of Llewem, and the old mill of Kilford, had all been burned by rebels. Also, although actual destruction was not specified, a new fulling mill had been built at Ystrad, and the mills of Sgeibion, Llewesog and Prys were being repaired, as also were houses on the manor of Kilford.[28]

Despite these raids, whose impact on the economy will be further discussed, the tide in the lordship of Denbigh was slowly turning against Glyn Dŵr. In 1407 and 1408, fines levied on various administrative units in north-east Wales amounted to a total sum of £1,471 14s. 2d, of which £1,079 7s. 3d, or 73.3 per cent, was spent on military excursions in north-west Wales. The revenue in 1407 of £229, derived from fines collected in the lordship of Denbigh, was spent on the maintenance of a force, comprising four men-at-arms and thirty-six archers, to defend the castle from 3 May 1406 until 10 July 1407.[29] The small size of this force again emphasised the limited extent of the impact of the uprising on the lordship at this time.

Whereas a sum of £200 10s. had been charged in 1407, but not actually collected, and that included truces drawn up between Henry IV and inhabitants of the lordships of Denbigh and Ruthin, a sum of £596 1s. was actually raised from the lordship of Denbigh in this year and comprised general fines levied on communities in the various commotes.[30] Fines were also paid by some of the residents who were enumerated in the first section of this document. In contrast to the general settlement involving all the inhabitants of the island of Anglesey in 1406, the relevant section in the Denbigh document contained only fifty-three entries. These clearly referred to specific offences, with two entries referring specifically to the capture of outlaws. A sum of 20s. out of a total fine of 40s. was paid by Alfred Peake, William Billyng, Thomas Romworth and John Throscull, who had brought Gronw Gethyn before the Justice at Denbigh. Also, 10 marks were rendered by John Conway of Rhuddlan castle, who had handed over Gruffudd ap Bleddyn ap Einion Llwyd, a priest from Abergele. The remaining entries were less informative and referred to the payment of fines for various rebellions, felonies, transgressions and misdeeds. Individuals who had flirted with the rebellion now seemed to be returning to their traditional allegiance, and in two exceptional cases, the capture or handing over of outlaws was part of the amnesty.[31]

The 1407 list, with the sole exception of Alfred Peake, failed to refer to any of the more prominent families of the lordship, both of native and settler origin. Whereas Alfred Peake was described in 1410 as the former joint occupant with William Swynemore and John Fraunces of a water mill in the Park of Segrwyd, that he leased in the same year, in the Park of Lleweni, three plots of 20 acres, 4.5 acres and 2.5 acres. He also served as bailiff of the Englishry in the period 1409–11, and again in 1424.[32]

The involvement of some of the other individuals named in 1407 may well have resulted from dissatisfaction with land transactions, and it is therefore significant that several of them appeared in the 'decayed rents section of the 1397 and 1402 accounts as the former occupants of lands that had later escheated. Gronw ap Einion Llwyd was described in 1397 as the late occupant of 3.5 acres in Cernenyfed.[33] Also, the accounts for ' Clisserin' in 1397 and 1402 reveal that Gronw Gethyn had formerly held here 2 acres, while Gruffudd ap Bleddyn ap Einion Llwyd was described in 1402 as the former occupant in this township of one parcel of land valued at 3s. 9½d and another five plots amounting to 7.5 acres.[34] The loss of five distinct plots suggests that Gruffudd had some cause for discontent, and that this may well have motivated his support of Glyn Dŵr.

Other contributors of fines were in a more favourable position. Margaret Lawrence hailed from a leading Abergele family. John Lawrence, the bailiff of Abergele in 1380, had been named in 1375 as a former bailiff of this borough.[35] Richard Lawrence was similarly described in 1402, while Thomas Lawrence held this office in 1407.[36] Some of the contributors had succeeded in restoring their fortunes after the rebellion. William Billyng, the lessee in 1402 of several plots of escheated lands, leased in 1410 an identical plot, amounting to 46 acres in the Park of Lleweni, and also a further 14 acres in the Park of Segrwyd.[37] Cona Ddu, who had been sergeant of the peace in Is Dulas before 1402, held the same office in 1408–10.[38] Whereas Alfred Peake was described in 1410 as the former joint occupant with John Frances of a watermill in the Park of Segrwyd, he also leased in the same year, in the Park of Lleweni, three plots of 20 acres, 4.5 acres and 2.5 acres. Furthermore, he also served as bailiff of the Englishry in the period 1409–11, and again in 1421.[39]

On 1 May 1411, the steward of Ruthin, significantly named Henry Salusbury, was instructed by the Justice of Chester, in an order issued at Bala, to return from his lordship to the lordship of Denbigh all the tenants of the Prince of Wales, and was also empowered to arrest those who refused to return and seize their property.[40] However, many of Glyn Dwr's adherents within the lordship seem to have prospered after the rebellion had subsided. They most probably belonged to a depressed economic and social class, but after the rebellion some of these appeared as office-holders and occupants of plots of land. It is possible that a connection existed between one of the known rebels of 1400, Ieuan Llwyd, who was named as the son of Ednyfed and father of Dafydd, and Gruffydd ap Ieuan Llwyd, raglot of Is Aled in 1411.[41] Also, whereas Deicus ab Einion, who was listed in 1407 among those who paid fines, and described in 1402 as the former occupant of 6.5 acres in Sgeibion, was ringild of Ceinmeirch in 1424 and 1426; his name was presented in 1437 as 'Deicus ab Einion ap Ieuan Lloyd', the occupant of 4 acres in Bachymbyd, and his son 'Einion ap Ieuan Llwyd', the tenant of 7 acres in Cernenyfed.[42]

Moreover, the few rebels who were identified as members of the more prominent families, succeeded in recovering and consolidating their positions. Two families whose members participated in the rebellion also seem to have avoided being penalised. Gronw Goch, ringild of Uwch Dulas in 1398, held the same office in 1410, as did his son Llywelyn in 1415. Therefore, the complicity of his other son, Einion, in the 1400 raid does not seem to have prejudiced the involvement of this family in local government.[43] In 1437, Deicus Penllwyd, one of Einion's fellow rebels, held 1 acre and half an acre on twenty-year leases in Sgeibion. He also occupied in Bachymbyd, 9 acres on a forty-year lease, 5.5 acres on a twenty-year lease and, together with his wife Matilda 16.5 acres.[44]

The restoration and acquisition of local influence by individuals who had formerly been attracted to Glyn Dŵr's cause revealed his waning influence in the lordship. A crucial factor was probably the tight grip exerted on the lordship by the Prince of Wales, with the lordship henceforth a base from which other areas in Wales could be reconquered. He succeeded to the throne as Henry V on 20 March 1413, and soon afterwards, on 9 June, delivered the Mortimer lands, including the lordship of Denbigh, to Edmund Mortimer, the fifth earl of March, who remained loyal to the monarchy, despite the plotting of his uncle, Edmund, who had formed an alliance with Glyn Dŵr.[45] However, his brother-in-law, Richard, second son of Edmund of York and newly created earl of Cambridge, conspired to depose Henry and proclaim the earl of March as king, who had been the heir-presumptive to Richard II. The plot was disclosed to Henry by Edmund and Richard was executed.[46] Edmund's claim to the throne continued to attract the attention of anti-Plantagenet sentiment, and he was described in 1422 as being 'still the hope of the discontented'.[47] He died on 18 January 1425 without a direct heir, and his lands passed to Richard, the son of his sister Anne and the late earl of Cambridge.

Notes

1   R. R. Davies, *The Revolt of Owain Glyn Dŵr* (Oxford, 1995), p. 9, referred to 'a sense of bustling activity at Denbigh in the 1390s ... Denbigh had not been as lively for many a long year'; Hopkinson and Speight, *The Mortimers*, p. 117; Dafydd Johnston, *Gwaith Iolo Goch* (Caerdydd, 1988), pp. 84–90, 292–303;

Dafydd Johnston, *Iolo Goch* (Caernarfon, 1989), pp. 16–17; Dafydd Johnston (ed.), *Iolo Goch: Poems* (Llandysul, 1993), pp. 82–9, 173–5: 'Earl of March   best cul in the world / Iarll Mars – gorau iarll ym myd'; *CPR 1391–6*, p. 375.

2   Davies, *The Revolt of Owain Glyn Dŵr*, pp. 42–3; Davies, *Lordship and Society*, pp. 214–15; BL Egerton Roll, 8732. Hopkinson and Speight, *The Mortimers*, pp. 152–3.

3   Davies, *Lordship and Society*, pp. 205–6, TNA SC 6 1182/2; Hopkinson and Speight, *The Mortimers*, p. 153; Adam Chapman, 'Rebels, Uchelwyr and Parvenus: Welsh Knights in the Fourteenth Century', in Adrian R. Bell and Anne Curry, with Adam Chapman, Andy Knight and David Simkins (eds), *The Soldier Experience in the Fourteenth Century* (Woodbridge, 2011), pp. 152–3, referred to the appointment of Philip, who was possibly a patron of Iolo Goch, as chancellor of the duchy of Normandy in 1418, and also his consecration as Bishop of Worcester in 1419 and Bishop of Ely in 1426.

4   Richardson and Sayles (eds), *Rotuli Parliamentorum Angliae hactenus inedita*, vol. 3, p. 342; Davies, *The Revolt of Owain Glyn Dŵr*, pp. 80–1; Nigel Saul, *Richard II* (London, 1997), p. 397.

5   Edward Maunde Thompson (ed.), *Chronicon Adae de Usk, A.D. 1377–1421*, 2nd edn (London, 1904), p. 165, n. 3, for reference to the suggestion in the chronicle of Wigmore Abbey that the main reason for Mortimer's attendance at Shrewsbury was to defend his title to the lordship of Denbigh; Chirs Given-Wilson (ed. and trans.), *Chronicle of Adam of Usk, 1377–1421* (Oxford, 1977), pp. 32–6; Chris Given-Wilson, 'Chronicles of the Mortimer family, c. 1250-1450', in Richard Eales and Shaun Tyas (eds), *Family and Dynasty in Late-Medieval England, Proceedings of the 1997 Harlaxton Symposium* (Donington, 2003), p. 75.

6   M. McKisack, *The Fourteenth Century, 1307–1399* (Oxford, 1959), pp. 484–5; Hopkinson and Speight, *The Mortimers*, pp. 117–9.

7   *CCR 1396–9*, pp. 278–9.

8   *CPR 1401–5*, p. 412; Davies, *The Revolt of Owain Glyn Dŵr*, p. 80; Hopkinson and Speight, *The Mortimers*, p. 120.

9   TNA SC 6/1185/4; Saul, *Richard II*, pp. 288–92, 409–10.

10 Anthony Steel, *Richard II* (Cambridge, 1941), pp. 263–6; James Sherborne, 'Richard II's return to Wales, July 1399', *WHR*, 7/4 (December 1975), 389–402.

11 McKisack, *Fourteenth Century*, p. 493.

12 *CCR 1399–1402*, pp. 437–8; McKisack, *Fourteenth Century*, pp. 491–6; J. M. W. Bean, 'Henry IV and the Percies', *History*, 44 (1959), 219–24; Ralph A. Griffiths, *Conquerors and Conquered in Medieval Wale*s (Stroud, 1994), pp. 92–101, 102–38; Davies, *The Revolt of Owain Glyn Dŵr*, pp. 81–3.

13 J. E. Lloyd, *Owen Glendower* (Oxford, 1931), pp. 28–32; Davies, *The Revolt of Owain Glyn Dŵr*, pp. 102–3; 'De Oweino Glendworedy', in Michael Livingstone and John K. Bollard (eds), *Owain Glyndwr: A Casebook* (Liverpool, 2013), p. 11, 36–9, 299–303.

14 TNA SC 2/221/m.9d.

15 *SD*, p. 71. In 1334 Alicia Verdon held one plot in the 'Acre' of Lleweni for which she rendered 4s. Its measurements were not specified but it was called 'Gathmeilyr'.
16 Keith Williams-Jones, 'The Taking of Conwy Castle, 1401', *TCHS*, 39 (1978), 7–43; J. Goronwy Edwards, 'Edward I's Castle Building in Wales', *Proceedings of the British Academy*, 32 (1946), 38, described Conwy castle as 'the most magnificent of Edward I's Welsh fortresses'.
17 H. Nicholas (ed.), *Proceedings and Ordinances of the Privy Council of England*, vol. 1 (London, 1834), p. 153.
18 Lloyd, *Owen Glendower*, p. 60; Davies, *The Revolt of Owain Glyn Dŵr*, p. 181; Livingstone and Bolland, *Owain Glyndwr*, pp. 54–6, 308–9.
19 Livingstone and Bolland, *Owain Glyndwr*, p. 108; TNA SC 6/1185/4; E 101/43/9.
20 *Statutes of the Realm*, vol. 2 (London, 1810–28), pp. 128–9, 140–1; Bowen, *Statutes of Wales*, pp. 31–7.
21 TNA SC 6/1185/4.
22 Thompson, *Chronicon Adae de Usk*, p. 71; *Chronicle of Adam of Usk*, pp. 148–9; *Calendar of Recognizance Rolls of the Palatinate of Chester, Appendix ii to the Annual Report of the Deputy Keeper of the Public Records* (London, 1875), p. 415.
23 Davies, *The Revolt of Owain Glyn Dŵr*, p. 109; TNA SC 6/1185/4.
24 J. A. Giles (ed.), *Incerti Scriptoria Chronicon Angliae* (London, 1848), p. 31.
25 Lloyd, *Owen Glendower*, pp. 59–60; Davies, *The Revolt of Owain Glyn Dŵr*, pp. 180–4; Bean, *Henry IV*, p. 224.
26 Hopkinson and Speight, *The Mortimers*, p. 123.
27 Davies, *The Revolt of Owain Glyn Dŵr*, pp. 242–3, 246–55.
28 NLW Wynnstay 86, 69v – 72v, 76r–78r, 84v–86r.
29 TNA SC 6 775/7; 775/8.
30 TNA SC 6/775/7.
31 NLW Peniarth, 405 D, ff. 516–44; and *Bodewryd*, 103(a); Glyn Roberts, 'The Anglesey Submissions of 1406', *BBCS*, 15 (1954), 39–61; TNA SC 6/775/7.
32 TNA SC 6/1185/10; 1185/11; 1185/13.
33 TNA SC 6/1184/22.
34 TNA SC 6/1184/22; 1185/4.
35 TNA SC 6/1183/15; 1184/13.
36 TNA SC 6/1185/4; 1185/10.
37 TNA SC 6/1185/4; /11.
38 TNA SC 6/1185/4; /9 ; /11.
39 TNA SC 6/1185/10, /11; /13; /15.
40 NLW Lleweni, 663.
41 TNA SC 6/1185/13.
42 TNA SC 6/1185/4.
43 TNA 1185/3; 1185/11; 1112/24.
44 NLW Wynnstay, 86, 68–9, 71–3.
45 *CPR 1413–16*, p. 45.

46 S. B. Chrimes, *Lancastrians, Yorkists and Henry VII* (London, 1964), p. 46, described the 1415 plot as 'a last flicker of the Mortimer spectre rather than the first presage of the Yorkist nightmare'.
47 E. F. Jacob, *The Fifteenth Century, 1399–1485* (Oxford, 1961), p. 218.

10

THE LAND MARKET, 1334–1437

The examination of the tenurial structure of the lordship of Denbigh in the century after the compilation of the 1334 Survey has been confined to the commotes of Ceinmeirch and Is Aled, the two commotes most subject to immigration after the conquest. The two crucial sources are the 1334 Survey and the 1437 Rental: the latter is incomplete but does contain significant information relating to Ceinmeirch and the greater part of Is Aled.[1]

A study of the changes affecting these two commotes is complicated by the absence of references to clan holdings in the 1437 Rental. This should certainly not be considered as proof of their total disappearance and later financial accounts, in the early sixteenth century, indicate their continued existence.[2] It is certainly true that they had diminished by the early fifteenth century, but they continued to function, and in 1426 respites were made on customs due from all five commotes.[3] The rents actually collected, in proportion to the sums charged, varied from 83.9 per cent in Ceinmeirch, to 51.95 per cent in Is Aled, 47 per cent in Is Dulas, 34.4 per cent in Uwch Dulas and 22.7 per cent in Uwch Aled. No detailed evidence was provided concerning the clan groupings but the reduction in revenue suggests a steady disintegration of the clan lands. As a result of both outbreaks of plague and rebellion, the possibilities of acquiring recently vacated lands naturally presented opportunities for ambitious clansmen to discard traditional restrictions on the acquisition and disposal of land.

The consequent increase in the number of Welsh tenants by 1437 was probably a corollary of this trend, with former clansmen increasingly in possession of individual plots of land. However, clan lands, albeit in a state of decline, seem to have continued to be occupied despite their omission from the 1437 Rental. To prevent the presentation of a distorted image of townships wherein clans might have functioned in this year, the study of changes in the period 1334–1437 distinguishes between those townships that did and those that did not contain clan lands in 1334.

On the whole, the acreage of townships that had contained clan lands in 1334 remained stable, although there was a sharp reduction in Prion and Llewesog.[4] However, in some townships in Is Aled the acreage increased during the period in question. In Ereifiad, therefore there was an increase of 13.5 acres and 4 perches; in Berain, of 15 acres, 1 rood and 19 perches; and in Bodysgawen of 34.5 acres, half a rood and 13 perches.[5] In these instances, it is of interest to note that these three townships in 1334 contained both free and bond clans, and that not one of the free clans was especially powerful. It is therefore possible to suggest, on the basis of these examples, that between 1334 and 1437 the farmed-land plots had been augmented following the incorporation of clan lands that had fallen vacant following the disruption of clan groupings.

On the other hand, a different pattern of development characterised those townships that were associated with the more prominent clans. Therefore, there was little change over the period 1334–1437 in the farmed-land entries of the townships of Ystrad Cynan, Nantglyn Cynan and Nantglyn 'Sanctorum', founded by the clan of Braint Hir,[6] and Alltfaenan and Penporchell associated with the clan of Rhys Gryg[7]; it is possible that these stronger clans were able to survive the pressures that had overcome the clansmen of Ereifiad, Berain and Bodysgawen.

When one considers the revenue derived from individual holdings, this was largely maintained in Ceinmeirch, and reductions by 1437 resulted directly from the policy of leasing. A typical reference was the reduction in this year of 11d in the payment for the fifth year of a six-year lease by Roger Knowsely for 2 acres and 1 rood in the Park of Segrwyd, and this represented a clear illustration of the action of an administration prepared to accept a lower payment in order to guarantee receiving a regular income.[8] The farmed plots of Alltfaenan, in Is Aled, were valued at £7 7s. ½d in 1334 but only £5 5s. ½d in 1437, but significantly, in the latter year, a sum of £4 7s. 1½d had been deducted following the leasing of certain lands.[9] In this commote, the township of Berain was exceptional in that, whereas £13 9s. ½d had been rendered in 1334, the sum had increased to £14 17s. 9d by 1437, with leases resulting in a reduction of a further £4 17s. 1½d from former valuations.[10]

On the other hand, the position in Ceinmeirch was far less stable. The income from Postin fell from £1 0s. 4d to 2s., and this reflected the decrease in this township's acreage.[11] In Llewesog, however, the increase in the acreage of 7.5 acres, 1 rood and 2 perches was accompanied by a rise in the revenue of 8s. 1d, whil3 the compilation of nine leases resulted in a deficit of £2 5s. 11d on these transactions.[12] A slight rise in the acreages of Segrwyd and Prion was accompanied by a substantial increase in revenue, while in these two townships the absence of leasing meant that no deductions were made from the specified valuations. In Segrwyd, rents increased from £3 1s. 2½d to £6 6s. 11d and in Prion from 17s. to £1 5s. 3d.[13]

It is possible that the proliferation of tenants, and the resulting disintegration of individual holdings, was responsible for this increased revenue. Similar trends may be observed in other townships in the two commotes, with the exception of Postin, whose acreage fell from 37 acres, 1.5 roods and 10 perches to 4 acres.[14] Nantglyn 'Sanctorum', whose acreage remained practically unchanged, may therefore be considered as a typical example in that the number of entries rose from twenty-three to forty.[15] At the same time, the average size of the individual plots of land fell from 7.5 acres, 1.5 roods and 13 perches to 4.5 acres and 10 perches.

This fragmentation of farmed-land holdings was accompanied by an increase in the number of Welsh tenants. A comparison of entries in the 1334 Survey and 1437 Rental, clearly indicates the success of Welsh tenants in obtaining lands in townships from which they had been excluded in 1334, and in consolidating their positions where a minority had formerly settled. Whereas ninety-one plots in the Park of Segrwyd had all been occupied by English tenants in 1334, the 108 holdings in 1437 were occupied by seventy-four English and thirty-four Welsh tenants.[16] Also, in Sgeibion, whose tenants in 1334 consisted of forty Welsh and forty-two English tenants, the ratio in favour of the Welsh individuals by 1437 had risen to 137:22.[17] On the other hand, Welsh persons had failed to penetrate certain townships that had incorporated clan-lands in 1334, and they continued to be excluded from the township of Gwenynog 'Wyntus' despite the increase of entries in this township.[18]

It is clear that the townships that provided scope and opportunities for tenants to occupy plots of farmed-lands were those that contained no clans in 1334. The amount of land farmed out was roughly identical and the increases noted above in Ereifiad, Berain and Bodysgawen represented exceptional examples,[19] with this trend suggesting the continued existence of clans in these townships. They were favourably situated, and following the Conquest were occupied largely by immigrant settlers: in the following century they seem to have attracted the ambitious element among the native population.

Another noteworthy feature of the evidence presented by the 1437 Rental was that a comparison with the 1334 Survey and 'decayed rents' entries in fourteenth-century accounts reveals that some lands, although lying vacant for some time, were eventually recovered by members of the family of the original tenant. In 1334 Roger Peake had occupied 11 acres and 16 perches in Cernenyfed for 5s. 6¼d.[20] An entry in the escheator's roll for Cernenyfed in 1370 referred to the 3 acres and one parcel of land formerly held by Reginald Peake for 1s. 7d.[21] The same plot remained among the 'decayed rents' until 1402,²² but the 1437 Rental recorded that Richard Peake held here 3 acres and one parcel for an annual rent of 1s. 7d. This plot, which had lain vacant for at least thirty-two years, had by 1437 been recovered by a member of the family that had been its former occupant.²³

Other families, whose names were absent from certain townships in the 1334 Survey, were mentioned as the former occupants of escheated plots of land in the 'decayed rents' entries of fourteenth-century accounts. The plots, which were described as being vacant, often corresponded to units held by the same family in 1437. In the period between 1334 and 1375, Thomas Holland had secured possession of 20 acres of land, for a rent of £1 in the Park of Segrwyd.²⁴ This plot lay vacant from 1376 until 1402,²⁵ but the 1437 Rental recorded that Elis Holland rendered £1 for 20 acres, and this land had therefore been recovered by the Holland family.²⁶ The plot of 3.5 acres and 10 perches held by William Mody in Bachymbyd, in 1437, was probably the same one as the 3.5 acres described in 1361 as being vacant but formerly occupied by a member of the Mody family.²⁷ Moreover, another Cernenyfed entry in 1437, recording the 10.5 acres that William Pigot held for 5s. 3d in 1437, may be traced back to the family's occupation of it before 1363.²⁸

Reference was made in Chapter 9 to the predominance of Welsh individuals when one considers the payment of fines.²⁹ While members of the three English families named above in the 1373 escheator's account as contributors of fines – John Stockeley, Thomas Lauton and William Evyas – were described in 1437 as the former occupants of various plots of land,³⁰ only representatives of the Evyas family continued to be active tenants. William Evyas held in the Acre of Lleweni two plots amounting to 3 acres and 15 perches and he was named as the previous occupant of a plot of 3.5 acres and also probably of another plot of 6 acres with the former tenant named as 'Wiliam ap Ieuan Evyas'.³¹ Also, Thomas Evyas occupied here two plots of 4 acres and 1 rood, and 1 acre at rents of 4s. 3d, and 12d, and he was the tenant, on a forty-year lease, of two tofts and 4.5 acres, on which he paid a rent of 2s. 11½d. In another two entries, named as Thomas, the son of Richard Evyas, he was described as the tenant of 4 acres, 1 acre and 1 rood.[32]

The 1437 Rental recorded a considerable amount of land occupied on leases, including those in five townships in the commote of Ceinmeirch that extended over 200 acres; namely, the Park of Segrwyd, Cernenyfed, Sgeibion, Bachymbyd and Llewesog. In all five, a large amount of the total acreage consisted of leased land, varying from 12.1 per cent in Sgeibion to 26.5 per cent in the Park of Segrwyd and 39.2 per cent in Bachymbyd.[33] The duration of the leases varied from four years to 100 years, and the average for this commote was 16.7 per cent, with most of the leases operative for twenty years or fewer. However, the tendency was for the length of leases to extend, with lessors seeking to guarantee a stable income for a long period. In this respect, it is of interest to note the three 100-year leases held by Llywelyn Corves in the Park of Segrwyd, for plots of 26 acres, 12 acres and 1 rood, and 6 acres.[34]

This reference to Llywelyn Corves, emphasises the involvement of Welsh persons as lessees: of the ten leases recorded in Sgeibion in 1437, eight were held by Welshmen; namely, Deicus Penllwyd, Ieuan ap Bleddyn ap Gronw, Dafydd ap Ieuan ap Dafydd, Hwfa ap Einion Bannwr, Ieuan ap Meilyr, Bleddyn ap Meilyr, Deicus ap Ieuan ap Bleddyn and Dafydd ap Iorwerth Sais. In the same township, two Welshmen – Robert ap Dafydd ap Iorwerth and Deicus ab Einion ap Iorwerth – leased a mill for 30s.[35] The general prevalence of leases in 1437 was in contrast to the situation in 1334 when leases represented privileged grants to favoured individuals.[36] In the intervening century, references to leases as a more regular feature of land tenure appeared increasingly in the escheat entries of receivers' accounts, and by 1437 a significant number of Welsh persons occupied small plots of land on leases.

Another Welsh person named as a substantial landholder in the lordship of Denbigh in 1437 was Thomas Llannerch. In the

Acre of Lleweni he held four plots amounting to 21 acres and 1.33 roods, and he was also named as the former occupant of eight plots amounting to 104 acres and 1.5 roods which were held in the fifth year of eight-year leases by Robert Bridlington. Other references to the family in this township included the naming of Christina Llannerch as the lessee of two plots amounting to 40 acres in this township; and Adam Llannerch as the former tenant of two plots amounting to 10.5 acres in this township, together with a plot of 2 acres later occupied by William Swynemore. Another six entries identified William Llannerch as the occupant of 21 acres and 1 rood and he was also the former occupant of 30 acres, 1 rood and 10 perches leased by Morys ap Wilcok and his son John. Also, John the son of Robert Llannerch was named as a former tenant of a plot of 6.5 acres held by Dafydd ap Ieuan ap Ithel in the final year of a four-year lease.[37] Llywelyn Corves and Gronw ap Iorwerth ap Ithel also leased substantial areas in the Park of Segrwyd in 1437, with the former leasing four plots, together amounting to 55.5 acres and the largest one of 26 acres on a 100-year lease, while the latter leased three units of 14 acres, 14 acres and 10 acres.[38] However, on the whole, Welsh persons leased plots of under 10 acres. Dafydd ap Llywelyn ap Goronwy was the lessee of six plots in Gwenynog Cynon amounting to 12 acres and 1 rood: the previous owner in five instances was stated to have been William Kilford, and the sixth, amounting to 3 acres, was described as having formerly been in the possession of Agnes, the late wife of William Kilford.[39]

Yet another Welsh lessee in 1437 was William ap Iankyn ap Bleddyn, who occupied in the Park of Lleweni twelve plots, which together amounted to 32.5 acres and 10 perches. These plots were all under 4 acres with the exception of one, which measured 7.5 acres, 1 rood and 12 perches and that was held in the fifth year of a six-year lease with the former owner named as Robert Birchinshaw. He also held in the adjoining Acre of Lleweni, two plots of 7 acres and 7.5 acres, both on six-year leases.[40] A possibly related entry for the Acre of Lleweni referred to a person described as 'the said

Yankyn'. He may well have been William's father, and was the tenant of four plots in this township, whose measurements ranged from 4 acres to 5.5 acres. These were described as having been held by a person named as 'Iankyn ap Bleddyn ab Einion', with one plot held on a six-year lease and another one on a four-year lease.[41] Two other plots in the Park of Lleweni were associated with this same family. One, measuring 3 acres, was held by a certain Robert ap Yankyn ap Bleddyn, and another, amounting to 5.5 acres and 1.5 roods, by probably the same person but now named as Robyn ap Yankyn ap Bleddyn.[42] Also, William's daughter Margaret was described as a tenant in the Acre of Lleweni where she held a small plot, measuring 1 acre and 1 rood.[43] These members of the same family, together with the forementioned Dafydd ap Llywelyn, seem to have been more typical representatives of the Welsh lessees recorded in the 1437 Rental.

The reference to Margaret, and also those in the entries for the Acre of Lleweni to Christina Llannerch and Angharad *ferch* ('daughter of') Dafydd, illustrate the roles of Welsh females as landholders in 1437. Christina held two plots of 12 acres and 28.5 acres in the fourth year of six-year leases. While Angharad *ferch* Dafydd, together with Gr' ap Ieuan Ddu, occupied three plots of 7 acres, 5 acres, and 4 acres and 7 perches: the latter had previously been the property of Dafydd ap Iorwerth Ddu and his wife Angharad.[44] Also, several other examples were provided of plots of land occupied in the commote of Ceinmeirch by Welsh women tenants, again citing the word '*verch*' (*ferch*) for 'daughter'. These included references to the tenure of 8 acres in the Park of Segrwyd by Mali, the daughter of Iollyn ap Gruffudd ap Madog (this plot was held jointly with Gruffudd ap Madog), and 5.5 acres in Cernenyfed by Gwenllian, the daughter of Ieuan ap Einion.[45]

In Sgeibion, three plots of 9 acres, 7 acres and 38 perches, and 2 acres, 1.5 roods were held by Matilda the daughter of Philip ap Rhys; two plots of 5 acres, and 3 acres and 1 rood were occupied by Efa, the daughter of Dafydd Bannwr and another plot of 5.5 acres and one 1.5 roods was held by Gwenllian the daughter of

Einion ap Llywarch.[46] Moreover, Lleucu, the daughter of Einion Bannwr, held here two plots comprising one parcel of land and 1 acre and 29 perches, together with another two plots of 6.5 acres, and 4 acres and 1.5 roods in Bachymbyd. In this township Nest, the daughter of Llywelyn, held two plots of 11 acres and 1 rood, and 2.5 acres and 1 rood: the latter had previously been held by Gwladus, the daughter of 'Hankok' and her son Owain.[47]

Joint tenancies involving slightly larger plots of land included those whereby Gwenllian and Morfudd, the daughters of Dafydd ap Ieuan ap Dafydd, were the tenants of two plots of 14 acres and 6 acres in the Park of Segrwyd.[48] In Bachymbyd, 8 acres were held by Juliana and her husband Tudur ap Hywel ap Madog: the former occupant was named as Margaret, the daughter of Ednyfed 'Taillour' ('the Tailor'), and another plot of 16.5 acres and 15 perches was occupied by Mali and her husband Deicus Penllwyd. Deicus alone held here a further 9 acres in the fourth year of a forty-year lease, the former occupant of this plot was stated to have been John Ramsbothom; and also another 5.5 acres in the fourth year of a twenty-year lease with the former occupant being Thomas Honeydrop. Another 10.5 acres and 1 rood were occupied by Margaret and her husband John, the son of Robert Goch and Margaret his wife, and in this case the former occupant was named as William the son of Alan.[49]

Alice, the wife of Einion ap Dafydd jointly held with Dafydd ap Madog ap Gwyn 9.5 acres and 1 rood in Llewesog. Also, a tenancy involving three individuals in this township enabled Christina, the daughter of Einion ap Tudur, together with Gruffudd ap Deicus ap Llywelyn and Einion ap Tudur ap Heilyn to hold here three plots of 29 acres, 8 acres and 4 acres, half a rood and 20 perches.[50] A family comprising four persons, Richard Spenn, his wife Lleucu and sons Thomas and Iankyn were named as the tenants of 4.5 acres in Bachymbyd. In this township, an exceptional example in the commote of a female lessee was recorded here, whereby Morfudd, the daughter of Gruffudd ap Gr', occupied 6 acres of a plot of land formerly held by Gr.' ap Gr'. ap Tud and Gwenllian his wife in the fourteenth year of a twenty-year lease for which a rent of 12s. was paid. this represented a decrease of 8s. 3d from the previous payment of 19s. 3d.[51] Also, an unusual example of a grant for a term of life was the one in Sgeibion, whereby Mali, the wife of a certain Ieuan ap Rhirid, held a plot of 1.5 acres.[52]

This expansion of the Welsh tenancies, even though they often referred to plots of land that were generally smaller than those held by settler families, appears to be the most significant change affecting the tenurial structure of the lordship by 1437. That year, Welsh tenants held lands in townships that had been occupied exclusively by English persons in 1334, and during the intervening period, the tenurial segregation caused by the post-conquest settlement had been partially reversed. It is clear that no conscious policy had been adopted, even after the Glyn Dŵr rebellion, of restricting the participation of Welsh persons in the land market. Throughout the period covered by this chapter Welsh persons appeared frequently in lists of lessees of land, and thereby continued the tradition of enterprise in the furtherance of personal self-interest, illustrated by the activities of Iorwerth ap Llywarch in the early fourteenth century.[53]

When one considers the descendants of the English settlers attracted to the lordship of Denbigh in the post-conquest period, there was evidently a certain amount of continuity within the territorial township framework with some individuals occupying the same territorial units as their forebears did in 1334. Whereas in 1334 William Duckworth held one bovate for 3s. 4d in Lleweni, his descendant, bearing the same name, held a similar plot in 1437,[54] and a number of other examples illustrate the way families maintained their hold on the same plot of land over the whole period. Also, in certain instances, the connection of a family, which had held a certain plot of land in 1334, with the same plot in 1437 is indicated by the statement that members had formerly occupied it. In 1334 William, the son of John Romworth, held in the Park of Lleweni 6.5 acres, 1.5 roods and 7 perches at a rent of 6s. 11d.[55] A fairly similar plot in the Park, measuring 6.5 acres, 1.5 roods and 18.5 perches, was occupied in 1437 by Henry Salusbury in the fourth year of a ten-year lease, with the rental of that year recording that the former occupants were Annabel, Agnes and their brother John, whose father was Robert Romworth. This lease yielded an annual rent of 2s., which was stated to be 4s. 11d short of the original valuation, which corresponded to the 1334 rent.[56]

Other plots in the Acre of Lleweni associated with Annabel, Agnes and John Romworth included the substantial one of 34.5 acres, previously held by them but occupied in 1437 on a twenty-year lease by Henry Romworth, who was also named, together with Wiliam Lloyd, as the previous occupant of a plot of 12.5 acres and 1 rood occupied in 1437 by Gr.' ap Tudur Ddu. Annabel, Agnes and John were identified as the previous occupants of another three plots amounting to 7 acres held here by the forementioned William ap Ienkyn ap Bleddyn, and they were also named as the tenants of 3 acres held by them for a rent of 3s. In addition, Agnes and Anabel held here 7.5 acres and 1 rood for a rent of 7s. 9d, while Annabel and John were named as the previous occupant of a plot of 3 acres, 1.5 roods and 10 perches held in 1437 by William Llannerch. Other members of the Romworth family named as current or former landholders in the Acre and Park of Lleweni included Elene, John and William.[57]

A further example of an association between one family and a specific plot of land was provided in entries relating to the township of Cilcedig. Whereas in 1334 Thomas Billyng had rendered 12s. 10d for 24.5 acres in Cilcedig, in 1437 Henry, the son of William Billyng, had leased 13 acres that yielded 12s. for a forty-year period.[58] The usual format of recording leases in the 1437 Rental, wherein the former occupant was named, was not adopted in this entry, but it is probable that the land had remained in the possession of the Billyng family. However, as a rule, references to former tenants who had occupied units of land since 1334, at least, were contained not in leases but in entries where new tenants seemed to have had a more secure right to their lands. In these entries, also, a rent similar to that of 1334 was levied. Henry Heton held 4 acres in Polflat in 1334, and, although this same unit in 1437 was occupied by William Bridlington and his wife Katherine, its former tenants were named in the Rental as Llywelyn Heton and his wife Alice.[59]

These references to Katherine Bridlington and Alice Heton emphasise, as was also the case with Welsh families, that female members of settler families featured prominently as landholders in the lordship in 1437. Agnes, wife of Henry Salusbury occupied 166 acres and 1 rood in three plots in the Park of Segrwyd, in the commote of Ceinmeirch, and also, in another two plots, 2 acres and a 'hafod' in Oakwood.[60] Again, in the Acre of Lleweni, another 13 acres were stated to have been formerly held by her but then became the property of four individuals; namely, Rhys ap Iorwerth, Wiliam ap Llywelyn, Dafydd ap Ieuan and William Rossindale.[61] Agnes Salusbury held 19 acres in Ystrad Cynon,[62] and she and her husband Radulf held a plot of 4 acres and 1 rood in the Acre of Lleweni.[63] Also, Isabel, the daughter of Thomas Salusbury and another female member of this predominant family recorded in the 1437 Rental, was the former occupant of a plot of 1 acre and 1.5 roods held in 1437 in the Park of Lleweni by the forementioned William ap Yankyn ap Bleddyn.[64]

Four entries in the Acre of Lleweni referred to members of the Hilton family. Alice, the daughter of Thomas Hilton, held two plots of 16 acres, and 5.5 acres and 1 rood; Margaret, the daughter of Robert Hilton, held a plot of 18 acres formerly occupied by the said Robert; and Katerina was described as the former occupant of 3 acres held by William Holland.[65] Five plots amounting to 93.5 acres, 1 rood and 20 perches were held in the Acre of Lleweni by Isabel, the daughter of Richard Peake, and she was also the tenant of a substantial plot of 25 acres and half a perch formerly held by her father in the associated Park.[66] In Ystrad Cynon Margery the wife of Henry Henbury held two plots that amounted to 5.5 acres, and Alice, the daughter of Henry Westmorland together with her daughter Angela, occupied here a plot of 9 acres.[67]

Other entries in the 1334 Survey and 1437 Rental illustrated a strong degree of continuity in the tenurial structure of the lordship, with the size of many family estates fluctuating only slightly in the intervening period. In Bachymbyd, the lands associated with the Plesyngton family increased from 85.5 acres and 13 perches to 88 acres and 1 perch over the whole period. This latter total in 1437 included a plot of 17 acres, 1.5 roods and 10 perches, whose former tenant was Robert Plesyngton, but that was now occupied by Madog ap Meilyr on payment of a fine of 11s. 11¼d. Madog also leased for 2s. 6d another plot of 39.5 acres and 1 rood of land, formerly occupied by 'Godryth' de Spenne and then by Henry Plesyngton, which had previously yielded 20s. 3d, with this year being the final year of a twenty-year lease.[68] The 1334 family estate included an entry of 3 acres, 1 rood and 8 perches of meadow held by Cecilia Plesyngton for 6s. 1¼d, and this plot had fallen vacant by 1361, when it was stated to have formerly been in the possession of Richard, the son of John Plesyngton.[69]

The plot remained among the 'decayed rents' until 1397, although the specification, from 1375 onwards, was stated to have been 4 acres, 1 rood and 8 perches.[70] Another entry of 8.5 acres and 1 perch, which cannot be identified with a specific unit in 1334, was also included among the 'decayed rents' in 1370.[71] The latter does not re-appear, but it is significant that the meadow-land of 4 acres, 1 rood and 8 perches, which had lain vacant from 1361 until 1397, had been restored to the family possessions by 1437, with Henry Plesyngton paying a sum of 4s. 6d for this property, previously held by Richard Plesyngton, for the first year of a four-year lease: a previous payment of 9s. was recorded, and this therefore represented a deficit of 4s. 6d. As the entry was missing from the 'decayed rents' of 1402, it is possible that the Plesyngton family recovered this meadow-land in the period from 1397 until 1402.[72]

The overall position of the Swynemore family in Llewesog changed only slightly during the 103 years from 1334 until 1437. The 40 acres and 23 perches, which had been held exclusively by this family in 1334, together with the share of 24 acres held jointly with John Pigot, had by 1437 fallen to 22.5 acres, 1 rood and 7 perches; the rental also recorded that another 15.5 acres had formerly been in the possession of Reginald Swynemore but was now held by Dykun Mershe on a forty-year lease, with this being the fourth year and the payment of 3s. representing a deficit of 7s. 7d on the required sum of 10s. 7d.[73] However, in this instance, a superficial comparison of the acreages in 1334 and 1437 conceals remarkable fluctuations in the territorial fortunes of the Swynemore family. It is therefore significant that the 1363 account recorded that over 140 acres of land held by the Swynemore family had fallen vacant in Llewesog: of this amount William de Swynemore had occupied 30 acres and John de Swynemore 114.5 acres.[74]

In 1334, the leading landowner in Llewesog was John Pigot, who held exclusively in three plots 75 acres and 15 perches in addition to his forementioned share of 24 acres with John de Swynemore.[75] This shared tenure of 24 acres, together with the disappearance of this family from the township by 1437, suggests that the Swynemores might have obtained this land at the expense of John Pigot. The Swynemore lands appearing among the 'decayed rents' gradually fell to 146 acres in 1370,[76] 81.5 acres in 1375,[77] and 27.5 acres in 1397[78] and 1402,[79] and they seem to have been gradually disposed of in this period. Considerable changes had therefore affected the Swynemore estate in the township of Llewesog, and in fact, despite certain indications of continuity in the landholding structure, the possessions of some families in the lordship within certain townships had changed dramatically in the 103-year period.

This was especially true of the Salusbury estate, which in 1334 had consisted of only 44.5 acres and 1.5 roods in Lleweni,[80] but which in 1437 amounted to 660 acres, 1.5 roods and 1 perch. In this year the base of the estate lay in the Acre of Lleweni, with 152 acres and half a rood held in this township, and 31 acres, 1 rood and 1 perch in the associated Park.[81] The 1437 Rental also referred to another 160 acres held in Is Aled,[82] and although the actual township was not specified, it is probable, in view of the previous and future concentration of the estate at Lleweni, that this also was the same township.

Land was also held in a number of other townships in the commotes of Ceinmeirch and Is Aled. Reference has already been made to the property held by Agnes, wife of Henry Salusbury, in the commote of Ceinmeirch, while Henry was one of the lessees of the manor of Kilford.[83] In addition, lands had been held in Is Aled in the townships of Ystrad Cynan, Alltfaenan and Gwenynog 'Wyntus': the entry for the latter township referred to a plot of 10 acres held by Thomas Salusbury and this plot had also been recorded in the accounts for 1397 and 1402.[84] The relative sparsity of references in the entries of 'decayed' and 'decreased' rents indicates the strength of the Salusbury family, and with regard to the latter, the temporary nature of a lease must also be kept in mind. An appreciation of the viability of the Salusbury estate in 1437 is heightened by the relative absence of leased plots of land in the Acre of Lleweni with only one entry referring to this being the nineteenth year of the twenty-year lease held by Henry Salusbury and Alex Henbury for the new mill of the Clwyd that had been burned during the rebellion. Also, in the adjoining Park of Lleweni, three entries recorded that this was the fourth year of ten-year leases held by Henry Salusbury for plots amounting to 18.5 acres and previously occupied by Henry le Peake, William Romworth, and John, Annabel and Agnes, the children of Robert Romworth.[85]

Earlier in the fourteenth century, members of this family representing successive generations were married to local Welsh women. A graveyard inscription commemorated the death in 1400 of Henry Salusbury and his wife Agnes, daughter and heiress of John Curteys, whose forefather William held in 1334 nearly 200 acres in Segrwyd, Archwedlog and Ystrad, and two burgages in Llanrwst.[86] One genealogical source referred to the marriage of Henry Salusbury and Nest, daughter and heiress of

Cynwrig Fychan ap Cynwrig Sais, and Edward I's grant to him of Lleweni, described as 'a hunting seat of the princes of Wales'. Cynwrig was probably a representative of the Marchweithian clan and other sources refer significantly to Llywarch's court at Lleweni (*'a'i lys yn Lleweni'*) and to 'Llysmarchweithian' as an earlier name for Lleweni.[87] Henry's son William married Margaret, the daughter and heiress of David, the son of Cynwrig ap Philip 'Phighton', while the wife of his eldest son Rawling was Margaret, the daughter and heiress of Ieuan ap Cadwgan ap Llywarch, a descendant of Llywarch Holbwrch ('Lewarch Olbwrch'), 'lord of Meriadog', who has been described as a 'tribal' founder and may possibly have been the chamberlain and treasurer of the powerful Welsh ruler, Gruffudd ap Llywelyn (d. 1063).[88]

Whereas attention is concentrated on the lordship of Denbigh, members of the Salusbury family also featured as landholders in neighbouring localities. On 2 November 1399, Henry leased for a rent of 100s. per annum for a two-year period, from Henry, Prince of Wales, the pleas and perquisites of the courts of the town of Flint, together with the tolls of fairs and markets held there.[89] Also, on 1 May 1411, in his role as steward of the lordship of Ruthin, he was instructed by Gilbert lord Talbot, the Justice of Chester and deputy of the Prince of Wales, to send back to the lordship of Denbigh all the tenants of the Prince of Wales from this lordship, and any opposition to this order would lead to their imprisonment and seizure of their property.[90]

In contrast to the expansion of the Salusbury estate as recorded in the 1437 Rental, the lands associated with members of the Curteys family in the Park of Segrwyd fell from the 127 acres held in 1334: 120 acres occupied by William, which had been granted in exchange for the townships of Penmaen and Llysfaen, and also the 7 acres held by him for an annual rent of 3s. 6d.[91] By 1437, the Curteys lands in the Park had decreased to 42.5 acres, of which 16 acres were held in joint occupation with other tenants. John Curteys occupied five plots, which together amounted to 26.5 acres, while William was a co-tenant of 6 acres with John Walshe and 10 acres with William Wood.[92]

The names of John and William Curteys had appeared regularly in the 'decreased rents' entries of the 1397, 1402 and 1410 accounts,[93] and it is certainly possible that, whereas the privileged possession of the 120 acres recorded in 1334 had been lost, the family estate in 1437 had been amassed largely as the result of the leasing of escheated plots of land in the late fourteenth century and early fifteenth century. William Curteys, who jointly occupied 16 acres here in 1437, had leased 7 acres of escheated land in 1397, and the amount leased, having increased to 41 acres and half a rood in 1402, stood at 13 acres and 1 rood in 1410. Two of the entries recorded in 1402, referring to 10 acres and 6 acres, corresponded to plots held in 1437, but that for some reason were absent from the 1410 account, when William was described as the tenant of 6 acres and 1 rood, and 7 acres of escheated land. In addition, the 16 acres were held in partnership with John Walshe and William Wood, and no other evidence was provided to explain William Curteys's connection with these two individuals.[94] However, more positive information was presented to explain John Curteys's accumulation of lands by 1437. That year's rental recorded that he occupied in the Park of Segrwyd three plots, amounting to 6 acres, 12 acres and 2 acres, which had been held in 1334 by Henry Frodesham, John Hoghton and John Pontefract.[95] Whereas the 12 acres held by John Hoghton only appeared in the 1375 account, the two other entries were consistently recorded among the 'decayed rents' from 1362 until 1375.[96] They did not appear in the next surviving account, compiled in 1397, yet in this document, in the section relating to 'decreased rents', John Curteys was described as the lessee of five plots that amounted to 26.5 acres. He leased 1 acre for 6d, 5.5 acres for 4s. 6d and 20 acres in three unspecified units for 16s. 8d.[97] He continued to occupy the 26.5 acres, on the same terms, in 1402, and probably again in 1410.[98] The 26.5 acres corresponded to his estate in 1437, for which a rent of 26s. 6d was paid. With regard to the fore-mentioned 20 acres occupied in 1334 by members of the Frodesham, Hoghton and Pontefract families, the rent paid in 1437 was identical to the 1334 valuation.[99] This represents an illustration of rents being maintained at the same level in the 1334–1437 period, and also of a change in ownership being accompanied by the leasing of plots when they became vacant during the fourteenth century.

The Ramsbothom family also experienced a dramatic fall in its possessions in Cernenyfed, although in this case new plots were temporarily acquired through the leasing of escheated land. In 1334, lands totalling 39 acres, 1 rood and 6 perches were held, with 28.5 acres and 37 perches held in two plots by William Ramsbothom and another 11.5 acres and 9 perches held by Margery Ramsbothom. Also, 22.5 acres, 1 rood and 16 perches were occupied jointly by William Ramsbothom and Simon Whiteacre: this land had formerly been held by Richard Turner, whose family held a total of 142 acres and 10 perches in nine plots in this township.[100] In 1363, John Ramsbothom had leased 30.5 acres and 1 rood of escheated land at the nominal rent of 2s. 10½d, but the entry, by 1366, had disappeared, and, in view of the evidence of the rental, seems to have passed permanently from the hands of this family. In 1363, John's holding of 11 acres had fallen vacant, and the coincidence of these two entries suggests that the hereditary holdings had been allowed to fall into decay, so that a larger property could possibly be developed on a short-term lease.[101] By 1437, the Ramsbothom family was in possession here of 11 acres, which formed their only estate in Cernenyfed in 1437.[102]

Members of certain families, described as tenants in 1437, and who had not held land in a particular township in 1334, obtained plots by means of the leasing of escheated lands. In 1437, Robert Dolben leased in the Park of Segrwyd three plots of 4 acres, 4 acres, and four acres and half a rood, and he also rented 7 acres and half a rood. Richard Dolben also held 12 acres, and another 2 acres were occupied by his father William Dolben.[103] All four plots held by Robert Dolben had been leased by him from the escheat lands of the Park in 1410, together with another plot of 10.5 acres, thereby amounting to a total holding of 30 acres and 1 rood.[104]

The background to the Rossindale estate in the same Park may be traced to the escheat entries in the accounts of the late fourteenth century. The 1437 Rental recorded that John Wood leased 4 acres that had formerly belonged to Robert Rossindale, whose occupation of this plot resulted from John Rossindale's leasing of 4 acres of escheat land in 1397.[105] In addition, while Thomas Rossindale was recorded as being the occupant of 10 acres and 3 roods in 1437 for a payment of 10s. 9d, an identical plot had appeared among the 'decayed rents' in 1375 and was described significantly as having been formerly in the possession of Thomas Rossindale.[106] The initial occupation of this unit of land evidently occurred between 1334 and 1375 as the family did not appear in the 1334 Survey as tenants in the Park of Segrwyd.[107]

While it is evident that the fortunes of some settler families fluctuated considerably in the period 1334–1437, on the whole their stronger tenurial positions may be traced back to the immediate post-conquest period when the Englishry was established and immigrant English families favoured by extensive and privileged grants of land. The extent of assimilation, by 1437, should therefore not be over-emphasised and the 1437 Rental clearly indicated that the extent of fusion had not yet been completed. A racial dualism could therefore be observed in the landholding structure of the lordship, and to a certain extent this was heightened by the Glyn Dŵr rebellion, with a number of native inhabitants of the lordship attracted to Glyn Dŵr's cause and consequently forfeiting their lands. Also, the absence of fines after 1397, and the continuing popularity of leases of escheated lands, indicated that the short-term acquisition of land, involving smaller sums of capital, was preferred by many local inhabitants. At the same time, the more prominent settler families seem to have been better able to survive contemporary financial difficulties and exploit the opportunities that presented themselves after the uprising. In this respect the biased land settlement adopted after the creation of the lordship of Denbigh may be considered to be a vital factor responsible for the emergence in 1437 of settler families as an embryonic gentry class.

Notes

1. *SD*; NLW Wynnstay, 86.
2. For example, TNA, Henry VIII 4974, m.2v.
3. TNA SC 6/1185/15.
4. *SD*, pp. 18–20; NLW Wynnstay, 86, ff. 68 r, 72 v, 73 r.
5. *SD*, pp. 109, 131, 120; NLW Wynnstay, 86, ff. 81v, 82 r and v, 83 r and v, 84 v, 85 r and v, 86 r and v.
6. *SD*, pp. 83–5, 92–3, 94–6; NLW Wynnstay, 86, ff. 80 r and v; 81 r and v.
7. *SD*, pp. 86–7, 140–2; NLW Wynnstay, 86, ff. 80 v, 84 r and v.
8. NLW Wynnstay, 86, f. 66 v.
9. *SD*, p. 87; NLW Wynnstay, 86, f.80 v.
10. *SD*, p. 135; NLW Wynnstay, 86, ff. 84 v, 85 r and v, 86 r.
11. *SD*, p. 27; NLW Wynnstay, 86, ff. 68 r, 66 r.
12. *SD*, p. 39; NLW Wynnstay, 86, ff. 72 v, 73 r.
13. *SD*, pp. 10, 20; NLW Wynnstay, 86, 66 r, 68 v.
14. *SD*, pp. 27, 141–2; NLW Wynnstay, 86, ff. 66 r and v, 67 r and v. A problem of comparison has been presented in the evidence for some townships, as in Penporchell (NLW Wynnstay, 86, 84 r and v) where the acreage in 1437 was not provided in some entries.
15. *SD*, pp. 94–6; NLW Wynnstay, 86, ff. 81 r and v.
16. *SD*, pp. 12–16; NLW Wynnstay, 86, ff. 66 r, 67 r and v.
17. *SD*, pp. 28–32; NLW Wynnstay, 86, ff. 69 v, 70 r and v, 71 r.
18. *SD*, p. 89; NLW Wynnstay, 86, ff. 80 v; 81 r. One of the tenants here was John Holland, who occupied a plot of 31.5 acres previously held by Robert Holland: the Anglicised character of this township suggests that he should be recognised as an English person in contrast to those with a similar surname identified as Welsh persons in another locality and in a slightly later period.
19. *SD*, see n. 5 above.
20. *SD*, pp. 23, 21; TNA, SC 6/1183/3.
21. TNA SC 6/1183/3.
22. TNA, 1185 / 4.
23. NLW Wynnstay, 86, f. 69 r.
24. TNA SC 6/1183/20.
25. TNA SC 6/1185/4.
26. NLW Wynnstay, 86, f. 67 v.

27 NLW Wynnstay, 86, f. 72 r; TNA SC 6/1182/4.
28 NLW Wynnstay, 86, f. 69 r; TNA SC 6/1182/5.
29 *Supra*, pp. 132–4, 143.
30 TNA SC 6/1233/5; NLW Wynnstay, 86, ff. 77 v, 78 r and v.
31 NLW Wynnstay, 86, ff. 77 r and v, 78 v.
32 NLW Wynnstay, 86, ff. 77 v, 78 r and v.
33 NLW Wynnstay, 86, ff. 69 v–71 v; 66 r–67 v; 71v–72 r.
34 NLW Wynnstay, 86, f. 66 r.
35 NLW Wynnstay, 86, ff. 69 v, 70 v, 71 v.
36 *Supra*, pp. 135, 141, 144–6, 149, 157, 171.
37 NLW Wynnstay, 86, ff. 76r–78r.
38 NLW Wynnstay, 86, ff. 66 r and v.
39 NLW Wynnstay, 86, f. 81 r.
40 NLW Wynnstay, 86, ff. 77 v, 78 r and v.
41 NLW Wynnstay, 86, ff. 76 v, 77 r, 78 r.
42 NLW Wynnstay, 86, f. 78 v.
43 NLW Wynnstay, 86, f. 78 r.
44 NLW Wynnstay, 86, ff. 76 v, 78 r.
45 NLW Wynnstay, 86, ff. 67 v; 68 v.
46 NLW Wynnstay, 86, 69 v, 70 r, 71 r.
47 NLW Wynnstay, 86, 69 v, 70 v,71 v, 72 r.
48 NLW Wynnstay, 86, 66 v.
49 NLW Wynnstay, 86, 71 v, 72 r.
50 NLW Wynnstay, 86, 72 v.
51 NLW Wynnstay, 86, f. 72 r.
52 NLW Wynnstay, 86, f. 70 v.
53 *Supra*, pp. 39–42, 73.
54 *SD*, p. 63, NLW Wynnstay, 86, f. 75 r.
55 *SD*, p. 75, NLW Wynnstay, 86, f. 79 r.
56 NLW Wynnstay, 86, f. 79 r.
57 NLW Wynnstay, 86, ff. 77 r and v, 78 r and v, 79 r.
58 *SD*, p. 43; NLW Wynnstay, 86, f. 73 r.
59 *SD*, p. 80; NLW Wynnstay, 86, f. 80.
60 NLW Wynnstay, 86, ff. 66 r, 67 r, 68 r.
61 NLW Wynnstay, 86, 77 r and v.
62 NLW Wynnstay, 86, 80 r.
63 NLW Wynnstay, 86 f. 77 v.
64 NLW Wynnstay, 86, f f. 78 v.
65 NLW Wynnstay, 86, ff. 77 r and v, 76 v.
66 NLW Wynnstay, 86, ff. 76 r, 77 r and v; 79 r.
67 NLW Wynnstay, 86, f. 80 r.
68 *SD*, pp. 34–6; NLW Wynnstay, 86, ff. 71 v, 72 r.
69 *SD*, p. 36; TNA SC 6/1182/4.
70 TNA SC 6/1183/18; 1184/22.
71 TNA, SC 6/1183/2.

72 TNA SC 6, 1184/22; 1185/4; NLW Wynnstay, 86, f. 72 r.
73 *SD*, p. 38; NLW Wynnstay, 86, f. 72 v.
74 TNA SC 6/1182/6.
75 *SD*, p. 38.
76 TNA SC 6/1183/2.
77 TNA SC 6/1183/18.
78 TNA SC 6/1184/22.
79 TNA SC 6/1185/4.
80 *SD*, pp. 63, 66, 69.
81 NLW Wynnstay, 86, ff. 76 r and v, 77 r and v, 78 r and v; 79 r and v.
82 NLW Wynnstay, 86, ff. 79 v, 80 r and v.
83 NLW Wynnstay, 86, f. 73 v.
84 NLW Wynnstay, 86, ff. 84 r and v; TNA SC 6/1184/22; 1185/4.
85 NLW Wynnstay, 86, ff. 78 v, 79 r.
86 *Calendar of Salusbury Correspondence*, 6; *SD*, pp. 12, 13, 84, 204, 281.
87 J. Y. W. Lloyd, *History of Powys Fadog*, vol. 4 (London, 1884), p. 331; *Heraldic Visitations of Wales and Part of the Marches*, vol.2, ed. by S. R. Meyrick (Llandovery, 1846), p. 114; Williams, *Ancient and Modern Denbigh*, p. 165; *WG, 1400–1500* (Aberystwyth, 1983), IX, O-Sandde, 1569.
88 Dwnn, *Heraldic Visitations of Wales*, vol. 2, p. 331; *WG, 1400–1500*, IX, O-Sandde, 1569; *Idem*, 'Pedigrees of the Welsh Tribal Patriarchs', *NLW Journal*, 13 (1963–4), 95, 129; D. S. Evans (ed.), *Historia Gruffud vab Kenan* (Cardiff, 1977), pp. 7, 62–3.
89 NLW Lleweni, 407.
90 NLW Lleweni, 663.
91 *SD*, pp. 12–13.
92 NLW Wynnstay, 86, ff. 66 v, 67 r and v.
93 TNA SC 6/1184/22; 1185/4/11.
94 NLW Wynnstay, 86, f.67 r; TNA SC 6/1184/22; 1185/4/11.
95 NLW Wynnstay, 86, f. 66 v; *SD*, p. 13.
96 TNA SC 6/1182/5; 1183/18.
97 TNA SC 6/1184/22.
98 TNA SC 6/1185/4/11.
99 NLW Wynnstay, 86, ff. 66 r and v, 67 v; *SD*, p. 13.
100 NLW Wynnstay, 86.
101 TNA SC 6/1182/6/8.
102 NLW Wynnstay, 86, f. 69 r.
103 NLW Wynnstay, 86, ff. 66 v, 67 r and v.
104 TNA, SC 6/1185/11.
105 NLW Wynnstay, 86, f. 67 r.
106 TNA SC 6/1183/18.
107 *SD*, pp. 12–16.

11

THE ECONOMY, 1334–1425

This chapter is concerned primarily with identifying the various sources of seignorial revenue generated by the lordship, and the methods whereby they were raised. Payments to the central receiver will also be examined carefully as these provide an indication of the value of the lordship to its various lords, The main sources are the 1334 Survey,[1] the 1437 Rental[2] and a series of receivers and ministers' accounts[3] that, though not forming an unbroken sequence, provide relevant and valuable information. Whereas the dilemma of reconciling divergent social and economic policies, combined with fluctuations in possession, had previously resulted in considerable pressure being placed on its economy, the lordship of Denbigh was a high-yielding financial unit within the various estates in which it was incorporated for the remainder of the fourteenth century. However, this changed in the early fifteenth century as a result of the adverse impact of the Glyn Dŵr rebellion on the various sources of revenue.

For a more complete understanding of economic developments in the lordship, the various aspects, considered from the evidence of ministers' accounts, have been related to the more complete information contained in the receivers' accounts. The nature of the accounts and the economic background that they reflected prompt one to divide the era from 1334 to 1425 into three periods; namely, 1334–60, 1360–1402 and 1402–25. The sources available for the first period are limited to the receivers' account for 1345 and series of ministers' accounts from 1354 to 1358, with attention focused on the implications of outbreaks of the Black Death. The second period, extending from 1360 to 1402, constituted one of high seigneurial profits, with payments to the central receiver maintained at a high level. A consideration of the third period, 1402–25, enables one to assess the immediate impact of the Glyn Dŵr rebellion on the sources of seigneurial revenue and on the economy itself.

1334–60

Only one receiver's account, the one compiled in 1345 by John Pirye, has survived from this period.[4] A balance sheet compiled from the 1345 account revealed a considerable reduction from the valuation recorded in the 1334 Survey. In the three commotes of Ceinmeirch, Is Aled and Uwch Dulas (the other two commotes were not included) a sum of £206 16s. 7½d was obtained from land rents and £18 18s. from court profits. When these sums are considered in relation to the payments recorded in the 1334 Survey, it is evident that, in 1345, only 30.9 per cent was rendered from Is Aled, 28.9 per cent from Uwch Dulas and 17.9 per cent from Ceinmeirch. Moreover, the income in 1345 from court profits amounted to only 22.7 per cent of the 1334 assessment for these three commotes. On the debit side, it was recorded that wages amounting to £18 17s. 10¾d were paid to various officials, and various expenses amounted to £33 18s. 1¾d. The payment to the central administration of £43 3s. 9d resulted in a credit balance of £132 4s. 10d, and an additional note referred to the payment of debts amounting to £140 5s. 10½d.

A number of ministers' accounts are available for the period 1355–8 for the commotes of Ceinmeirch, Is Aled, Uwch Aled and Uwch Dulas, and interest is focused immediately on Uwch Aled, whose economic development from 1354 until 1358 is traced by four accounts.[5] Unfortunately, certain sections of these accounts are blurred, especially the entries of *Firme ballivi* ('Farm of the bailiff') in 1354 and 1358, and this presents problems in seeking to correlate the evidence and compile balance sheets, as will later be attempted for this commote. However, the totals of the various entries may be read and utilised for a more general comparative study of the stipulated four years.

The financial accounts are particularly important as they include a specific reference to the initial outbreak of the plague on the lordship in 1349. This appeared in the account, for the period from Michaelmas 1354 until Michaelmas 1355, which declared that an allowance of £2 14s. 1d had been granted at Easter for twenty-two weeks, on account of the deaths, at the time of the plague ('*tempore Pestilentiae*') of tenants in the townships of Petrual and Barrog, in the commote of Uwch Aled. Although the plague was not specifically mentioned, there was also a loss of revenue, amounting to £4 4s.1d, from *twnc* and other customary renders in these two townships.[6] Further evidence had also been provided in the court roll compiled when the sessions of William Montagu, earl of Salisbury, were held at Denbigh on 3 September 1352. This document, recording the admission of Thomas, the son of Roger Lawton to 80 acres of land in Lleweni, also referred to the failure of the heirs of the previous tenant, Adam, the son of John Blackburn, who had died of the plague, to appear at the lord's court to pay a relief. This was despite a 'proclamation made among the English and Welsh tenants of the lordship in the year after the plague' with the result that the land had escheated to the lord.[7] The plague seems to have had a greater impact than the paucity of references would suggest, especially as it severely afflicted neighbouring Ruthin in 1349, where seventy persons are believed to have died in June 1349.[8]

Payments from the ringildries of Uwch Aled, Is Dulas and Uwch Dulas to the receiver in the period 1354–60 were below those rendered from 1360 until the outbreak of the Glyn Dŵr rebellion. In Uwch Aled, the ringild's payments from 1355 to 1380 were generally in the region of £60 to £90, but in 1357, only £49 13s. 5d was rendered, and in 1361 the ringild's contribution had fallen to £13 2s. 1d.[9] Payments were also at a low level in Is Aled, Is Dulas and the Englishry.[10] In Is Aled, where payments from 1363 until 1380 generally ranged from £74 to £112, £57 13s. 4d was handed over in 1361, and the corresponding amount in Is Dulas, whereas renders from 1372 until 1398, were usually between £59 and £75, only £17 18s. 9d had been delivered in 1361. Moreover, the bailiff of the Englishry rendered only £5 4s. in 1361, while his contribution, as a rule, varied between £20 and £55. Unfortunately, the absence of accounts from an earlier period prevents an assessment of the real impact of the plague. It could also be argued that the increased payments were the result of rigorous action by the officials of the Black Prince, who had received custody of the lordship in 1360, and it is therefore surely significant that payments from Ceinmeirch and Uwch Dulas showed a dramatic increase after 1360.

1360–1402

The era of high seignorial profits, extending from 1360 until 1402, is covered by both receivers' and ministers' accounts. Payments to the central receiver were generally maintained. In 1370, the first year for which accounts of all five commotes survive, a sum of £1,123 was delivered to the Receiver-General and the Chamberlain of Chester, and in 1398, the lordship contributed £903 10s. 6¼d to the central coffers of the Mortimer estate.[11] As late as 1402 a payment of £928 17s. 4d was made from the lordship of Denbigh.[12] The revenue from land had fallen from £551 9s. 9¼d in 1375 to £455 6s. 10¼d in 1402, while in the same period renders from officials fell from £690 2s. 2¼d to £489 9s. 4¼d.[13] At the same time, expenditure within the lordship was at a high level in 1402, indicating that, in this year, despite the maintenance of considerable payments to the central authority, the lordship was beset by financial difficulties, and that the era of high seignorial profits was coming to an end.

This period is covered by both receivers' and ministers' accounts, which respectively throw light on the nature of lordship and commotal accounting. In the accounts under consideration in this section, those compiled by both the receiver and by various officials, survive in the period 1360–70 for only three commotes; namely, Ceinmeirch, Is Aled and Uwch Dulas. These, however, provide information for a period when two severe outbreaks of plague – the Second Pestilence of 1361 and the Third Pestilence of 1369 – affected certain areas of the country. Unfortunately, there is a gap in the surviving accounts from 1384 until 1397, and this restricts study of the financial organisation in the immediate pre-Glyn Dŵr period. However, the position in 1379–80 may be compared with that prevailing in 1397–8, and for this purpose, the accounts for these three commotes have been analysed.

In the decade from 1360 to 1370 an impression of stability is conveyed by the accounts for the three commotes. The 1361 plague seems to have had some effect, and there was therefore an increase in the 'decayed' and 'decreased' rents of Ceinmeirch in the year 1362–3, from £9 1s. 5¼d to £22 7s. 6¼d, and in Is Aled from £21 5s. 1¼d to £29 18s. 0¼d.[14] Also, payments from the receiver to the Receiver-General increased during this decade and, whereas they amounted to £ 471 10s. (or 73.8 per cent of the total expenditure) in 1362, they had increased to £1,123 (or 90 per cent) in 1370.[15] It is clear that, as far as the central administration was concerned, the lordship of Denbigh was in a healthy economic condition during this decade.

The following decade, from 1370 to 1380, may be studied in greater depth, as these three commotes are covered by accounts that run successively for a number of years. There are nine ringild's accounts for the period 1372–80 for Uwch Aled; four for Is Aled in the period 1373–6; and seven for 1372–5 and 1378–80 for Uwch Dulas. The office of ringild was generally farmed out and the main sources of revenue were court profits and customary dues. The debit side of the roll recorded payments to the receiver (the '*liberaciones*') together with a fee for the farm. In those years when the office was held in the lord's hands, the ringild was paid a wage, which has been added to the credit side.

The complete series of accounts for Uwch Aled in this decade indicated a fluctuating pattern of final balance, court profits and payments to the receiver. On the whole, a credit balance was achieved, and this varied from £3 18s. 5¾d in 1373 to £39 12s. 2¾d in 1375.[16] During this decade a total profit of over £200 was derived from this commote, but a substantial proportion of this net profit was rendered by the ringild in years subsequent to the tenure of this office. A debit balance was only recorded in two years. In 1374, when the ringildry of the commote was farmed to Iorwerth ap Einion Traws, there was a debit balance of £12 0s. 8¼d, and Maredudd ap Iorwerth's account for 1380 recorded a debit balance of £3 2s. 8¾d.[17] In both cases, the cause for this was the high level of payments to the receiver, and the renders in these two years were greater than in those years when there was a credit balance.

In 1374, whereas the ringild collected £38 11s. 7¾d from traditional customs and court fines, he rendered to the receiver £44 2s. 4d: this sum excluded the payment of arrears by himself and other officials. He also paid £5 10s. for the farm of the office.[18] This was in contrast to the position in the previous two years when, with the farm levied at the lower rate of £5 3s. 4d, he rendered sums of only £21 16s. 8d and £25 10s. 4d to the receiver.[19] In the following year, 1375, the ringildry was granted to Thomas Schutlesworth, who was paid a wage of £2 5s. 7½d. In this year, the only sum rendered to the receiver was £18 13s. 4d, consisting of the arrears of Iorwerth ab Einion Traws, the former ringild, and therefore no money forming part of that year's actual income was handed over to the receiver.[20]

The position was similar in the following two years, when sums of £21 5s. 8d and £12 7s. 6d were paid to the receiver.[21] In 1378 the commote was again farmed, to Dafydd ap Hywel ap Cynwrig, for £4 10s. This lower rate, which was emphasised in the account by a reference to a former payment of £5 10s. ('*solebat affirmari £5 10s. 0d*') suggests a difficulty in enlisting suitable officials at the local commotal level.[22] In the following two years the commote was again held in the lord's hands, with payments of £29 13s. 4d and £40 9s. 8d, respectively, of the current revenue being paid to the central treasury.[23] The latter figure, indeed, was the highest payment since 1374, and the debit balance in these two years, that is 1374 and 1380, suggests that the final balance was determined largely by sums rendered by the ringild to the central receiver.

A study of the collection of seignorial revenue in the pre-rebellion period has been attempted by an analysis of ministers' accounts for Ceinmeirch, Uwch Aled and Uwch Dulas in the years 1379–98. All three commotes showed an increase in the amount of arrears recorded, but other aspects of the accounts revealed fluctuating trends, and each commote will therefore be considered separately. In Ceinmeirch a comparison of the revenue from customs and payments to the receiver, as recorded in the ringilds' accounts in the period from 1379 to 1398, revealed that the former fell from £10 1s. 10d to £6 3s. 11d, and the latter from £14 8s. to £5 13s. 4d. A debit balance of £15 11s. 1¼d had been converted into a credit balance of £2 17s. ½d.[24] Whereas there was an overall increase in the arrears and final debt in Uwch Aled, the payments to the receiver ('*liberaciones*') fell from £29 11s. 4d in 1379 to £21 12s. 9d in 1398. In the same period arrears increased substantially from £48 6s. 1½d to £89 13s. 56d. Another significant feature of the 1379 and 1398 accounts was the increase in the *twnc* payments levied in the various townships, and an attempt therefore seems to have been made in Uwch Aled, despite the general decrease, to increase the financial demands made upon local inhabitants with regard to the revenue derived from traditional Welsh customs[25]

Differing trends therefore emerged in a study of the three commotes in the period leading up to the Glyn Dŵr rebellion. When considered together, however, they reflect the attempt by the administration to maintain the level of financial renders despite a fall in land values. In Ceinmeirch and Uwch Dulas, payments were maintained by the strenuous collection of arrears, whereas in Uwch Aled, an inability to secure the payment of arrears resulted in an attempt to increase *twnc* payments. Financial pressure was evidently inflicted on the inhabitants of the lordship, and probably constituted a grievance which induced support for Glyn Dŵr's cause.

In 1400, Owain Glyn Dŵr led the rebellion bearing his name, and for a number of years the economy of the lordship was disturbed by the spasmodic outbreak of hostilities. The financial contributions received from the lordship of Denbigh were not immediately affected by the rebellion. In 1399, the lordship was the largest single unit in the Mortimer estate, and the sum of £903 10s. 6¼d handed over to the central receiver represented 26 per cent of the total revenue of £3,398 17s. 4½d.[26] When considering that the next highest payment was only 51.7 per cent of the Denbigh render, the economic importance of the lordship within the Mortimer complex is emphasised. Moreover, by 1402 payments from the lordship had increased to £928 17s. 4d.[27]

1402–25

Despite the continued high yield in 1402, the financial organisation of the lordship was subject to strain, and this year, in fact witnessed a fall in the revenue derived from both land rents and officials. Also, 1402 was the only year in the period extending from 1362 to 1420 that had a debit balance. In view of the lordship not having suffered excessively from the hostilities by this time,[28] the debit balance seems to have been caused by the reluctance of some tenants to contribute their dues, rather than their inability to do so. However, the immunity of the lordship ceased after the death of Henry Percy and the grant of the lordship to Henry, Prince of Wales. A letter patent, dated 25 April 1405, recorded that no issues had been levied on lands belonging to the manor of Ystrad during the previous two-and-a-half years 'on account of the Welsh rebels'.[29] Also, on 29 November 1405, Thomas Sandewath was granted custody of lands valued at 6 marks in peace time but which, at that time, were of small or no value 'because of the Welsh rebellion'.[30] Authority was soon restored in the lordship, and in 1407 and 1408 fines were imposed on communities and individuals. In 1407, a sum of £596 1s. was collected from fines levied in the lordship,[31] and in the following year, £229 was again contributed from the same source.[32] It is certainly true that the fines seem to represent a political penalty rather than an economic assessment, but the considerable sums involved represent an intensification of the pressure imposed on the inhabitants of the lordship.

These sums may be considered to have arisen from the temporary and abnormal conditions created by the rebellion, one must now turn to the more permanent results of the uprising. The deterioration of the economy was reflected in the 1410 account, which reveals that few individuals were prepared to take advantage of the increasing number of holdings vacated as a result of the rebellion. Therefore, the 'decayed rents' of Is Aled rose from £55 3s. 8¾d in 1402 to £179 16s. 5½d in 1410, that is, when set against the total rent charge, from 24.3 per cent to 61 per cent. Also, payments to the central receiver fell from £928 17s. 4d to £110 in the same period. When considered in relation to the total expenditure, these payments represented a reduction from 73.9 per cent to 38.4 per cent, a remarkable decrease explained by the increased payments on wages that in 1410 constituted 47.5 per cent of the receiver's expenditure. The fall in land rents and payments to the central receiver represent clear evidence of the impact of the rebellion on the lordship's economy. At the same time, the revenue derived from the various officials decreased less markedly. While the actual sums fell from £489 9s. 9¾d in 1402 to £155 12s. in 1410, the percentage, in relation to the total income, was maintained, and the 44.9 per cent recorded in 1402 had risen slightly to 46 per cent in 1410.[33] It is true that the ratio had increased to 80.8 per cent in 1415,[34] but the absence of any reference to income from land prompts one to avoid overemphasising this statistic. The evidence relating to the accounts for 1402 and 1410 suggests that the administration's attempt to retrieve a rapidly deteriorating situation was dependent on the cash obtained from various officials, and a study of the extant accounts of these officials is therefore necessary.

The ringilds' accounts for Ceinmeirch, for 1407 and 1408, and Uwch Dulas for 1407-9 have survived,[35] and these have been compared to the pre-rebellion accounts for the same commotes in 1398.[36] An assessment has consequently been attempted of changes that affected the seignorial revenue of the two commotes in this period from 1398-1411. In both commotes the revenue from Welsh customs fell drastically. In Ceinmeirch, neither *tunc* nor the other customs was rendered in 1407, and also no revenue was received from the other customs (the '*Consuetudines*') that had contributed £6 3s. 11d in 1398. Difficulties continued to be encountered in recruiting local inhabitants for commotal offices, and the farm of the office of collector of *amobr* in Ceinmeirch was reduced from the sum of £1 3s. 4d, paid by William Swynemore in 1410 to the 16s. 8d paid by Llywelyn ap Iorwerth Sais in 1411.[37] In Uwch Dulas, the farm of this office fell from the £4 0s. 9d paid by Einion Fychan in 1398 to the 13s. 4d rendered in 1408 and 1409, and the 10s. in 1410 paid in 1410 by Bleddyn ap Cynwrig Goch.[38] Varying trends may be observed with regard to the court profits derived during these years from the two commotes. In Ceinmeirch fluctuations were of a moderate extent and ranged from £2 16s. 6d in 1398 to £1 12s. 8d in 1411.[39] On the other hand, there was a dramatic fall in Uwch Dulas, from £46 18s. 9d in 1398 to £1 15s. 6d in 1411.[40]

The relative success of attempts to restore the economy to a healthier condition was revealed by the favourable credit balance discernible in the receivers' accounts for 1410 and 1420. In 1410, in addition to the payment of £110 to the Receiver-General of the Mortimer estate, together with expenditure on wages and miscellaneous expenses, there remained a credit balance of £61 16s. 10d.[41] The contribution to the Receiver-General had increased to £352 2s. 2d by 1420, and an analysis of the account reveals that in this year, after the payment of wages and various expenses, there was a favourable balance of £431 13s. 10d.[42] These statistics suggest a degree of economic recovery, and this impression is also conveyed by the number of leases drawn up from 1417 onwards. The 1437 Rental revealed that only a small amount of escheated land was leased out, and forty-year leases, compiled in 1398, governed the occupation in 1437 of 4 acres in the 'Acre' of Lleweni by Robert ap Iorwerth, and of 43 acres in Tal-y-bryn by Hywel Meifod.[43] The rental does not provide evidence of other leases being compiled before 1417, and numerous examples in the rental reveal the compilation of leases in the period following 1417, and it is probable that it was only in this year that the enterprising section of the lordship's inhabitants considered that it was propitious to lease plots of land. In the following year Henry Salusbury, together with Alex Henbury, occupied on a twenty-year lease the new mill of Clwyd, which had been burned down during the rebellion.[44]

Payments to the central receiver for the Mortimer lands continued to be below the pre-rebellion level in the period 1415–20, and this was again confirmed by the evidence of an account compiled at Michaelmas, 1425, relating to the preceding period since the death of Edmund, earl of March, on 18 January.[45] In the whole period considered in this chapter there was a decline in the value of the lordship of Denbigh. In 1334 the lordship was evaluated at £1,100 7s. 1¾d,[46] but lower sums of £ 778 6s. 8d and £812 12s. 11d were quoted, respectively, in the *valors* of 1422 and 1424.[47] These sums in the two latter valuations, and the difference between them, indicate a degree of recovery from the dislocation caused by the rebellion. Indeed, the permanent effect of the rebellion should not be overstated, and the fall in the figures of the early fifteenth century, in comparison with those of the previous century, may be explained partly by the permanence of some of the damage inflicted during the rebellion and partly as an admission of deeper difficulties. It is not easy to explain this but there is little doubt that, despite the apparent recovery revealed after two outbreaks of the pestilence, the latter was at least an important contributory factor to the progressive economic malaise. The high yields made to the seignorial lords before 1400 were achieved despite these difficulties, but they were never again achieved to the same extent. Even so, the contribution made to the Mortimer coffers at the end of this period shows that the lordship of Denbigh continued to be one of its most valuable financial assets.

Notes

1. *Infra*, pp. 208–9, 235.
2. NLW Wynnstay, 86
3. See below for numerous examples cited and including those listed below in nos 9 and 36.
4. TNA SC 6/1182/2.
5. TNA SC 6/1182/3.
6. TNA SC 6.
7. *Cal. Inq. P.M.*, x, 533.
8. Gareth Evans and Arnold Hughes (eds), *The History of Ruthin* (Ruthin, 2014), p. 27.
9. TNA SC 6/1182/3; 1182/4.
10. TNA SC 6/1182/4; 17.
11. TNA 1183/3; TNA SC 11/23.
12. TNA SC 6/1185/4.
13. TNA SC 6/1183/20; 1185/4.
14. TNA SC 6/1182/5; 1182/7.
15. TNA SC 6/1182/5; 1183/3.
16. TNA SC 6/1183/8; 1183/17.
17. TNA SC 6/1183/12; 1184/19.
18. TNA SC 6/1183/12.
19. TNA SC 6/1183/6; 1183/8.
20. TNA SC 6/1183/17.
21. TNA SC 6/1183/21; 1184/2.
22. TNA SC 6/1184/7.
23. TNA SC 6/1183/11; 1183/15.
24. TNA SC 6/1184/8; 1185/2.
25. TNA SC 6/1184/11; 1185/1.
26. TNA SC 6/11/23.
27. TNA SC 6/1185/4.
28. *Supra*, pp. 130–1.

29 *CPR 1405–8*, p. 7.
30 *CPR*, p. 103–4.
31 TNA SC 6/775/7.
32 TNA SC 6/775/8.
33 TNA SC 6/1185/4; 1185/12.
34 TNA SC 6/1185/14.
35 TNA SC 6/1185/6; 1185/8; 1185/7.
36 TNA SC 6/1185/2; 1185/3.
37 TNA SC 6/1185/11; 1185/13.
38 TNA SC 6/1185/3; 1185/7; 1185/11.
39 TNA SC 6/1185/2; 1185/13.
40 TNA SC 6/1185/3; 1185/13.
41 TNA SC 6/1185/12.
42 TNA SC 6/1185/13.
43 NLW Wynnstay, 86.
44 NLW Wynnstay, 86.
45 TNA SC 6/1305/8.
46 *SD*, p. 323.
47 TNA E 142/38; E 142/39; A. C. Reeves, *The Marcher Lords* (Llandybie, 1983), p. 131, referred to the permanent reduction, following the Glyn Dŵr rebellion, in the revenues of the lordships of Chirk, Oswestry, Denbigh, Glamorgan, Newport, and other lordships.

12

ADMINISTRATION, 1334–1543

The administrative system established in the immediate post-conquest period continued to operate throughout the history of the lordship until its replacement by the shire system introduced as a result of the sixteenth-century Union legislation.[1] Throughout the period extending from 1334 to 1543 the steward, receiver and constable continued to be the premier members of the central administration of the lordship. In 1363 the steward received an annual payment of £30, the receiver £20 and the constable £6 3s. 4d; and the corresponding amounts in 1397 were £40, £13 6s, 8d. and £5, and in 1410 it was £40, £20 and £10.[2] Their responsibilities were discharged throughout the later history of the lordship and this was also the case with the more local officials with the continued operation of the commote court as the local judicial unit. Welsh law seems to have survived in this court, with its interpretation by the *iudex*, whose presence emphasised the continuity of the post-conquest judicial system, and this official continuing to function in the lordship until the early sixteenth century.[3] He was paid an annual salary that increased from £1 6s. 8d in 1362 to £5 in 1397 and 1402,[4] and he also received a substantial share of the court profits. In 1380, he received a sum of £3 11s. 4d from the court profits of Is Aled, which amounted to £24 13s. 6½d.[5] He was assisted in the execution of verdicts by the raglot and ringild, and this is indicated by payments to these officials at those times when they received an annual fee. In Is Dulas in 1380 the raglot received a fee of £6 10s. and the ringild one of £3 0s. 10d for their services at the commote court.[6]

It is probable that the commote court was the only court to which the lord's tenants had recourse. There is no reference to a central court for the lordship, and despite the lack of any specific evidence, one may tentatively suggest that tenants would have only had the right of appeal to the lord's council. The two references in the Black Prince's Register to actions in 1361 in 'the court of Denbigh' probably refer to the court of the Englishry. On 31 March 1361, John Delves was ordered to respite the process made against John Swynemore in 'the court of Denbigh' and in September, of the same year, it was recorded that a judgment had been brought against Adam Salusbury 'in the court of Denbigh'.[7] The absence of further references in the register, enrolled letters and accounts suggest that the 'court of Denbigh' was the court of the Englishry rather than a central court for the lordship, and that, despite the lack of concrete evidence, the tenants would have had leave of appeal only to the lord's council.[8]

The lordship, which was by this time attached to the principality, had become part of a more centralised organisation, and officials were frequently interchanged with those of the royal government.[9] A number of new appointments were made to the central administrative structure of the lordship, and John Brunham, the younger, the chamberlain of Chester from 1346 to 1370, who had formerly served as steward of the lordship, was appointed as the receiver on 23 May 1360.[10] Associated with the administration of the nearby earldom of Chester, he had served as the chamberlain of Chester from 1346 to 1370.[11] Also, John Delves, the member of an apparently modest Staffordshire family who became a considerable landowner in Cheshire, and, having served as Deputy Justice of North Wales and Chester since 29 September 1348, was nominated on 23 May 1360 as both steward and constable of the lordship of Denbigh.[12] Within a month, on 5 June, he had been replaced as constable by Thomas Statham, but Delves was sufficiently prominent to become the governor of the prince's council in 1363.[13] On 13 July 1360, Thomas Chaundeller and Robert Houghton were appointed respectively as master forester and escheator.[14]

The frequency of these appointments in the summer of 1360 was symptomatic of a determination to overhaul an administration, which appears to have been considered disorganised. Following Robert Houghton's succession to the office of escheator, he was pardoned on 13 July 1360 for removing, during the period when the lordship was part of the earldom of March, certain rolls and muniments that belonged to the lordship.[15] Also, on 16 February 1361 and 4 February 1364, commissions were appointed to investigate various errors in the records of the lordship, and this represented a further indication of the inefficient administration inherited by Edward, Prince of Wales, known as the Black Prince.[16]

A significant innovation in the judicial system was the holding of sessions in eyre at Denbigh on 17 March 1362 with Sir William Banastre and Sir William Shareshull, both prominent officials in the Prince's council, requested to serve at Denbigh as chief justices in eyre.[17] John Brunham, the receiver of the lordship, was ordered to pay their expenses, which amounted to £35 19s. 9½d.[18] The sessions were also held in the following two years, in October 1363 and February 1364, with the same two officials again responsible for their functioning.[19] Cases involving prominent individuals from the lordship were tried at the sessions. Thomas Puttenham master forester in 1362 and 1363, was required in 1362, together with his wife Alice, to appear before the sessions, and John de Brunham had been ordered to take out a writ against them on 20 March 1362.[20] The defendants in 1364 included Adam Winchester and Henry Salusbury, together with other members of the latter's family.[21] The sessions continued to be held in 1379 and in 1380 after possession of the lordship was restored to the earldom of March, and in the latter year, the account of the ringild of Is Aled recorded that the *iudex*, raglot and ringild of this commote were all in attendance at the sessions.[22] No further evidence is available concerning the holding of sessions, but in 1443 a fine was paid by the inhabitants so that the sessions would not be held. This was common practice in south Wales with fines for the redemption of Great Sessions an important source of revenue for the marcher lords, but the absence of references in Denbigh to the sessions from 1380 to 1443 should not be taken as proof that none was held as there is a similar lack of evidence for the marcher lordships generally in the later Middle Ages.[23]

In addition to the central and commote courts other judicial institutions were also established, with the boroughs, Englishry and the woodwards of the five commotes holding their own courts. In Is Aled the forest court was divided on racial grounds, as indeed was the commote court itself, and in 1363 the woodward of this commote accounted for a forest court *inter Wallenses*, whose profits amounted to 43s. 6d, and also a forest court, *inter Anglicos*, which yielded 8s. 10½d.[24] Also, the escheator held a court and the fines and reliefs that appear in appendages to some of his accounts were levied on tenants assuming possession of their lands. Substantial payments from the escheator were recorded in various accounts, including those compiled in 1397, 1422 and 1424.[25]

The racial basis underlying the establishment of administrative and judicial units also resulted in a distinction in legal procedures with the Conquest accompanied by the widespread introduction of English criminal law.[26] However, Welsh law (*'cyfraith Hywel'*) was clearly administered in the commote courts and 'Welsh' forest courts where the *ynad* was responsible for its interpretation, with Welsh law continuing to operate in real actions relating to land.[27] On 27 May 1362, John de Delves, the steward was ordered to render satisfaction to Thomas ap Iorwerth ap Llywarch concerning the latter's complaint that Henry Salusbury prevented him from occupying his lands. Thomas, as plaintiff, had claimed that he was summoned in those assemblies, *cymanfas*, when the earl of March held the lordship, that is from 1355 to 1366, for non-payment of rent. As a result of his non-appearance, his lands had been seized by Welsh law. However, he had later paid a fine to the prince for his non-appearance and therefore, according to Welsh law, was entitled to the restitution of his lands.[28]

This manipulation of Welsh law by a member of the Salusbury family, which was rapidly extending its landed possessions, illustrates the tendency for English settler families to use Welsh law when it profited them.[29] Similarly, the petition, presented on 23 February 1361 by two-thirds of the 'commonalty' of the lordship, requested that boundary disputes be settled not by arbitrary 'unjust ministers' but by 'the law of those parts'.[30] The use of Welsh law in criminal actions was more restricted, but the one surviving example again involved the Salusbury family. On 4 February 1364, Sir William Shareshull and his fellow justices of eyre were ordered by the prince's council to proceed on a case against Henry Salusbury according to 'the laws and customs of those parts'.[31]

Whereas payments from escheator to receiver in some years were at a high level, amounting to £139 14s. 5½d in 1375, and £227 6s. 2d in 1397, with the latter sum representing 19 per cent of the total revenue of the lordship, an intensification of financial difficulties may be observed by this time.[32] The tenure of commotal offices seems to have become decreasingly lucrative. In 1380, Thomas Schutlesworth, ringild of Is Aled, was responsible for the profits derived from the commote courts and sessions, and also, as the commotal accountant, for the payments from free and bond clansmen, together with fees to the *iudex* and raglot, as well as to himself. The office of raglot was retained in the lord's hands, because of a scarcity of possible office-holders (*'defectus firmarii'*) and Gruffudd ap Cynwrig Routh paid £10 for the office of sergeant of the peace in Is Aled; an office for which a sum of £17 had been paid in 1376, and his son Ednyfed rendered £7 for the office of *amobr* for which £8 had been paid in 1376.[33] There was also a tendency again for the farms to fall towards the end of the fourteenth century, and in Uwch Aled, the farm of the sergeantry of the peace, which had been maintained at £7 13s. 4d from 1377 until 1380, had fallen to £5 13s. 4d in 1397 and to £4 11s. 6d in 1398.[34]

Severe problems were experienced during and as a consequence of the Glyn Dŵr rebellion, and in this period both Welsh and settler families contributed to the administrative service provided in the lordship. John Swynemore served as constable of Denbigh castle in 1344 and 1345, and William Curteys occupied the same position from 1402 until 1410.[35] John Curteys was the capital forester in 1374 and 1375, while Henry Salusbury held this office in 1366, 1368 and 1402.[36] Also, William Swynemore was the escheator from 1407 until 1411.[37] After the outbreak of the Glyn Dŵr rebellion, William Fletcher, John Heton, Richard Peake and John Pigot served as archers, and Robert Swynemore as custodian in the castle garrison in 1402.[38]

A firm grip on several local administrative posts was maintained by the settler families, and the office of bailiff of the Englishry was held by John Peake from 1375 until 1380, and by Alfred Peake from 1409 until 1411 and again in 1424.[39] Thomas Salusbury was the parker of Postin 1363, and Robert Pigot the parker of Moel-y wig and Garsnodiog in 1375 and Postin in 1398.[40] Offices within the commote included those of *amobr* of Ceinmeirch and Is Aled occupied by William Swynemore in 1408.[41] Also, while Reginald Heton was the *raglot advocariae* of Uwch Aled in 1354, his descendant Richard held this office in the period 1377–9.[42]

It is however certainly the case that commotal offices were generally held by members of the local Welsh community, with some families closely associated with the administration over a considerable length of time, and significantly including the period when the lordship was in the throes of the Glyn Dŵr rebellion. The descendants of Cynwrig Routh regularly served as commotal officials, with Llywelyn ap Cynwrig Routh occupying, in the commote of Is Aled, the offices of raglot, in 1374 and 1375; ringild in 1362; *raglot advocariae* in 1366 and woodward in 1361 and 1368.[43] Cynwrig Routh's other son, Gruffudd, was raglot of Ceinmeirch in 1360 and 1363, and *amobr* in 1366, and he also served as ringild of Is Aled from 1366 until 1370.[44] Moreover, Gruffudd's son Ednyfed in 1380 was the *amobr* of Is Aled.[45]

Similarly, the family of Llywelyn Chwith was closely associated with the administration of Uwch Aled. Llywelyn Chwith was the raglot from 1372 until 1378, and again in 1397, and the *amobr* in 1398.⁴⁶ The family tradition was maintained by his son Ieuan, who served as sergeant of the peace in 1402, raglot, *amobr* and woodward in 1379, 1380 and 1408, and *amobr* again in 1409.⁴⁷

Other members of prominent local families included Llywelyn Bottreys, the ringild of Is Aled in 1424 and 1426, who in 1437 occupied 66 acres in Nantglyn 'Sanctorum' and 2.5 acres together with rights in the water and fulling mills of Nantglyn Cynan.⁴⁸ Another family that played a prominent role in commotal adminstration in this period was the Iorwerth Sais family. Iorwerth served in Ceinmeirch as the *amobr* in 1374 and 1375, and the woodward in 1379 and 1380.⁴⁹ His son Dafydd was the woodward in 1398 and his other sons Tudur and Llywelyn respectively occupied the posts of *amobr* in 1402 and 1411.⁵⁰ Moreover, Llywelyn ap Iorwerth Sais, who also served as ringild of Ceinmeirch in 1410, had leased 5 acres of escheated land in Cernenyfed in 1397, while his brother Dafydd was the lessee in 1397, 1402 and 1411 of a *tyddyn* and 3.5 acres in Sgeibion.⁵¹ The family estate had been considerably extended by 1437 when the *tyddyn* and a plot of 3.5 acres in Sgeibion were occupied by Dafydd's son Tudur, while in Cernenyfed Dafydd and Llywelyn each held plots of 9 acres, while the two brothers also jointly held 38.5 acres in the same township.⁵²

The more significant offices, however, continued to be reserved for members of settler families or for persons who do not seem to have any close association with this locality. The latter seems to have prevailed with the two appointments made on 12 March 1425 to the central administration following the death of Edmund Mortimer, earl of March, and the subsequent integration of the lordship into royal custody because of the minority of Richard duke of York. Thomas Eltonhed was appointed as receiver of the lordship, and Thomas Newenham as auditor of Denbigh together with a number of other lordships including Builth, Ewyas and

Narberth.[53] In 1439, Roger Wigmore served as steward in the administration of Richard duke of York and earl of March and Ulster.[54] An even more prominent individual, William Burley of Boncroft, Shropshire, who had occupied the post of speaker of parliament in 1437 and in 1445–6, member of parliament in the period 1417–56, and steward of the lordships of Montgomery and Oswestry, held the office of steward of the lordship of Denbigh in the 1440s.[55] A person with local associations, Thomas Salusbury was the constable of Denbigh castle in 1454 when he reached an agreement with Thomas Dutton, and a pardon granted in December 1460 to William Stanley of Hooton, Chester referred to his previous tenure of the office of receiver of the lordship.[56]

A number of administrative developments had accompanied the forfeiture of the lordship and its acceptance into royal hands in 1460. One immediate result was the grant for life, on 5 January 1460 to the king's brother Jasper Tudor of the offices of constable of Denbigh castle and steward and master forester of the lordship: this grant referred to his immense contribution to the successful besieging of the castle of Denbigh and crushing the rebels therein.[57] On 13 September 1460, the post of constable was granted for life to Robert Bolde, and while this grant had been confirmed on 1 July 1461, in slightly over a month, on 7 August 1461, Robert Leghe had been issued with a similar grant.[58] Thomas Salusbury became the steward and receiver of the lordship on 28 July 1465, and in the following year, on 23 January, identified as 'the younger', he was granted for life the office of constable.[59] The increasing influence in Wales of William Herbert was reflected by his appointment as steward on 28 August 1467, in addition to his post as constable of Denbigh castle.[60] Sir William Stanley, who had been created steward for life on 14 February 1469, became the chamberlain of the household in 1491, with Thomas Salusbury the elder serving as his deputy from 1469 until 1481.[61] Members of the Salusbury family continued to play a significant role in the administration of the lordship, and Roger Salusbury, who had been granted for life the post of chief forester on 12

May 1461, was appointed as steward, together with that of porter in 1506, and he also served as steward again in 1508.[62] In 1501 Thomas Salusbury served as woodward and *rhaglaw*, and in 1503 he was a member of a commission comprising four individuals appointed to survey the castle, borough, town and lordship of Denbigh.[63] Thomas's kinsman, Henry Salusbury had served as receiver in 1490, and escheator and attorney in 1492; and the office of receiver was also held by Randolph Brereton in 1493.[64]

A notable feature of the above-named office-holders is the absence of distinctive Welsh names, and a significant exception to this trend is the name of Owen Tudor, a member of the Ednyfed Fychan family, and grandfather of Henry VII.[65] He was identified, in a grant for life dated 5 February 1460, as the 'king's esquire', who served as woodward, and also parker of the parks of Moelywig, Garsnodiog, Kilford and Postin.[66] Robert Lloyd, described as 'a yeoman of the Crown', was named in 1492 as escheator and attorney, in 1499 as keeper of the park of Galghull and bailiff itinerant, and also in 1504 as clerk of the king's works and keeper of the gaol called the 'Cheker gate and Burgess gate': the latter posts were vacant because of the deaths of Robert's brother William Lloyd and Henry Strynger.[67]

When one turns to the more local offices at the commotal level, a number of distinctive Welsh names appear. These included in 1460 Nicholas ap Rhys, granted the office of *rhaglaw* in the five commotes of the lordship 'for good service and labour for the king in repressing rebellion'; and Huw ap Hywel, appointed the *rhaglaw* of advowry and amobrage, again in the five commotes.[68] Also, Cadwaladr ap Rhys, described as 'the king's servant' was in 1498 appointed as *rhaglaw* for life in the lordship.[69] John and Morgan Holland seem to have been members of a prominent local family. In August 1497 John, described as 'yeoman of the Crown', was appointed keeper of the Little Park instead of Nicholas Manley who had forfeited the post because of his absence from the battle of Blackheath and from the royal expedition to Boulogne.[70] Morgan Holland, described as one of the marshals of the king's hall, became the keeper of Moelywig park; and the latter post was again occupied by him in the following year.[71] Intriguing references in 1499 were the naming of William Almer, one of the yeomen of the Crown, as the keeper of the Little Park and also as the *ynad*, the person responsible for interpreting various aspects of Welsh law.[72]

Notes

1   *Supra*, pp. 189, 208–9.
2   TNA SC 6/1182/6; 1184/22; 1185/10.
3   J. Beverley Smith, 'Crown and Community in the Principality of North Wales in the Reign of Henry Tudor', *WHR*, 3 (1966), 170; TNA SC 6/HEN VII/1670-1.
4   TNA SC 6/1182/5; 1184/22; 1185/4.
5   TNA SC 6/1183/16.
6   TNA SC 6/1184/13.
7   *BPR*, iii, 412.
8   *BPR*, 422.
9   Tout, *Chapters in the Administrative History of Medieval England*, vol. 5, pp. 294–5, described the promotion, in 1367, to the king's privy seal of Peter Lacy, the Prince's Receiver-General and Keeper of the Great Seal, while retaining the latter two posts as a 'Gilbertian height of absurdity'; Booth, *The Financial Administration of the Lordship and County of Chester*, pp. 65–7.
10 *BPR*, iii, 381.
11 Tout, *Chapters in the Administrative History of Medieval England*, vol. 5, pp. 316, n. 2; Booth, *The Financial Administration of the Lordship and County of Chester*, p. 66, assessed Brunham as 'a complete success'.
12 G. Ormerod, *The History of the County Palatine and City of Chester*, 2nd edn, vol. 3 (London, 1882), p. 518; Tout, *Chapters in the Administrative History of Medieval England*, vol. 6, p. 60; Booth, *The Financial Administration of the Lordship and County of Chester*, p. 66, considered Delves's career to be ' a compelling example of the rewards open to a trusted administrator in the Black Prince's service, even to someone from a relatively humble background'.
13 Tout, *Chapters in the Administrative History of Medieval England*, vol. 5, p. 389.
14 *BPR*, iii, 387, 388.
15 *BPR*, 387.
16 *BPR*, 406, 463.
17 Tout, *Chapters in the Administrative History of Medieval England*, vol. 5, p. 385, n. 6, pp. 322, 344, n. 7, p. 385 , n. 6; B. H., Putnam, *The Place in Legal History of Sir William Shareshull* (Cambridge, 1950); T. B. Pugh (ed.), *The Marcher Lordships of South Wales, 1415–1536: Select Documents* (Cardiff, 1963), p. 39: 'It is difficult to see why the marcher lords of north Wales did not follow the example of the lords of eyre,

and oblige the inhabitants to redeem them'; Booth, *The Financial Administration of the Lordship and County of Chester*, p. 120, described Shareshull as a key figure in the development of financial policy in the royal government as well as in the prince's administration during these years.

18 *BPR*, iii, 446; TNA SC 6/1182/5.
19 *BPR*, iii, 461, 463.
20 *BPR*, 441.
21 *BPR*, 467–8.
22 TNA SC 6/1184/8; /10; TNA SC 6.
23 TNA SC 11/818; Pugh, *Marcher Lordships*, pp. 37–9.
24 *Supra*, p. 42.
25 TNA SC 6, 1184/22; E 142/38; E 142/39.
26 R. R. Davies, 'The Twilight of Welsh Law, 1284–1536', *History*, 51 (June 1966), 156, for reference to compilation, in the neighbouring lordship of Dyffryn Clwyd, of separate rentals for the Englishry and Welshry, with the prevalence of different customs of inheritance, services and duties.
27 Davies, 'The Twilight of Welsh Law', 147, and 156 for the comment that 'no one would want to deny that Welsh land law and tenure were quite distinctive'.
28 *BPR*, iii, 446.
29 Davies, 'The Twilight of Welsh Law', 160, for a comment that such 'unlikely person as Roger Mortimer, of Wigmore, Gruffydd ap Gwenwynyn of Powys and the Lord Grey of Ruthin could occasionally resort to Welsh law when it suited them'.
30 *BPR*, iii, 410 and *supra*.
31 *BPR*, iii, 463.
32 TNA SC 6/1183/20; 1184/22.
33 TNA SC 6/1184/16; 1183/16.
34 TNA SC 6/1184/2; /7; /11; /15; /20; /1185/1.
35 TNA E 101, 612/1; SC 6/1182/2; 1185/4; /9; /10; /12.
36 TNA 1183/15; /20; 1182/10; /11; 1185/4.
37 TNA 1185/9/12.
38 TNA 1185/4.
39 TNA 1183/16; 1184/16; 1185/10–13; 1305/8.
40 TNA 1182/7; 1183/20; 1185/2.
41 TNA 1185/8–11.
42 TNA 1182/3; 1184/2.
43 *Supra*, pp. 146, 150.
44 TNA 1182/4; /6; /8; /10; /11; 1183/3.
45 TNA 1184/16.
46 TNA1182/6; /8; /12; 17; /21; /1184/2; /7; /22; 1185/1.
47 TNA 1185/4; /9; /10.
48 TNA 1112/24; 1185/16; NLW Wynnstay, 86.
49 TNA 1183/14; /18; 1184/8; /12.
50 TNA 1185/2; /4; /13.
51 TNA 1184/22; 1185/4; /11; /13.

52 NLW Wynnstay, 86.
53 *CPR 1422–9*, pp. 272–3.
54 NLW Plas-yn-cefn, 1583.
55 Reeves, *Marcher Lords*, pp. 80–1.
56 NLW Bachymbyd, 521.
57 *CPR 1452–61*, p. 534.
58 *CPR 1461–7*, pp. 51, 60, 421–2.
59 NLW Lleweni Deeds, 361; *CPR 1461–7*, pp. 421–2.
60 *CPR 1467–77*, p. 22.
61 *CPR*, p. 183.
62 *CPR 1461–7*, p. 24; *CPR 1494–1509*, pp. 483, 605.
63 *CPR*, pp. 266, 332.
64 *CPR 1485–94*, pp. 313, 380.
65 Roberts, *Aspects of Welsh History*, pp. 193, 240, 241, 242, 307, 316.
66 *CPR 1452–61*, p. 547.
67 *CPR 1485–94*, p. 379; *CPR 1494–1509*, p. 385.
68 *CPR 1452–61*, pp. 543; 567.
69 *CPR 1494–1509*, pp. 14, 124, 266.
70 *CPR*, p. 110.
71 *CPR*, p. 158.
72 *CPR*, p. 188.

13

POLITICAL CONTROL AND LAND TENURE, 1425–1485

The death on 18 January 1425 of Edmund Mortimer, the fifth earl of March, who left no direct heirs, resulted in his extensive estates, including the lordship of Denbigh, being inherited by Richard, duke of York, the son of Edmund's sister Anne and her deceased husband, the earl of Cambridge. The lands placed under his direct control extended southwards from Denbigh to Caerleon and Usk in south-east Wales, and it has been estimated that the revenue from his Welsh lands, amounting to £3,430 per annum, exceeded that derived from his English estates, valued at £2,230 per annum.[1]

Following the death of Duke Humphrey in 1447 and because the king, Henry VI, was at that time childless, the duke of York was the heir apparent to the throne. However, the king's weakness and the bitter rivalry of a number of magnates resulted in fierce competition for political control. Having been sent to Ireland in 1449, the duke of York returned in September the following year and is known to have reached Denbigh by 8 September.[2] The birth of a male heir to the throne in 1453 was countered by the deteriorating mental health of the king. The duke of York was appointed Protector in March 1454, and his powerful supporters included Richard, earl of Warwick and lord of Glamorgan; Sir Walter Devereux, his chief steward; and his son-in-law, Sir William Herbert.[3] However, Henry VI's recovery later in 1454 brought to an end York's protectorate and ushered in a protracted period of civil war between the rival supporters of the houses of

York and Lancaster, with the conflict having a direct impact on various areas of Wales, including the lordship of Denbigh.

Whereas the duke of York was successful at the opening skirmish fought at St Albans in 1455, the Lancastrian success in 1459 at Ludford Bridge, near Ludlow, led to the imposition of a payment of 500 marks by several pro-Yorkist families to ensure that those lordships that had previously supported the duke of York might be 'brought back the more speedily to the king's obedience'.[4] The lordship of Denbigh presented the most severe opposition to the royal forces. Jasper Tudor's appointment on 5 January 1460 as constable of the castle and steward of the lordship was accompanied by the grant to him of the authority to enforce its obedience, enlist more troops in Wales and pardon or execute rebels.[5] After seven weeks, the garrison continued to offer resistance and on 22 February Jasper Tudor was granted a special commission with extensive powers to ensure its rapid surrender. After this had been achieved, he was to occupy the town 'as of our gift', receive all the movable goods that had been held by the garrison and then grant them among the soldiers. He was also granted a force of soldiers and archers with authority to enlist more troops in Wales, pardon or execute the rebels 'and receive into our favour any rebels of the castle of Denbigh, or outside, except certain English and Irish holding and defending the same castle against us; except also certain Welshmen outlawed and attainted'.[6]

The effectiveness of these measure was reflected by the surrender of the castle of Denbigh in early March 1460, and on 13 March a special grant of £1,000 was provided, to be raised from the Welsh estates of the duke of York and the earl of Warwick, because of the expenses incurred in the capture of this town and other places in Wales.[7] Denbigh was now in the custody of Roger Puleston, Jasper Tudor's deputy, and possibly housed some Lancastrian supporters.[8] Later in the year, on 30 December, the duke of York was killed at the battle of Wakefield where his armies were defeated.[9] The Yorkist cause was now led by the duke's son Edward, earl of March, who immediately set about recruiting troops from his estates in the Welsh marches, probably including the lordship of Denbigh.[10] This force defeated the Lancastrian opposition at the battle of Mortimer's Cross on 2 February 1461, and Edward then proceeded to London where he was crowned on 3 March as Edward IV, the king of England.[11]

The accession of Edward IV led to the incorporation of the lordship into the English realm and this was its status until the creation of the shire of Denbigh in the Union legislation of 1536–43. Following the battle of Mortimer's Cross, Jasper Tudor wrote on 25 February to Roger Puleston and John Eyton, his stewards at Denbigh, encouraging them to be faithful and in this letter he referred to the earl of March and Sir William Herbert as 'traitors'.[12] The garrison of Denbigh now fully supported the Lancastrian cause and this was reflected in another letter sent by Jasper Tudor on 23 July to Roger Puleston, described as 'Keeper of the castle of Denbigh', in which he was encouraged to defend the castle of Denbigh: 'do your faithful diligence for the safeguard of it.'[13] Lancastrian supporters, who had suffered another defeat at Towton on 29 March, experienced a further reverse at Tuthill, near Caernarfon on 16 October.[14] In January 1462, the borough of Denbigh surrendered to Yorkist pressure, and on 23 February it was awarded a sum of £1,000 by the monarch for the reconstruction of buildings destroyed 'by occasion of burning of the same town, violently done'.[15] By this time, William Herbert was in a very powerful position, and in 1463 became the chief justice and chamberlain of Merioneth.[16] However, supporters of the Lancastrian cause continued to operate and an attempt to oppose their intentions was the decision to send John, duke of Norfolk, to Denbigh. He was recorded as being in the town on 1 March 1464, discussing the situation with rebels, and it was stated that it would take another fortnight for this task to be completed, that pardons would be granted to most of the troublemakers, 'and as far as I can understand they shall have grace'.[17]

In 1468, a Lancastrian force, led by Jasper Tudor, attacked the town of Denbigh, where a considerable amount of damage was caused, with the town plundered and set on fire.[18] However, he failed to capture the castle, whose defence was organised by Lord Herbert. Twenty of Tudor's men were executed, yet Jasper Tudor succeeded in holding sessions here in the name of Henry VI.[19] This led to the mobilisation of a large army recruited from the marches and the border counties, led by William Herbert and his brother Richard, which defeated Jasper's troops in a battle fought between Denbigh and the Conwy valley. Several prisoners were captured and a considerable amount of damage seems to have been caused.[20] Sir John Wynn, writing in the early seventeenth century, stated that the Lancastrian forces 'wasted with fire and sword the suburbs of the town of Denbigh and all the lordship of Denbigh' and that the desolation caused by Herbert's supporters 'consumed the whole borough of Llanrwst and all the vale of Conwy'.[21]

In 1469, the defeat of the Yorkist force at Banbury and execution of William Herbert were followed by the Yorkist success at Tewkesbury with Edward IV thereby enabled to rule his kingdom until his death in 1483.[22] Following the tumultuous events of the period 1483–5, Henry Tudor secured the throne at the battle of Bosworth and reigned as Henry VII during the period 1485–1509. The supporters who contributed significantly to his military success included Rhys ap Maredudd (Rhys Fawr), whose father, Maredudd ap Tudur, had served as the steward of the monastic lands of Aberconwy at Hiraethog, and also of the lands of the Knights of St John, the Order of Hospitallers.[23] This had been established towards the end of the twelfth century at Dôl Gynwal, which was thereafter known as Ysbyty Ifan.[24] Rhys Fawr is reputed to have fought at Bosworth and to have taken possession of the banner displaying the Red Dragon, following the death of Sir William Brandon. He is also held to have waved it triumphantly for several hours, and been responsible, according to the poet Tudur Penllyn, for the death of Richard III.[25]

By this time, significant developments in the tenurial framework of the lordship had been reflected in the rentals of 1450/1[26] and 1476/7,[27] and these would again be confirmed in the rental compiled in 1491/2[28] – these three documents, in contrast to the 1437 Rental, contained information relating to the entire lordship. One noteworthy feature of the landholding structure in Ceinmeirch in 1451 was the numerous instances of plots of land held on leasehold terms. The first entry for Cerneonyfed recorded the tenure of 38.5 acres by Gruffudd ap Ieuan ap Iorwerth in the second year of a two-year lease for a rent of 15s., with the former tenant named as John ap Ieuan who had previously paid a rent of 19s. 3d.[29] Another substantial plot, amounting to 27 acres in Sgeibion, and previously occupied by Agnes Chaddesley, was held by Ieuan ap Meilyr in the eighth year of a twenty-year lease, for a payment of 3s. 4d: a reduction of 10s. 2d on the previous payment of 13s. 6d.[30] Similar examples may also be cited from the township of Bachymbyd, where Madog ap Meilyr paid a sum of 10s. 1½d in the fourteenth year of a twenty-year lease for a plot of 29.5 acres and 1 rood: the two former occupants were named as Henry Plesyngton – who had rendered a sum of 20s. 3d for this plot – and Edith Spenne. The latter's probable kinsman, William Spenne, was named as the former occupant of three plots amounting to 44.5 acres and 2 perches held in the second year of twenty-year leases by the substantial landholder Iankyn ap Ieuan ap Bleddyn.[31]

The above references to Agnes Chaddesley and Edith Spenne, illustrate the active role played by female landholders in Ceinmeirch. Other examples identified in this rental included Gwenllian the daughter of Ieuan ap Einion who occupied a plot of 5.5 acres in Cerneonyfed;[32] Gwenllian *ferch* ('the daughter of') Einion ap Llywarch, was the tenant of 5.5 acres and 1.5 roods in Sgeibion; Matilda, the daughter of Philip ap Rhys who held three plots of 9 acres, 7 acres and 38 perches, and 2 acres and 1.5 roods; and Efa, the daughter of Dafydd Pannwr, who occupied two plots, one of 3 acres and 1 rood and the other one of 5 acres whose previous occupant was her father, Dafydd Pannwr.[33]

Several of the females identified as landholders in 1451 were again named in 1477 and 1492, and included the forementioned Gwenllian, Matilda and Efa as landholders in Sgeibion.[34] However, a number of significant additional leases were recorded in the 1477 rental, and these included the tenure in Bachymbyd by Mali, the daughter of Madog ap Meilir, of a plot of 7 acres, 1.5 roods and 10 perches, formerly held by Robert Plesyngton, in the fourth year of a twenty-year lease; this was held in addition to her tenure with Edward ap Cynwrig ap Dafydd of a plot of 5.5 acres for a rent of 2s. ¼d.[35] Male members of settler families occupying land on leases in Ceinmeirch in 1477 included Thomas Salusbury junior who held in Sgeibion for the payment of 12d, a plot of 10 acres and 25 perches in the eighth year of a forty-year lease.[36] He also held in Bachymbyd, in the eighth year of forty-year leases, three plots of 7.5 acres; 28.5 acres, 1 rood and 2 perches; and 7.5 acres, 1 rood and 1 *placea*, previously held by William Spenne for payments of 2s. 4d, 5s. 4d and 3s. 4d, respectively.[37]

In 1451 Thomas Salusbury and John Huxley had leased for £10 the mill of Kilford, which had formerly yielded a payment of £15, in the fifth year of a six-year lease. Thomas Sandyway was responsible, in the sixth year of a ten-year lease, for the payment of 53s. 4d for the old mill, which had been burned during the Welsh rebellion and had been newly rebuilt. Thomas was also the lessee of the manor of Ystrad, for a payment of £6 13s. 4d in the eleventh year of a fifteen-year lease.[38] By 1477 Thomas Salusbury senior was the lessee, on payment of a sum of £10, of the manor of Kilford in the seventh year of a twenty-one-year lease. The newly rebuilt old mill was also leased by him for 33s. 4d; and Thomas Salusbury junior leased the water mill in the seventh year of a twenty-one-year lease for 66s. 8d. The manor of Ystrad was leased by Alice Sandyway in the final year of a twenty-year period for £8, while John, the son of Henry Salusbury paid 12d for the newly built fulling mill.[39] The 1492 Rental recorded the nineteenth year of Thomas Salusbury senior's lease of the manor of Kilford, and the eighteenth year of Thomas Salusbury lease of the water mill, while the occupant of the water mill was named as Robert ap Gruffudd. David Myddelton and his wife Elen held the manor of Ystrad in the ninth year of a twenty-year lease, while a sum of 12d was paid by John Mody for the fulling mill.[40]

In the commote of Is Aled, Welsh female tenants named in the 1451 rental included Alys who had been the wife of Wiliam ap Llywelyn and was the occupant in the Acre of Lleweni of two plots: one of 8 acres and 1 rood, which had previously been occupied by John, the son of Simon; and another 1-acre plot for which she paid a rent of 12d. Three other plots amounting to 16 acres, formerly held by Dafydd ap Iorwerth Ddu and Angharad his wife, were currently occupied here by Angharad, the daughter of Dafydd, and Gruffudd ap Ieuan Ddu.[41] The numerous Welsh landholders in Ereifiad included five females: namely, Isabel Lloyd, the leaseholder of 11 acres and 26 perches in the eighth year of a twelve-year lease; Joanna, the daughter of Tudur ap Ithel; Gwenllian, the daughter of Ieuan ap Carewid, Lleucu the daughter of Ieuan Llwyn; and Efa, the daughter of Iorwerth, who together with Ednyfed ap Ithel ap Dafydd was named as the occupant of two plots, of which one was held for a payment of 6s.[42]

Members of the Yankyn ap Bleddyn family, previously noted as landholders in 1437,[43] again featured prominently in the 1451 Rental. Yankyn ap Bleddyn ap Einion was named as the occupier in the Acre of Lleweni of 23 acres in five plots, and his son, Wiliam ap Yankyn ap Bleddyn held another three plots amounting to 13.5 acres and 1 rood, with the largest one, comprising 6.5 acres and 1 rood formerly in the possession of Robert Birchinshaw. In the nearby Park of Lleweni he held a plot of 3.5 acres and 10 perches, and also a plot of 2.5 acres and 1 rood in the first year of a ten-year lease. Tomos, the son of Wiliam ap Yankyn ap Bleddyn, occupied in the Acre of Lleweni 2.5 acres previously held by John Annabel and Agnes, the children of Robert Romworth, in the thirteenth year of a twenty-year lease. Wiliam's brother, Robyn, held here a plot of 1 acre formerly occupied by John Huxley, and Wiliam's daughter Margaret was again named in 1451, as she had been in 1437, as the occupant here of a plot of 1 acre and 1 rood. Also, another probable brother, Wilcok ap Yankyn ap Bleddyn, was the tenant of six very small plots in the Park, together amounting to 7 acres and 11 perches.[44]

Prominent female landholders in the commote of Is Aled who were clearly members of settler families included Isabel, the daughter of Richard Peake who in 1451 held 80 acres in the Acre of Lleweni, and 25.5 acres in the Park of Lleweni.[45] Female members of the Salusbury family, which was rapidly expanding its landed possessions at this time, again featured as landholders in the Acre of Lleweni. Alice and her husband Radulf occupied a plot of 4 acres and 1 rood and one plot formerly held by Adam Hynde. In addition, Agnes, wife of Henry Salusbury,, was described as the tenant of 2 acres previously held by William Curteys and his wife Matilda; and she was also named as the former occupant of plots of 13 acres and 3 acres.[46]

An important figure among the members of settler families who were landholders in Is Aled was Roger Salusbury, who was named in seventy-two entries in the Acre of Lleweni as the occupant of 414.5 acres 1.5 roods and 13.5 perches. Thomas Salusbury junior occupied in the Acre of Lleweni plots of 6 acres in the tenth year, 7 acres in the twenty-fourt year and 22.5 acres and 1 rood in the third year of forty-year leases. He also held the new mill of the Clwyd that had been burned during the rebellion in the seventh year of a 100-year lease.[47] In the Park of Lleweni Thomas Salusbury senior held a substantial plot of 46 acres for a rent of 11s. in the sixteenth year of a forty-year lease. He also held another plot of 6 acres with Henry Salusbury for which they paid 6s., and the latter also rendered a sum of 4s. 8d for a plot described as 'terre [the land of] Iorwerth ap Llywarch', and 9d for a plot of 3 roods. Another two properties held formerly by Henry Salusbury and amounting to 20 acres and 10 acres were held by

John Salusbury and his son John for payments respectively of 4s. and 2s. 8d. Roger Salusbury was named here as the sole occupant of eleven plots amounting to 60 acres, 1.5 roods and 9 perches, and he also held with Margaret the daughter of John Russhes, a plot of 5 acres.[48]

Three members of the Salusbury family also held property in nearby townships. Roger Salusbury held one substantial parcel of escheated land, together with eight very small plots of land in the 'New borough' of Lleweni, and also a substantial property amounting to 80 acres in Ystrad Cynon, where Thomas Salusbury occupied a plot of 12 acres that had formerly been held by Thomas Heton and his wife Marjorie.[49] Thomas also occupied a plot of 10 acres in Gwenynog Wyntus, and Alex Salusbury held a plot of 10.5 acres in Alltfaenan that had formerly been occupied by Dafydd ap Ieuan ap Ithel.[50]

Whereas the lands held by members of the Salusbury family were located in several townships, those occupied by Henry Wynnaway were to a large extent concentrated in onelocation; namely, the Park of Lleweni where he was a dominant figure. He leased here eight plots, amounting to 46 acres and 1 rood, and they were all occupied on forty-year leases with 1451 being the fourteenth year.[51] Henry Wynnaway also held in Ystrad Cynon two small plots each of 1 acre for a payment of 8d, which had previously been occupied by Alex Swynemore and Reginald Swynemore.[52]

The 1477 Rental recorded that a significant figure among Welsh landholders in the commote of Is Aled was Ieuan ap Llywelyn Fychan. He leased thirteen plots amounting to 143 acres, 1 rood and 7 perches in the Acre of Lleweni in the tenth year of a forty year-lease, with the largest one of 38.5 acres and 1 rood, together with another three amounting to 20 acres previously held by Thomas Llannerch. He also leased a plot of 21 acres formerly held by Elen Holand in the fifteenth year of another forty-year agreement.[53] Another major landholder was Dafydd Myddelton, whose property in Gwenynog Cynon was listed in nine entries.

Eight of these recorded plots comprised 48.5 acres and 1.5 roods, with the largest one, amounting to 21.5 acres and 1.5 roods formerly held by John Paget, was held in the twenty-third year of a thirty-year lease for a payment of 3s. Another plot, measuring 14 acres, 1.5 roods and 15 perches, formerly occupied by Henry Fletcher, was held for a payment of 4s. 2d in the fourth year of a twelve-year lease. A final compound entry comprised five entries, listing Myddelton's occupation of another 50.5 acres, with one recording his occupation of a plot of 26.5 acres formerly held by Thomas Pigot, and another one to a plot of 9 acres in the Park of Segrwyd previously occupied by Thomas Pigot.[54]

Welsh persons predominated among the tenants in the three commotes of Uwch Aled, Is Dulas and Uwch Dulas. The eighteen entries recorded for the township of Chwibren, in Uwch Aled in 1451, included those identifying Llywelyn Fychan ap Ieuan ap Llywelyn as the occupant, for a total payment of 16s. 6d, of a plot of 13 acres, two plots of 1 acre each, certain specified rights and a water mill in the eighth year of a twenty-year lease.[55] In Arllwyd members of the Pigot family were major landholders. Six entries recorded Gronw Pigot's tenure of 23 acres and he was also named as the occupant, in the second year of a five-year lease, of land for which a payment of 8s. 4d was rendered.[56] This family continued to feature prominently in this commote in 1477 with Gronw Pigot the tenant in Arllwyd of two plots which amounted to 10.5 acres and 1 rood, and Richard, the son of John Pigot, named as the occupant of a plot of 8 acres and the previous tenant of a plot of 34.5 acres and 1.5 roods held by Einion ap Yankyn ap Dafydd.[57]

In the commote of Is Dulas the eighty-four plots in the township of Wigfair were all occupied in 1451 by Welsh tenants. The largest plot, amounting to 26.5 acres, was held by Goronwy Ddu ap Ithel, with the former tenant, probably his father, named as Ithel ap Iorwerth Ddu. Five plots in the township of Dinorben Fawr, amounting to 39 acres and a half share of a *gwely* were occupied by Thomas Lawrence for a rent of £1 1s. 8d, and the Welsh tenants included Gruffudd ap Dafydd Holand who held lands here in the ninth year of a twenty-year lease for a payment of 13s. 4d. The previous occupants of this plot were named as Ieuan ap Dafydd Holand and Ralph Holand and the latter also held the manor of Dinorben Fawr in the fourth year of a five-year lease for a payment of £8.[58]

The 1477 Rental named Henry Salusbury as the tenant of the manor of Dinorben Fawr in the eighth year of a forty-year lease, and also Gruffudd ap Dafydd Holand's continued tenure in this township of escheat lands, for a rental of 13s. 4d, in the twenty-second year of a forty-year lease.[59] Another significant feature of this rental was the inclusion of references, in the *Acre Anglie et Wallie* of Abergele, to Elizabeth Holland as the previous occupant of four plots of land amounting to 31 acres. These entries recorded that the present occupant was Goronwy ap Llywelyn ap Cynwrig, who also rendered a sum of 15s. 4d for various parcels of land previously held here by Elizabeth Holland. Despite the absence of Elizabeth Holland, a number of females were again named as landholders in this commote. They included, in Wigfair, Katerina who held a plot of 2 acres and, with Yankyn ap Moris Glyn, further plots of 1 acre and 3 acres; Lleucu, the daughter of Llywelyn ap Gruffudd Chwith, the occupant of 7 acres and 1 rood, Angharad, the daughter of Gruffudd ap Tudur ap Ithel, the tenant of 3 acres, and Gwenllian, the daughter of Einion, the joint occupant of a plot of 3.5 acres and 1 rood.[60]

Entries for the commote of Uwch Dulas in 1451 had again drawn attention to the prominence of Elizabeth Holland as a significant landholder. She held five plots of land in the township of Tŷ-brith amounting to a total of 53 acres and 10 perches for a payment of £2 9s. 9½d. All the other individuals named in the entry for this township had Welsh names and this was also largely true of the other townships in this commote. However, a significant exception was the occupation, for a payment of 15d, by Agnes, the wife of Henry Salusbury, of a plot of 3 acres and 1 rood in the township of 'Meiniog and Cefn'.[61] References to mills in this commote included those recording the payment of 20s.

by Goronwy Gethin for the water mill of Cilcennis, and also the render of 4s. by the abbot of Aberconwy for the mill of Llanfair.[62] Elizabeth Holland was again named in 1477 as the previous occupant of land in Tŷ-brith, in the commote of Uwch Dulas but the extent of her estate had by now increased to 73 acres and 10 perches. With regard to the other tenants in this township, Welsh male individuals clearly formed the vast majority of the landholders in this commote, but a significant exception was the occupation by Thomas Salusbury of plots of 7.5 acres in Tŷ-brith, and also 4 acres and 1 rood in Maencoch and Cefncastell, in the fifth year of two forty-year leases.[63] Several payments were recorded relating to mills. The abbot of Aberconwy was again responsible for the mill of Llanfair, and Gronw Gethin for the water mill of Cicennis; both of them for identical payments to those recorded in 1451.[64] In Erethlyn Ieuan ap Einion Tew paid in 1477 a sum of 23s. 4d as his contribution for two parts of the render for the mill.[65] Also, payments of 10s. were rendered by Hywel ap Conus ap Dafydd ap Gronw and Ieuan ap Llywelyn ap Ieuan Llwyd in the seventh year of a ten-year lease for the water mill of Tallwyn, and 23s. 4d by Hugh Conway in the seventh year of a twenty-one-year lease for the water mill of Rhiw.[66]

Notes

1. Glanmor Williams, *Recovery, Reorientation and Reformation: Wales c.1415–1642* (Cardiff, 1987), p. 178.
2. Ralph A Griffiths, 'Richard, Duke of York and the Royal Household in Wales, 1449–1550', *WHR*, 8/1 (June 1976), 14; J. T. Rosenthal, 'The Estates and Finances of Richard, Duke of York (1411–1460)', in W. M. Bowsky (ed.), *Studies in Medieval and Renaissance History*, vol. 2 (Lincoln NE, 1965), p. 198.
3. Williams, *Recovery, Reorientation and Reformation Wales*, pp. 180–1.
4. Ralph A. Griffiths, *The Reign of King Henry VI* (London, 1981), p. 821; Williams, *Recovery, Reorientation and Reformation Wales*, pp. 186–7.
5. Williams, *Recovery, Reorientation and Reformation Wales*, p. 187; H. T. Evans, *Wales and the Wars of the Roses* (Stroud, 1998 [1915]), p. 67; *CPR 1452–61*, p. 550.
6. Evans, *Wars of the Roses*, p. 67; Thomas Rymer, *Foedera, conventiones, litterae, et euiuscunque generis acta publica*, vol. 11 (London, 1816–69), p. 445.

7   Evans, *Wars of the Roses*, p. 67; Rymer, *Foedera, Conventiones, Litterae*, vol. 11, pp. 444–6; *CPR 1452–61*, pp. 574, 578.
8   Evans, *Wars of the Roses*, p. 72.
9   Evans, *Wars of the Roses*, p. 73; Williams, *Recovery, Reorientation and Reformation Wales*, pp. 187–8.
10 Evans, *Wars of the Roses*, p. 74; Williams, *Recovery, Reorientation and Reformation Wales*, p. 188.
11 Evans, *Wars of the Roses*, pp. 74–80.
12 Evans, *Wars of the Roses*, p. 84; Williams, *Ancient and Modern Denbigh*, pp. 86–7.
13 Evans, *Wars of the Roses*, p. 84; Williams, *Ancient and Modern Denbigh*, p. 87.
14 Evans, *Wars of the Roses*, pp. 80, 86.
15 Evans, *Wars of the Roses*, p. 86; Ralph A. Griffiths and Roger S. Thomas, *The Making of the Tudor Dynasty* (Stroud, 1985), p. 60, for reference to Denbigh as York's 'main channel of communication between England and Ireland'; Williams, *Recovery, Reorientation and Reformation Wales*, p. 192.
16 D. Huw Owen and J. Beverley Smith, 'Government and Society 1283–1536', in J. Beverley Smith and Llinos Beverley Smith (eds), *History of Merioneth, volume 2: The Middle Ages* (Cardiff, 2001), p. 122.
17 Williams, *Recovery, Reorientation and Reformation Wales*, p. 200; J. Gairdner (ed.), *Paston Letters*, vol. 2 (London, 1872), pp. 151–2.
18 Evans, *Wars of the Roses*, p. 99.
19 William Gregory, *Historical Collections of a London Citizen, 1189–1469*, Camden Society, New Series, no. 18, ed. by J. Gairdner (London, 1876), p. 237; C. D. Ross, *Edward IV* (London, 1997), 113n, 114n; Michael Hicks, *The Wars of the Roses* (New Haven CT, 2012), p. 179.
20 Evans, *Wars of the Roses*, p. 100; Williams, *Recovery, Reorientation and Reformation Wales*, p. 201.
21 Wynn, *History of the Gwydir Family*, p. 33.
22 Sara Elin Roberts, *Jasper, The Tudor Kingmaker* (Fonthill, 2015), pp. 68–9, 71–3.
23 J. Y. W. Lloyd, *History of Powys Fadog*, vol. 5 (London, 1885), p. 406; Enid Roberts, 'Teulu Plas Iolyn', *TDHS*, 13 (1964), 41.
24 *Supra*. p. 42.
25 Glanmor Williams, *Harri Tudur a Chymru/Henry Tudor and Wales* (Cardiff, 1985), pp. 58–9.
26 NLW MS 12647 F.
27 NLW MS 163 B.
28 TNA SC 12/27/24.
29 NLW MS 12647 F, f. 4 r.
30 NLW MS 12647 F, f. 6 r.
31 NLW MS 12647 F, f. 7 v.
32 NLW MS 12647 F, f. 4 r.
33 NLW MS 12647 F, ff. 7 r and v.
34 NLW MS 163 B, ff. 6 r and v; TNA, SC 12/27/24, ff. 4 v, 5 r.
35 NLW MS 163 B, ff. 8 v, 9 r and v.
36 NLW MS 163 B, f. 6 r.

37 NLW MS 163 B, f. 9 r.
38 NLW MS 163 B, ff. 9 r and v.
39 NLW MS 163 B, ff. 10 r and v.
40 TNA SC 12/27/24, 9 r and v.
41 NLW MS 12647 F, ff. 12 r, 13 r and v.
42 NLW MS 12647 F, 20 r and v.
43 *Supra.* pp. 146, 150.
44 NLW MS 12647 F, ff. 12 v, 13 v, 14 r and v, 15 r.
45 NLW MS 12647 F, ff.11 v.
46 NLW MS 12647 F, ff.12 v, 13 r.
47 NLW MS 12647 F, 13 v.
48 NLW MS 12647 F, 15 r and v.
49 NLW MS 12647 F, f. 16 r.
50 NLW MS 12647 F, 21 v, 22 r.
51 NLW MS 12647 F, 15 r and v.
52 NLW MS 12647 F, f. 16 r.
53 NLW MS 163 B, ff. 15 r and v, 16 r and v, 17 r and v, 18 r and v.
54 NLW MS 12647 F, ff. 22 r and v.
55 NLW MS 12647 F, f. 26 r.
56 NLW MS 12647 F, ff. 28 r and v.
57 NLW MS 163 B, ff. 45 v, 46 r.
58 NLW MS 12647 F, f. 31 r.
59 NLW MS 163 B, ff. 45 v, 46 r.
60 NLW MS 163 B, ff. 50 r and v, 51 r.
61 NLW MS 12647 F, f. 38 v.
62 NLW MS 12647 F.
63 NLW MS 163 B, ff. 50 r and v.
64 NLW MS 163 B, f. 51 r.
65 NLW MS 163 B, f. 52 v.
66 NLW MS 163 B, f. 53 r.

14

POLITICAL CONTROL AND LAND TENURE, 1485–1543

The widespread expectation in Wales that the successful campaign of Henry Tudor and his accession to the English throne would lead to the granting of many privileges for his fellow countrymen did not materialise, and Henry's actions were severely restricted. However, significant measures were taken with a series of charters of privileges granted in return for substantial sums of money to various communities, including the one to the lordship of Denbigh in 1506, in response to a payment of 1,000 marks. The privileges granted by these charters included the right to buy and occupy land, hold office in England and in the boroughs of Wales; inherit land according to English law by the custom of inheritance by the eldest son; and be freed from heavy financial payments initially imposed in the Middle Ages.[1]

Rhys ap Maredudd had been rewarded for his support of Henry Tudor by being granted extensive lands by Henry VII, and some of his possessions are listed in the Cernioge collection of estate papers, held at the National Library of Wales.[2] Rhys had married Lowri, the daughter and heiress of Hywel ap Gruffudd Goch, described as *arglwydd Rhos a Rhufoniog* ('lord of Rhos and Rhufoniog'), and effigies of the two, together with their son Robert, may be seen on their grave at the Ysbyty Ifan Church.[3] The lands of Rhys's brother, Rhobert, were inherited by their sister Lowri, who married John Salusbury, Bachymbyd, and this may well explain the later enmity between Sir Robert ap Rhys and members of the Salusbury, family.[4]

Rhys and Lowri had eleven children, and their second son, Morys Gethin, was granted, on 27 February 1501/2, a ninety-nine-year lease by Dafydd, the abbot of Aberconwy, conveying a plot of land for the construction of four houses and a fulling mill on the river Foelas. That same year, he was appointed steward for life of the lands of Hiraethog. He acquired, on 30 November 1506, lands and tenements in Hafod-y-maidd, in the township of Prys and in this deed he was described as or otherwise called 'Morys Gethyn, Cernioge'. He was granted by his father, Rhys ap Maredudd ap Tudur, a plot of land in this township on 10 July 1510; and on the same date, Rhys ap Maredudd ensured that his son would be granted possession of lands and property in the townships of Prys, in the commote of Is Aled, and Dinerth and Llwydcoed, in the commote of Uwch Dulas. A series of transactions were then recorded in the period 1513-46 which named Morys's sons, Ieuan Llwyd, Robert and Cadwaladr, and his grandsons Dafydd Llwyd and Robert Wyn.[5]

Sir Robert ap Rhys, the third son of Rhys Fawr and Lowri, held the offices of Chancellor and Vicar-General of the St Asaph diocese, as well as that of chaplain and cross-bearer to Cardinal Wolsey, for whom he served as his deputy in the dioceses of Bangor and St Asaph. In August 1506, he was granted by Dafydd Owain, abbot of Aberconwy, a ninety-nine-year lease on a tenement named Llyn y Cymer, in the commote of Is Aled. He had leased lands belonging to the Aberconwy, Basingwerk and Strata Marcella abbeys, together with property valued at £40 on lands at Dôl Gynwal belonging to the Hospitallers of St John. He was also the prebendary of Llanefydd, an office which was valued at £44 per annum.[6] He had evidently succeeded in accumulating immense wealth, and this was clearly reflected in the new house that he built at Plas Iolyn, where he maintained a court in some style and splendour. Poets were welcomed here, and the table and cellar were described as 'so delectably stocked as almost to sate that most knowledgeable of poetic gourmets, Tudur Aled'.[7]

Sir Robert and his son Dr Elis Prys '*Y Doctor Coch*' ('the Red Doctor'), played a prominent role in the dissolution of the monasteries, and were generous bardic patrons at their mansion, Plas Iolyn: Dr Prys's son Tomos Prys, the buccaneer, was also a gifted poet.[8] Both Sir Robert and Dr Elis Prys competed fiercely with the Salusbury family for land and power and the achievements and lineages of both families were highly praised by contemporary poets.[9] Sir Robert was involved in several disputes with members of the Salusbury family who brought unsuccessful legal actions against him in the Star Chamber, Court of the Marches and Chancery.[10]

While he could be shielded by Cardinal Wolsey, Sir Robert was fairly secure but following Wolsey's downfall in 1530, Sir John Salusbury, chamberlain of north Wales and steward of the lordship of Denbigh saw his opportunity. In his letter to Thomas Cromwell, dated 21 January 1533, Salusbury, declared that he was proceeding with his accusations against Henry Standish, the bishop of St Asaph and Sir Robert ap Rhys with the latter accused of extortion. In October, Sir Robert, summoned to appear at the Court of the Great Leet in the lordship of Denbigh, before Sir John Salusbury, steward of the lordship, was accused of maintaining 200 followers for six years, and being in possession of eighteen rectories and ecclesiastical lands worth 100 marks per annum. Sir John witnessed that the residents of the lordship were being oppressed by corruption up to 4,000 or 5,000 marks per annum, and this was declared to be the greatest extortion in Wales for 500 years. His complaints drew attention to Sir Robert's wealth, with his wild cattle, sheep and one 'deyres' ('deer') valued at more than 1,000 marks, and his ready money and silver dishes worth more than £2,000. In addition to his extensive lands, he also seems to have been in possession of a considerable amount of money, with substantial sums left to his sons and daughter and bequests also to the friary in Denbigh and to ten parish churches.[11]

Another prominent Welsh family was that of Dafydd ap Maredudd ap Dafydd Llwyd, which acquired a considerable estate in the period 1502/3–16, comprising lands largely located in the township of Llangernyw on land belonging to the Bishop of St Asaph, but also in the episcopal township of Branan and the secular townships of Barrog in Uwch Aled and Garthewin in Is Dulas, in the lordship of Denbigh.[12] This policy was continued by his son Ieuan Llwyd ap Dafydd ap Maredudd, who was named in a series of transactions, dating from 29 July 1524 until 14 March 1557/8, as the acquirer of plots of land, again predominantly in Llangernyw, but also in the townships of Erethlyn, Gwytherin, Llanfair and Maes-y-gwig in the commote of Is Dulas, as well as in Fodrach, 'Marchaled' and Hafod-un-nos in lands held by the Bishop of St Asaph.[13]

A number of settler families also became closely involved with local Welsh traditions during the course of the later Middle Ages. The dominant settler family in the late fifteenth century and early sixteenth century was undoubtedly the Salusbury family, which had greatly benefitted from propitious marriage alliances and whose members, holding several important offices, dominated the local administration. Thomas Salusbury (Hen), killed at the battle of Barnet (1471), was succeeded by Sir Thomas, the eldest son and heir, who inherited Lleweni, and who was married to Jonet, daughter of William Fychan ap Gwilym of the Marchudd clan; Robert to Gwenhwyfar, daughter and co-heiress of Rhys ab Einion Fychan, of Plas Isa, Llanrwst, who was reputedly worth 1,000 marks per annum and was also of the Marchudd clan; and John to Lowri, daughter and heiress of Robert ap Maredudd, the elder brother of Rhys Fawr, and of the Marchweithian clan, who seem to have settled at Bachymbyd.[14]

Sir Thomas Salusbury, who died in 1505, had been knighted by Henry VII following his exploits at the battle of Blackheath, fought in 1497. He was succeeded by his son Sir Roger Salusbury, who died in 1530, and his eldest surviving son, John Salusbury, was created a Knight of the Carpet by Edward VI at his coronation. He served as sheriff of Denbighshire in 1542 and in 1575, chamberlain of north Wales, and member of parliament for his county 1547–52, and again in the period 1553–55. His uncle, again named John Salusbury, the fourth son of the forenamed Thomas Salusbury and also known by the name 'Siôn y Bodiau' ('John of the Thumbs'), probably because of a physical infirmity, became a dominant figure in the local administration, serving as steward of the lordship of Denbigh, constable of Denbigh castle, first chamberlain of the newly formed shire of Denbigh, member of parliament in 1539, and sheriff in 1541.[15]

Another influential settler family in 1334 was the Pigot family, which occupied lands in the neighbourhood of Denbigh, and also in Archwedlog, the township in Uwch Aled where there was a considerable English settlement. Attention has also been drawn to the sixteenth-century statement that 'Wilcok Pigod', the son of Syr Robyn Pigot, was an architect reputed to have been involved in the Earl of Lincoln's reconstruction of Denbigh castle – *pennsaer Iarll Lincol*.[16] Another source from this period listed a line of descendants bearing the Welsh names of Hywel, Siancyn, Deio, Gwenllian, Tegwedd, Tudur, followed by Sion Tudur, the poet who was a Yeoman of the Guard and Yeoman of the Crown. He was described as the descendant of the tribal founder Llywarch Howlbwrch, and his great-grandmother was named as Gwenllian, the daughter of 'Deio ap Siangkyn pigod'.[17]

Wilcok Pigot's sister Ermin was married to Henry Rossindale the younger who, as his name suggests, was a member of a family that originally came to Denbigh from Lancashire, and settled at Foxhall, in Henllan, near the town of Denbigh. Their descendants adopted the name 'Lloyd', and William Lloyd, as previously noted, acted as an intermediary in the negotiations in 1403 between Owain Glyn Dŵr and Henry Percy. His kinsmen occasionally reverted to the original name, but a notable member of the family in the sixteenth century was Humphrey Llwyd, the cartographer who was born at Denbigh in 1527, and who, representing the borough in parliament in 1563, was largely responsible for the legislation that resulted in the translation of the Bible into the Welsh language.[18]

Another descendant of a settler family who was a staunch supporter of the Welsh language in the reign of Elizabeth was the poet Wiliam Byrcinsha whose forefathers Adam, Richard and Thomas Birchinshaw had occupied 83 acres in 1334.[19] A family connection linked the Birchinshaw and Pigot families in that Catrin, the daughter of Tomos ap Harri Birchinshaw had married Richard ap Jenkin Pigot, described as a squire to the duke of York who had been slain at Llansannan in the dynastic wars of the fifteenth century.[20]

Tudur Aled sang in praise of several members of the Salusbury family, and in his *cywydd* to Sir Roger Salusbury referred to his association with the Marchudd clan and with Brynffanugl.[21] Tudur Aled was especially closely associated with the Plas Iolyn family, and drew attention to Robert ap Rhys's descent from Braint Hir and Marchweithian.[22] Tudur Aled had also composed an elegy to Robert's father, Rhys ap Maredudd, whose wife Lowri, the subject of a poem by Tudur Penllyn, was the daughter and heiress of Hywel ap Gruffudd Goch, described as lord of Rhos and Rhufoniog.[23] Lewis Môn was another poet who sang in praise of Robert ap Rhys, referring to the Braint Hir and Marchudd clans in addition to that of Marchweithian as forming his family's pedigree.[24] Marchweithian and Marchudd were also named by Wiliam Llŷn and Gruffudd Hiraethog in their poems in praise of Robert's son Dr Elis Prys.[25]

Contemporary poetry also provided descriptions of heraldic devices that were highly valued by local inhabitants. The arms of Marchweithian have been defined as 'Gules, a lion rampant, Argent', and in his poem in praise of Tudur ap Robert of Berain, Gruffudd Hiraethog described a white lion on a field of Gules, the coat of Marchweithian, representing Tudur's paternal line, and the gryphon of Gruffudd Goch, of Rhos, from whom Tudur's grandmother was descended: 'gwyn llew ar gan llawes a llawr o goch ... griffwnt yn Rhos' ('white lion on many a sleeve on a field of red ... the gryphon of Rhos').[26] A further description was provided in Gruffudd's elegy to Ifan ap Rhys ap Dafydd of

Llanefydd in 1553, with the arms, which should appear on Ifan's grave, including the forementioned Marchweithian arms.[27]

Many of the renowned literary figures associated with this area were themselves descended from the leading 'tribal' groupings. The survey of Denbigh recorded that Iolo Goch's father, Ithel Goch, had been granted lands in Llechryd in exchange for the one-sixth of a *gafael* ('land held by a lineage group') that he had previously held in Lleweni.[28] He was descended from Hedd Molwynog, as also was Tudur Aled, the descendant of Llywelyn Chwith and Bleddyn Fychan. Through marriage there was also an association with the Marchudd ap Cynan clan in which Generys Fychan, the great-granddaughter of Ednyfed Fychan, was married to Llywelyn, the brother of Llywelyn Chwith's father.[29] Sion Tudur had family links with both the Hedd Molwynog and Marchweithian family groupings; the former through his descent from Gwenllian, the wife of Hywel Pigod, and the latter through Tegwedd the wife of Dafydd Llwyd ab Ednyfed.[30]

Wiliam Midleton, the poet and privateer, claimed descent from Rhirid Flaidd, another 'tribal' founder. His forefather Ririd ap Dafydd had married the heiress of Alexander Middleton, of Middleton, near Chirbury in Shropshire in the fourteenth century, and another forefather, David Middleton, had moved to the vale of Clwyd in the mid-fifteenth century and settled in Gwaenynog.[31] William Salesbury, the translator into Welsh of the New Testament, was the grandson of Robert and Gwenhwyfar Salesbury, and his wife was Catrin Llwyd, the daughter of Sir Robert ap Rhys of Plas Iolyn and a member of the Marchweithian clan.[32] There was a family connection between William Salesbury and Edmwnd Prys, the poet, humanist and metrical psalm translator. Born in Llanrwst, he was descended from Ednyfed Fychan and the Marchudd ap Cynan 'clan', as also, through his mother, was Bishop William Morgan, the translator of the Bible, who, through his father, claimed descent from Hedd Molwynog and yet another 'tribal' founder, Nefydd Hardd.[33]

The increasing interest in Welsh literary activities reflected the growing awareness of a Welsh national identity. Significant measures adopted by parliament aimed at an enhanced law enforcement and strengthening the authority of Rowland Lee, bishop of Coventry and Lichfield. Following his appointment in 1534 as president of the Council in the Marches, he adopted with immense enthusiasm in the following eight years his responsibility for enforcing law and order.[34] In this period, a modified policy had also been adopted with an act passed in 1536 that ensured the appointment of justices of peace in the six existing shires and also in Glamorgan and Pembroke.[35]

Figure 6: Part of map, Humphrey Llwyd, *Cambriae Typus* (1573)

Shortly afterwards, another act established shires in Wales, with the territory forming the lordship of Denbigh henceforth becoming part of the new shire of Denbigh. Its constitution was finalised by further legislation in 1543, with the two latter acts forming the Act of Union, 1536–43. This act established Denbigh as the shire-town of the new county of Denbigh, with its own parliamentary representative, and as the administrative focus of an even more extensive area as a chancery and exchequer were established at Denbigh to serve the shires of Denbigh, Flint and Montgomery. The Act of Union has been widely considered to have removed the surviving elements of Welsh law and marcher autonomy in Wales and to have imposed 'English' legal uniformity throughout Wales'.[36] It is also considered to have created within Wales 'unity of jurisdiction and administration for the first time'.[37] The establishment in 1543 of four circuits of courts of Great Sessions grouped Denbighshire, Flintshire and Montgomeryshire as part of the 'Chester circuit', which was closely associated with the administration of Cheshire in that the three Welsh shires 'Great Sessions' were presided over by the Chester chief justices.[38]

An immediate response to the Union legislation was illustrated at the market cross of Denbigh in May 1537, where it was recorded that a large number of the inhabitants of nearby rural areas had assembled with their leader proclaiming that 'Welshmen were as free as Englishmen and they shulde paye no stallage there'. Sir John Salusbury of Lleweni, a very prominent local figure, who had been ordered to ensure that the peace be maintained on that day, but yet had declared his opposition to the decision that local residents be forbidden from bearing arms This demonstration was clearly a direct response to the Union legislation of the previous year, with local persons evidently aware that they should henceforth enjoy the same legal rights 'as other the kynges subiectes'.[39]

Notes

1   TNA SC 6/Hen VIII, 5623; Smith, 'Crown and Community', 170; Williams, *Henry Tudor and Wales*, pp. 86–9.
2   NLW, A Schedule of Cernioge Deeds and Documents (1962).
3   Roberts, 'Teulu Plas Iolyn', 43; Williams, *The Welsh Church from Conquest to Reformation*, p. 321.
4   Roberts, 'Teulu Plas Iolyn', 43–4.

5   *Cernioge Deeds*, 1–3, 7–9; nos 48–9, 51–3, 55, 57, 179, 69.
6   *Cernioge Deeds*, 1–175; Roberts, 'Teulu Plas Iolyn', 55–7.
7   Roberts, 'Teulu Plas Iolyn', 60–1; Williams, *The Welsh Church from Conquest to Reformation*, p. 323.
8   *DWB, Welsh Biography Online*: Robert ap Rhys, Dr Elis Prys, Tomos Prys.
9   Roberts, 'Teulu Plas Iolyn', 55–8.
10 Williams, *The Welsh Church from Conquest to Reformation*, p. 311; Roberts, 'Teulu Plas Iolyn', p. 58.
11 *WG, 1400–1500*, IX, O-Sandde, 1569, 1570, 1573, 1577; Roberts, 'Teulu Plas Iolyn', 43–4, 57–62.
12 NLW Wigfair Deeds and Documents, nos 25–293, pp. 22–36.
13 NLW Wigfair Deeds and Documents, nos 315 *et seq*, pp. 46–108.
14 Lewis Dwnn, *Heraldic Visitations of Wales and Part of the Marches*, vol. 2, ed. by S. R. Meyrick (Llandovery, 1846), p. 331; Lloyd, *History of Powys Fadog*, vol. 4, p. 443, vol. 5, p. 406; *DWB*, p. 899; *WG, 1400–1500*, IX, O-Sandde, 1569, 1570, 1573, 1577; Llinos Beverley Smith, 'The Welsh Language before 1536', in Geraint H. Jenkins (ed.), *The Welsh Language before the Industrial Revolution* (Cardiff, 1997), p. 25, for a comment on significance of the manuscript *Cardiff MS 51* that recorded Rhys ab Einion's property transactions in the Welsh language.
15 *DWB*, pp. 899–900; *WG, 1400–1500*, IX, 1570, 1571.
16 *SD*, pp. 21, 29, 38, 42, 56, 90, 204.
17 Enid Pierce Roberts, 'Siôn Tudur', *Llên Cymru*, 2 (1952–3), 3–4; Enid Roberts, *Gwaith Siôn Tudur*, vol. 2 (Bangor, 1978), pp. xii–xiii, xv, 387; see n. 36 above for references in *WG, 1400–1500*, vol. 8; also *WG*, vol. 9, 1447.
18 Roberts, *Gwaith Siôn Tudur*, p. 387; Dwnn, *Heraldic Visitations of Wales*, vol. 2, p. 332; *supra*, p. 207. R. Geraint Gruffydd, 'Humphrey Llwyd of Denbigh: Some Documents and a Catalogue', *TDHS*, 17 (1968), 54; Geraint H. Jenkins, Richard Suggett and Eryn M. White, 'The Welsh Language in Early Modern Wales', in *Welsh Language before the Industrial Revolution*, pp. 56, 82–3, 100; Geraint Evans, 'Tudor London and the Origins of Welsh Writing in English', in Geraint Evans and Helen Fulton (eds), *The Cambridge History of Welsh Literature* (Cambridge, 2019), pp. 219–220; Jane Aaron and Sarah Prescott, *The Oxford Literary History of Wales, volume 3: Welsh Writing in English, 1536–1914* (Oxford, 2020), pp. 10–14.
19 Cledwyn Fychan, 'Wiliam Byrcinsha', *TDHS*, 26 (1977), 77–83.
20 *WG, 1400–1500*, IX, O-Sawdde, 1450, 1565.
21 T. Gwyn Jones (ed.), *Gwaith Tudur Aled* (Cardiff, 1926), pp. 98–9, lines 22 and 24 for references to Marchudd and Bryn Ffannugl, pp. 572–3.
22 Jones (ed.), *Gwaith Tudur Aled*, p. 201, line 9 for reference to Braint Hir; and p. 205, line 8 to Marchweithian; 585, 593–5.
23 Jones (ed.), *Gwaith Tudur Aled*, pp. 231–3, 599; Thomas Roberts (ed.), *Gwaith Tudur Penllyn ac Ieuan ap Tudur Penllyn* (Cardiff, 1958), pp. 22–3; J. E. Griffith, *Pedigrees of Anglesey and Caernarvonshire Families* (Horncastle, 1914), p. 326.
24 Eurys Rowlands (ed.), *Gwaith Lewis Môn* (Cardiff, 1975), pp. 179, 13–16.
25 J. C. Morrice (ed.), *Barddoniaeth Wiliam Llŷn* (Bangor, 1908), pp. 11, 13–14; D. J. Bowen (ed.), *Gwaith Gruffudd Hiraethog* (Cardiff, 1990), pp. 11, 35–6.

26 Michael P. Siddons, *The Development of Welsh Heraldry* (Aberystwyth, 1991), p. 147; Bowen, *Gwaith Gruffudd Hiraethog*, 5.
27 Siddons, The *Development Welsh Heraldry*; Bowen, *Gwaith Gruffudd Hiraethog*, p. 244.
28 *SD*, p. 118.
29 Cledwyn Fychan, 'Tudur Aled: ailystyried ei gynefin', *NLWJnl*, 33 (1983–4), 50–70.
30 Roberts, *Gwaith Siôn Tudur*, pp. xii–xiii, p. 387; see above.
31 Enid Pierce Roberts, 'Cywyddau Marwnad Rhisiart Miltwn', in J. E. C. Williams (ed.), *Ysgrifau Beirniadol*, vol. 2 (Denbigh, 1966), pp. 247–8; Gruffydd Aled Williams, 'Wiliam Midleton, bonheddwr, anturiwr a bardd', *TDHS*, 24 (1975), 75–7.
32 W. A. Mathias, 'William Salesbury, ei fywyd a'i waith', in Geraint Bowen, *Y Traddodiad Rhyddiaith, Darlithiau Rhydychen* (Llandysul, 1970), p. 27.
33 Gruffydd Aled Williams, 'Edmwnd Prys, un arall o enwogion Llanrwst', *TDHS*, 23 (1974), 294–8; Gruffydd Aled Williams, *Ymryson Edmwnd Prys a Wiliam Cynwal* (Cardiff, 1986), pp. xci–xciii; R. Geraint Gruffydd, 'William Morgan', in Bowen, *Y Traddodiad Rhyddiaith*, p. 161; Yorke, *Royal Tribes of Wales*, pp. 188–9.
34 Williams, *Recovery, Reorientation and Reformation Wales*, pp. 259–63; J. Gwynfor Jones, *Early Modern Wales, c.1525–1640* (Basingstoke 1994), pp. 58–65, 96–8.
35 Jones, *Early Modern Wales*, pp. 77–8, 99–100.
36 Bowen, *Statutes of Wales*, pp. 67–9, 75–93, 101–33; William Rees, *The Union of England and Wales* (Cardiff, 1947); Figure 6, Part of Humphrey Llwyd's map, *Cambriae Typus* (1573).
37 Williams, *Renewal and Reformation*, p. 273.
38 G. Milwyn Griffiths, 'Glimpses of Denbighshire in the Records of the Court of Great Sessions', *TDHS*, 22 (1973); Glyn Parry, *A Guide to Records of the Great Session in Wales* (Aberystwyth, 1995), pp. iv–vi; Sharon Howard, *Law and Disorder in Early Modern Wales* (Cardiff, 2008), pp. 30–1.
39 TNA SP 1/120/50; P. R. Roberts, 'The "Act of Union" in Welsh History, *THSC*, (1974), 63; Jones, *Early Modern Wales*, p. 96.

15

BOROUGHS, 1334–1543

The pattern of urban development revealed by the 1334 Survey was maintained throughout the later Middle Ages, with the close relationship between the borough and castle providing both a stimulus and obstacle to the development of the urban community at Denbigh. The Survey had recorded that the burgesses were holding the borough from the lord at a fee farm of £24 – '*Feodi Firme burgi*'. This reference provided information on the administrative machinery of the borough; a subject that had not featured in the foundation charters.[1] The grant of a fee farm of the borough's revenues to the burgesses for a fixed sum, ensuring their annual farming out, over a period of years, was a coveted privilege, and implies that, even if the right had previously been denied to them, the burgesses were now allowed to choose their own bailiff.[2] Accounts compiled throughout the period under review by the two bailiffs elected annually reveal that they were responsible for the collection of fines and other sources of borough revenue, and also their submission to the receiver of the lordship.[3] At a later date, the burgesses were allowed to elect aldermen from among their ranks, and this right was certainly being exercised by 1461, when John Henbury, alderman of Denbigh, was granted the offices of *rhaglaw* and woodward in the lordship.[4]

Financial records from 1361–80 had recorded an average render of over £34 per annum from the borough to the receiver of the lordship, and three main sources of revenue were burghal rights, court profits and leases of certain rights, such as the farm of the common oven and toll profits.[5] No accounts survived for a period of thirty years after 1380 but those for 1410 and 1411 illustrate the considerable impact of the Glyn Dŵr rebellion on the economy of the borough, with arrears at 70.5 per cent and 82.3 per cent representing a significant proportion of the anticipated payments to the receiver of the lordship.[6] The absence of arrears from the contribution in 1426 of £8 1s. 2d indicates that the economy was by then showing signs of recovery.[7] However, the level of payments attained in the second half of the fourteenth century was never repeated, and those recorded in a sequence of accounts from 1509 until 1521 averaged only £16 8s.[8]

With regard to the privileges enjoyed by the burgesses of Denbigh, they were allowed to maintain a prison but were denied separate legal rights: the emphasis in the earlier borough charters was on burgage tenure rather than an independent judicial system. However, a borough court had been established by 1361 and was probably held in the Burgess Tower of the castle.[9] Also, the existence of a separate judicial system was confirmed by the designation of Denbigh as a '*liber burgus*' in the 1379 charter. This charter ensured that the burgesses should not be convicted by any 'foreigners' within the lordship but should only face legal actions in a borough court 'according to the liberties anciently approved and used in the boroughs of Rhuddlan and Conway', respectively located on the north-eastern and north-western flanks of the lordship of Denbigh. Moreover, if they committed an offence outside the lordship but within the principality of Wales, the burgesses would only be required to face legal action in the 'English boroughs'.[10]

The close association forged by the foundation charters between the borough and castle of Denbigh, was reflected by the provision that each burgess was required to provide an armed man to guard and defend the town: *a la garde et la defens.*[11] This was illustrated during the Glyn Dŵr rebellion, and in 1402 the castle was garrisoned by representatives of the Dolben, Peake, Pigot, Salusbury and Swynemore families, which all featured prominently in the life of the borough.[12] In the same year, a series of parliamentary measures designed to penalise Welshmen included the provision that the garrisons of castles and walled towns in Wales were to be manned not only by Englishmen but also by strangers to the locality.[13] The recruitment of local persons in Denbigh illustrated the element of trust placed by the administration in the burgess families, and reference has been made to the tenure of significant offices by burgesses including John Swynemore and William Danney, who served as constables and Robert Backerne as escheator. Also, numerous members of the Salusbury family held important offices in the late fifteenth century and the sixteenth century, in the lordship and later in the new shire of Denbigh.[14] The burgesses named in 1476 included Roger and Thomas Salusbury, and Roger, at the time of his death in 1530, held seven burgages,[15] and two other members of the family – both named John Salusbury with the elder, also known as John 'y Bodiau' – were also listed as burgesses in Henry VIII's survey.[16]

The borough's close relationship with the castle had both stimulated and hindered the development of the urban community at Denbigh. The series of grants providing enhanced privileges effectively contributed towards the increasing stature of Denbigh as a commercial and administrative centre. However, at the same time, the borough suffered on account of its identification with the central administration of the lordship, and the privileged position of the burgesses, as previously outlined in the discussion on the tumultuous events of 1294–5, clearly aroused resentment among the inhabitants of the surrounding countryside.[17] The underlying sentiments of fear and hostility generated by the alien burgesses had again surfaced in 1345 following the murder of Henry Shaldeford,[18] and in 1400 when the lordship of Denbigh provided a sizeable proportion of the insurgents involved in the initial attack of the Glyn Dŵr rebellion on the borough of Ruthin.[19] The borough was again critically affected by the dynastic struggles of the fifteenth century with the lordship, which had been associated with the Mortimer family for many years, one of the main centres of the Yorkist cause in Wales.[20]

The two sixteenth-century authors John Leland and William Camden, distinguished between the old and new urban settlements located at Denbigh. Leland suggested that the new town was of recent origin – 'hath beene totally made of later tyme'[21] – while Camden stated that as a result of the turmoil of the 1460s, the residents had 'removed hence by degrees' from the old to the new town. Two reasons were proposed for this movement of the urban population; the inconvenience caused by the steep slope leading towards the fortified borough, and the deficiencies of the water supply.[22]

Camden's analysis seems to have some validity, yet the emphasis in these sixteenth-century writings on the recent growth of the urban centre located outside the walls is contradicted by earlier evidence. This may be clearly observed by an examination of the development of the 'old' and 'new' towns since the foundation of the borough, in terms of both size and composition. The expansion of the urban settlement, whose extent was recorded in the 1334 Survey, is reflected in the 1379 Charter, which stated that the boundaries of this urban settlement comprised a circuit of a mile and a half on every side from the high cross standing in the marketplace of the town.[23]

The original connection between burgages in the borough of Denbigh and bovates in the surrounding townships was maintained in the fifteenth century and partly compensated for the absence of burgess lists in the rentals. The 1476 Rental recorded that Ralph Billyng held two burgages, and also a bovate in the township of Berain.[24] The presence of his predecessors as landholders is indicated by a reference in the 1437 Rental to Henry Billyng,[25] and another in the 1451 Rental to Richard, the son of Henry Billyng, as the occupant of a bovate in Berain.[26]

Surviving deeds provide information on changes in the occupation of burgages. In 1418, Henry Salusbury was granted a burgage in the town's suburbs by Margaret, described as the former wife of William Aberbury.[27] Accounts compiled by bailiffs of the borough contain evidence relating to both the composition and size of Denbigh. The office of bailiff seems to have been the preserve of the burgess families, and of those who appeared for the first time on the 1476 list, members of the Rossindale, Dolben and Billyng families first held the office respectively in 1380, 1403 and 1404.[28] The 1380 account referred to the lease to Thomas de Heton of a burgage formerly held by Thomas Londesdale.[29] Neither of these families was represented in the second foundation charter, and there is no suggestion that they held burgages in 1334, even though members of both families appeared in the Survey as landholders.[30] Whereas Thomas de Heton had acquired a burgage in Denbigh by 1380, the 1476 Rental confirmed the prominence in this borough of the Heton family: John Heton held two burgages within the walls, and a parcel of land outside the walls, while Henry Heton occupied two burgages in Sowterlane and one burgage in High Street.[31]

The inhabitants of the surrounding areas, together with the burgesses, sustained shopkeepers and craftsmen at Denbigh. In 1476, the shop owners included Alicia and Roger Huxley, Hugh Smalwood and Philip Wood. The location of the shops was not specified but a deed dated 16 October 1501 referred to the grant of a shop in High Street, 'in the suburbs of Denbigh'.[32] Those involved in the latter transaction included members of the Huxley and Smalwood families named in 1476, and it has been suggested that High Street was probably the earliest shopping centre in Denbigh.

The residents of the neighbourhood of Denbigh seem to have been required from the outset to trade within the borough. The commercial monopoly enjoyed by the burgesses was confirmed on 22 February 1379 by the forementioned charter, which established at Denbigh a gild merchant: the latter has been defined as 'an urban institution ... [which] promoted the interests of the mercantile elite as opposed to those of the artisans or handicrafts and the non-burgess population'.[33] This document, cited in the charter of 14 May 1662, emphasised security of tenure for the burgesses with the provision that 'if burgesses die intestate, royal officials should not take possession of these lands, but these should pass to their heirs and executors'.³⁴ Also, the ordinance dated 10 December 1484, forbade the inhabitants of the commotes of Ceinmeirch, Is Aled and Uwch Aled from 'buying or selling victuals or merchandise except within Denbigh.³⁵

Precise information on the size of the borough was not provided by the surviving records, but the actual number of burgages may be conjectured. The 1373 financial account recorded that 6s. 3d was rendered for seventy-nine burgages within the walls, and 29s. 11d for burgages outside the walls. Earlier accounts had indicated that the standard payment for a burgage was 1d per annum, and on this possible basis the payment of 29s. 11d suggests the existence of 359 burgages. A yield of 6s. 3d from the seventy-nine intra-mural burgages indicates that a similar fixed payment was not demanded from these holdings, and a total of 438 burgages would therefore seem to have been occupied in 1373.³⁶ The 1411 account illustrates the impact of the Glyn Dŵr rebellion, with sums of 6s. 2d and £1 3s.1d charged respectively for the intra-mural and extra-mural burgages. There had been a reduction of one burgage occupied within the walls, and a statement that each extra-mural burgage was held for 1d suggests a total burgage count of 355. A note referring to 'decayed rents' suggests that as many as sixty-two-and-a-half burgages were vacant and that therefore the number of burgages actually occupied in 1411 was as low as 292.5.³⁷ There had been a further deterioration by 1426, and that although 440 burgages were recorded on this account, 260 of them seem to have been vacant with only 180 burgages occupied that year.³⁸

A measure of recovery had been achieved by 1476 despite the dislocation caused by the lordship's involvement in the dynastic struggles of this period. The 1476 Rental provided a comprehensive and detailed survey of the tenurial structure of the borough. The first section listed sixty-five burgages that were occupied within the walls. A rent of 1d was levied on each burgage, and a bovate, amounting to 10 or 20 acres was attached to each burgage. A total of 760 acres was held in this way by occupants of burgages located within the walls. These burgesses included representatives of several families who did not appear in the second foundation charter but who may be identified as landholders in the 1334 Survey. These included members of the Backerne, Billyng, Henbury, Heton, Rossindale and Salusbury families. The forefathers of other burgesses listed in 1476, including representatives of the Bolton, Dolben, Drihurst, Hicock and Knowsely families,[39] had not been named in the 1334 Survey.

In the suburbs, 276 burgages were occupied outside the town walls. Their location was specified with the largest number, 147.5 in High Street, which constituted the earliest shopping centre; forty, thirty-five-and-a-half, and thirty-four burgages were held respectively in Sowterlane, Park Lane and Love Lane. A rent of 1d was again the usual rent for a burgage and 12d was normally levied on each *placea*. Some of the burgesses held burgages both within and without the walls, with Ralph Drihurst occupying two burgages inside the walls, one burgage each in Sowterlane and Love Lane, and also five burgages in High Street. Similarly, Henry Henbury, the occupant of a burgage within the wall, also held three burgages in Sowterlane and two in each of High Street and Love Lane. There is some evidence of burgage consolidation by 1476, with Ralph Scaltok occupying five burgages and three *placeae* in Love Lane at a rent of 6s. 8d. No Welsh name appears among the holders of burgages within the town walls, but outside the walls Dafydd ap Llywelyn ap Gronw and his wife Ermelen held a burgage in Love Lane and two burgages in High Street. Another probable Welshman, John, the son of Robert Goch, held a burgage in Sowterlane.[40]

The survey compiled in the reign of Henry VIII is unfortunately not as specific as the 1476 Rental, but provides a detailed account of Denbigh castle 'built high upon a rock of stone very stately and beautifully' and the borough and castle 'being walled about with a strong wall standing high'. This wall was said to have 'two gates with portcullis' and with each one being two-storeyed, and the castle was described as being 'six-square and hath at every square a strong tower' and buildings within the stone castle included 'two great stately chambers', 'a great seven-square tower', hall, and 'fair large Green, wherein standeth a Chapel, to serve the Castle'.[41]

The names of the burgesses, together with additional information, were provided for the sixty-one burgages occupied within, and 225.5 burgages outside the walls.[42] However, intriguing references to other burgages located both within and outside the walls prevent the calculation with any certainty of their actual number. Those occupied within the walls were probably in the region of eighty, as John Leland, referring to the 'diverse rowes of streates withyn the wald toune', stated that 'there be scant 80 howsolders'.[43] This survey also revealed that some of the families associated with the borough from its earliest days were no longer present, and these included the Hilton and Swynemore families. On the other hand, newcomers to the burgess-list since the 1476 Rental represented some members of the early fourteenth century-generation of settlers, with the Latham and Fraunces families achieving this local distinction only in the sixteenth century.[44] Other families seem to have progressed gradually, and occupied burgages outside the town walls before acquiring burgages within the walls. In 1476 John Huxley held eight burgages in High Street, two burgages in Sowterlane and one each in Love Lane and Park Lane; and Richard, the son of William, the son of John Thomson occupied three burgages in Park Lane.[45] By the reign of Henry VIII, Robert Huxley and Thomas Thomson, respectively, held eight and two burgages within the walls of Denbigh.[46]

The series of accounts that survive for Abergele provide information on the various sources of the borough's revenue. The main element was clearly court profits, with the other sources (normally rents and manorial profits: *exitus manerii*) being of minimal value and reasonably constant. From 1372 to 1426 the farm only increased from 2s. 11d to 3s. ¼d, and the manorial profits, which increased from 1372 until 1379, were not mentioned afterwards. Also, the borough, from 1334 until 1426, was stated to have contained thirty burgages and seems to have experienced no growth.[47] The series of accounts from 1378 until 1398 reveal that a considerable proportion of the payments from bailiff to receiver consisted of arrears, and this again reflected the static nature of the borough of Abergele.[48] Actual payments had fallen by 1410 and 1411, and the intensification of this decrease by 1426 reflected the problems experienced by the borough officials in the early fifteenth century. Court profits increased from £3 13s. 1d in 1411 to £5 18s. 1d in 1426; the latter being only £1 10s. 11¾d less than the court profits collected in 1398. Therefore, although the valuation of £9 2s. 1¾d in 1422 seems to have been unrealistic in view of the total income in 1426 being only £6 0s. 1½d, the credit balance of £4 17s. 5½d in 1426 seems to indicate that the borough was slowly recovering from the dislocation caused by the Glyn Dŵr rebellion.[49]

The corresponding accounts for the borough of Llanrwst are less satisfactory, and although it was stated explicitly in its bailiff's account that details of the rent and farm appear in the account of the ringild of Uwch Dulas, they were in fact absent. It is therefore impossible to compile for Llanrwst a detailed balance sheet as has been attempted for the other two boroughs. The only relevant information contained in the Llanrwst bailiff's account related to court profits and payments to the receiver, yet these do throw some light on developments within the borough. Both these items tended to be erratic, with court profits ranging from £12 4s. 5½d in 1370 to £2 13s. in 1398, and payments to the receiver from £11 12s. 8d in 1378 to 6s. 8d in 1426.[50]

In 1361 court profits and payments to the receiver yielded low sums of £4 1s. 3d and £3 14s. 4d, and in 1366, of the sum of £7 7s. 4¼d rendered to the receiver, £5 11s. 9d, or 75.7 per cent of the total sum consisted of arrears.[51] These statistics suggest that the borough of Llanrwst suffered during these years from financial difficulties which may possibly have been caused by outbreaks of the plague. On the other hand, payments were at a high level in 1397 and 1398. It is certainly true that 73.1 per cent of the sum rendered in 1397, that is £10 15s. 10d, consisted of arrears, but yet in the following year, all the payments, amounting to £7 18s. 10d, had been collected in that year.[52] Therefore, in the absence of other evidence, payments to the receiver suggest that the economy of this borough was in a reasonably satisfactory condition on the eve of the Glyn Dŵr rebellion. On the other hand, the succeeding accounts, compiled during the rebellion, indicate a considerable degree of dislocation, with no income recorded in 1410 and 1411. Also, despite being valued at £11 2s. ½d in 1424, payments to the receiver amounted to only 6s. 8d in 1426,[53] and the borough of Llanrwst, by these years, had clearly not recovered from the effects of the years of rebellion. Further damage to the economy of Llanrwst and its neighbourhood was undoubtedly caused by the hostilities of the fifteenth-century dynastic wars and reference appears above to the comments made by Sir John Wynn on the desolation that afflicted 'the whole borough of Llanrwst and all the vale of Conwy'.[54]

Wynn had also referred to the devastation caused by the onslaught that had 'wasted with fire and sword the suburbs of the town of Denbigh, and all the lordship of Denbigh'.[55] However, the regulation of trade in the borough of Denbigh had been sufficiently extended by the sixteenth century for the establishment of various specialist craft guilds, including those of corvisers, glovers, shoe-makers and weavers.[56] At this time, Denbigh was renowned for its glovers and drapers, and an earlier reference described Robert Dolben, granted three parcels of land on 12 March 1491, as a draper.[57] Also, Sir Richard Clough referred to himself, in his will compiled on 20 March 1568, as 'Richard Clough of London, mercer, Sonne to Richard Clough of Denbeache, glover'.[58] At this time, a market was held once a week on a Wednesday and a fair twice a year, the first on 3 May and the second on 14 September.[59]

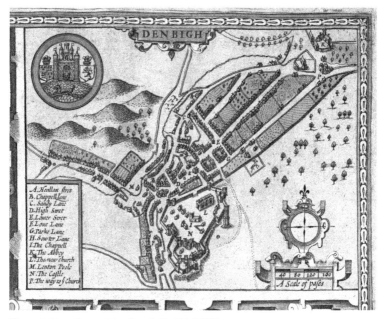

Figure 7: Part of map, John Speed, *Denbigh* (1610)

It is clear that the weekly market and biennial fairs served the prosperous agrarian community residing in the neighbourhood of Denbigh. John Leland in his Itinerary compiled *c*. 1536–9, described the parish of Denbigh as being 'plentiful of corn and gresse, with parts of the commote of Ceinmeirch containing' goodly corn and grasse', and the commote of Is Aled being 'goode for corne as whete, rye, peason and benes, and hath very good fine pasture and medois'.[60] A generation later Humphrey Llwyd described this locality as:

> aboundeth plentifully with all things that are necessarie to the use of man. The hilles yealdeth fleash and white meates. The most fertile valley: very good corne Corn and grasse … it is a greate market Towne, famous and much frequented with wares and people, from all partes of Northwales.[61]

The flourishing cattle market held at Denbigh in the sixteenth century is also reputed to have attracted English buyers and drovers.[62]

It is clear that there was a considerable delay before members of the local Welsh community succeeded in occupying burgages within the walls of the borough, and in this respect there was a striking resemblance between Henry VIII's survey and the 1476 Rental. They had as yet been evidently unable to take advantage of the provision in the charter of liberties, granted in 1506, which declared, as previously noted, that Welshmen of the lordship should be allowed 'to acquire in fee or otherwise land in England and English towns in Wales'.[63] A limited measure of success had been achieved in that two Welshmen had held the office of bailiff of the borough; Thomas ap William ap Henry in 1520 and Robert ap William ap Henry in 1521.[64]

These, however, were exceptions and on the whole members of settler families maintained their grip on this office and continued to assert their authority not only within the borough but also in the new administrative system established in 1536 and 1543. As noted in Chapter 14, this had resulted in the appointment of justices of peace in other areas of Wales, and the formation of the shire of Denbigh, with Denbigh as its shire town and as the administrative focus of a more extensive area comprising the shires of Denbigh, Flint and Montgomery. Also, formally constituted at this time to cater for local inhabitants were the Council in the Marches and the Court of Great Sessions.[65] The assembly of local inhabitants at the Denbigh market-cross in May 1537 illustrated the local response to the recent legislation, and the optimism and enthusiasm displayed emphasised the latent hostility of the rural Welsh inhabitants towards an urban community which had been fostered and succoured by an administration with which it had been closely identified since its creation.[65]

Notes

1. *Survey*, p. 52. See Figure 6, part of John Speed's plan of the town of Denbigh, 1610.
2. Lewis, *The Medieval Boroughs of Snowdonia*, p. 74; W. W. Stubbs, *The Constitutional History of England in its Origin and Development*, vol. 1 (Oxford, 1897), pp. 407–8; A. Ballard and J. Tait (eds), *British Borough Charters, 1216–1397* (Cambridge, 1923), p. xvii.
3. TNA LR 2/252.
4. For further information see p. 219 of this chapter.
5. TNA SC 6/1182/4, TNA SC 6/1184/12.
6. TNA SC 6/1185/11, 13.
7. TNA SC 6/1185/16.
8. TNA SC 6/Henry VIII/4974–81.
9. M. W. de Hemmeon, *Burgage Tenure in Medieval England* (Harvard, 1914), p. 157; and J. Tait, *The Medieval English Borough* (Manchester, 1936), p. 354, viewed burgage tenure as the distinguishing feature of a borough; SC 6/1182/4; Williams, *Ancient and Modern Denbigh*, pp. 300–1; Leland, *Itinerary*, p. 96.
10. Lewis, *Boroughs of Snowdonia*, p. 38, for a statement that each one of the nine boroughs of Gwynedd was considered a *liber burgus* or free borough, and p. 119 for comment that an independent judiciary 'was the essential feature of the *liber burgus*'.
11. Williams, *Records of Denbigh*, p. 122.
12. TNA SC 6/1185/4.
13. TNA, *Statutes of the Realm*, ii, 141; *The Chronicle of Adam Usk*, 1377–1421, ed. and trans. by Chris Given-Wilson, (Oxford, 1997); Williams, *Recovery, Reorientation and Reformation*, p. 10.
14. *Supra*, p. 130.
15. NLW Deposit, 163 B.; TNA LR 2/252.
16. *Supra*, p. 205.
17. *Supra*, p. 98.
18. *Supra*, pp. 115–17.
19. *Supra*, p. 129.
20. *Supra*. pp. 187–90.
21. Leland, *Itinerary*, p. 97.
22. *Supra*, p. 220.
23. *Supra*. p. 216.
24. NLW Deposit, 163 B.
25. NLW Wynnstay, 86.
26. NLW MS 12647.
27. NLW Lleweni Deeds and Documents, 351.
28. TNA SC 6/1184/16; 1185/9.
29. TNA SC 6/1184/16.
30. *SD*, pp. 106, 163, 165, 204; 16, 21, 35, 63, 76.
30. TNA SC 6/1184/16; NLW, Deposit 163 B.

31 NLW Lleweni Deeds and Documents, 328.
32 *Supra*, pp. 219–20.
33 The charter of 14 May 1662 is preserved among the borough records of Denbigh at the Denbighshire Record office in Ruthin: extracts have been translated in Williams, *Ancient and Modern Denbigh*, pp. 118–25.
34 *CPR 1476–1485*, p. 504.
35 TNA SC 6/1183/9.
36 TNA SC 6/1185/13.
37 TNA SC 6/1185/16.
38 NLW Deposit, 163 B.
39 NLW Deposit, 163 B.
40 TNA LR 2/252; Williams, *Ancient and Modern Denbigh*, pp. 89–91.
41 TNA LR 2/252.
42 Leland, *Itinerary*, p. 97.
43 TNA LR 2/252.
44 NLW Deposit, 163 B.
45 TNA LR 2/252.
46 TNA SC 6/1183/4; 1184/9; 1185/16; *Survey*, pp. 252–3.
47 TNA 1184/5; 1184/24.
48 TNA 1185/11; 1185/13; 1185/16.
49 TNA 1183/2; 1184/6; 1185/3; 1185/16.
50 TNA 1182/4; 1182/8.
51 TNA 1184/21; 1185/3.
52 TNA 1185/11; 1185/13; 1305/8; 1185/16.
53 Wynn, *The History of the Gwydir Family*, p. 33.
54 Wynn, *The History of the Gwydir Family*, pp. 33, 133.
55 Williams, *Ancient and Modern Denbigh*, pp. 126–40.
56 Williams, *Ancient and Modern Denbigh*, pp. 127–31; *Lleweni Deeds and Documents*, p. 384.
57 Robin Gwyndaf Jones, 'Sir Richard Clough of Denbigh, *c.* 1530–1570, Part 1', *TDHS*, 19 (1970).
58 TNA LR 2/252.
59 Leland, *Itinerary*, p. 94.
60 Llwyd, *The Breviary of Britayne*, ff. 66v, 67r; Llwyd, *'The Breviary of Britayn'*, p. 115. The main features of the town of Denbigh were represented on John Speed's detailed urban plan published in 1610; see Appendix 7.
61 G. D. Owen, *Elizabethan Wales: The Social Scene* (Cardiff, 1964), p. 83.
62 *Infra*, p. 235.
63 TNA SC 6/4980.
64 Bowen, *Statutes of Wales*, pp. 67–9, 75–93, 101–33; Rees, *Union of England and Wales*; Jones, *Early Modern Wales*, pp. 77–8, 99–100 [see also *supra*].
65 *Supra*, p. 209 for further details of this incident at Denbigh in May 1537, and additional references in Chapter 14, notes 38 and 39.

POSTSCRIPT

The term 'lordship of Denbigh' continued to be used after the creation of Denbighshire following the Union legislation of 1536–43. Robert Dudley, earl of Leicester, who was a significant figure in the history of Denbighshire in the second half of the sixteenth century, was granted the lordships of Denbigh and Chirk in June 1563. In June 1564, the lordship of Ruthin (Dyffryn Clwyd) was awarded to his brother Ambrose, earl of Warwick.[1] A survey of the lordship of Denbigh, compiled by Leicester's commissioners in the summer of 1563 revealed that the formal structure of the lordship was very similar to that recorded in 1334, with the core of the demesne comprising the four manors, six parks and seignorial mills. The parks, leased since the early fourteenth century, were associated with the leading families of the lordship: Ystrad with the Myddeltons, Dinorben Fawr with the Hollands and Kilford with the Salusburies of Lleweni. The close relationship of the latter family with the office of steward, from 1508 to 1563, was considered to be extremely significant with regard to both the tenurial and political framework of the lordship.[2]

On 26 September 1564, Leicester reached an agreement, termed the 'Composition', with the tenants of the lordship of Denbigh[3] and thereby succeeded in both reforming the tenurial structure of the lordship and in securing a considerable increase in its revenues. He also sought to regain control of leasehold lands that had been granted for very long periods by the Crown or its agents in the 1540s and 1550s. Tenurial confusion had been resolved following the granting to all tenants the freehold of their lands and an indication of its success was the request made by the tenants of the lordship of Chirk to be 'in the case that Denbighland be'.⁴

In the early 1580s, the lordship of Denbigh constituted by far the main source of Leicester's revenue in the annual rent roll compiled for his estates.⁵ A substantial contingent of the military force assembled for his expedition to the Netherlands in 1585-6 was comprised of prominent members of the Denbighshire gentry families, including Evan Lloyd of Bodidris, the high sheriff of Denbighshire in 1568 and 1583, MP for the shire in 1584-5 and farmer of lands in the lordship of Denbigh; Piers Holland, the son of Piers Holland of Kinmel, Abergele, the high sheriff of Denbighshire in 1578; Thomas Salusbury senior, the younger son of Sir John Salusbury of Lleweni and brother of John Salusbury (died in 1566); and William Midleton of Llansannan (c. 1550-c. 1600).⁶

In the eighteenth century, Humphrey Foulkes (1673-1737), a member of a prominent Denbighshire family, based at Plas Newydd, Meriadog, claimed that his qualification for writing a dissertation on marcher lordships was his residence for most of his life in the lordship of Denbigh. He referred to the list that he had compiled of English families, including the Salusbury, Heaton, Birchinshaw and Pigot families who had settled in this area. He also claimed to be descended from Marchweithian, who, as previously noted, was associated with one of the fifteen royal 'tribes 'of north Wales.⁷

Foulkes was one of the group of antiquarians who provided valuable information for the research project led by Edward Lhuyd (1660-1709), the eminent botanist, geologist, antiquary and philologist, and he also collected subscriptions for Lhuyd's *Archaeologia Britannica* (1707). Lhuyd was one of numerous individuals who had referred to memories of family associations with some of the Welsh 'tribal' groupings noted in this volume. He had asserted that he did not 'profess to be an Englishman, but an old Briton, and, according to our British genealogies, descended in the male line from Coel Godhebog, in the province of Riged, in Scotland, in the 4th century, before the Saxons came into Great-Britain'. His pedigree, in his own handwriting, preserved at the Ashmolean Museum, Oxford referred to his descent from Bleddyn Fychan and Coel Codebog, thereby associating him with the Hedd Molwynog clan.[8]

A possible relationship with Hedd Molwynog was also claimed in the early twentieth century by Annie Mary Davies who traced the family history of her grandfather Henry Rees, the eloquent preacher and Calvinistic Methodist leader who, with his brother, William Rees, 'Gwilym Hiraethog', the prolific author and influential editor, had been born and brought up in the Chwibren Isaf farmhouse, near Llansannan. Their ancestors had lived here for several centuries, and included the renowned poet, Tudur Aled. This volume's appendix, 'Genealogical Statement', named her forefathers on a list extending back to Hedd Molwynog, described as 'the founder of the ninth of the fifteen Noble Tribes of North Wales' and 'lord of Uwch Aled' who lived in this area 'about the beginning of the 12th century'. The long list of descendants were all closely associated with this area, and the one exception was Henry Rees's grandfather, Henry Rees, formerly of Carmarthenshire, who married Gwen Loyd of Chwibren Isaf.[9]

Annie Mary Davies thereby preserved and maintained a family tradition extending back to the medieval period. Combined with other experiences covering a wide chronological span, and despite the extensive social re-organisation in the period immediately following the Edwardian Conquest, this had a considerable influence on moulding the distinctive cultural character of this area, which has contributed significantly to the literary heritage of Wales.[10]

Notes

1   S. L. Adams, 'The Gentry of North Wales and the Earl of Leicester's Expedition to the Netherlands, 1585–1586', *WHR*, 7/2 (December 1974),129.
2   S. L. Adams, 'The Composition of 1564 and the Earl of Leicester's Tenurial Reformation in the Lordship of Denbigh', *BBCS*, 26/4 (May 1976), 485–9.

3   Galltfaenan Collection, MS 1074, Flintshire Record Office.
4   Adams, 'The Composition of 1564', 479–511.
5   Adams, 'The Gentry of North Wales', 129–30.
6   Adams, 'The Gentry of North Wales', 135–6, 140, 142; S. L. Adams, 'Military Obligations of Leasehold Tenants in Leicesterian Denbigh: A Footnote', *TDHS*, 24 (1975), 205–8; Gruffydd Aled Williams, 'Wiliam Midleton, bonheddwr, anturiwr a bardd', *TDHS*, 24 (1975), 82–3.
7   Mary Burdett-Jones, 'Humphrey Foulkes: uchelgais heb ei gyflawni', *Y Traethodydd* (Ionawr, 2009), 18–33; Mary Burdett-Jones, 'Humphrey Foulkes's Building the Palace, Dr Humphrey Foulkes's Attempt to Continue Edward Lhuyd's work', *TDHS*, 58 (2010), 11–22; NLW MS 10B; I wish to thank Mary Burdett-Jones for providing me with relevant information relating to the family background and career of Humphrey Foulkes.
8   D. W. Evans and Brynley F. Roberts (eds), *Edward Lhwyd: Archaeologia Britannica, Texts and Translations* (Aberystwyth, 2008); Brynley F. Roberts, *Edward Lhwyd, c.1660–1709: Naturalist, Antiquary, Philologist* (Cardiff, 2022). I am grateful to the late Dr Brynley F. Roberts for the following reference and for further information relating to the family background of Edward Lhuyd: Nicholas Owen, 'Memoirs of the Life of Edward Lhuyd' in *British Remains* (London, 1777), pp. 131–2.
9   Annie Mary Davies (trans.), *Life and Letters of Henry Rees* (Bangor, 1904), pp. 6–12, i–vii.
10 See p. 236.

CONCLUSION

Significant local developments in the area that in 1282 formed the lordship of Denbigh included the policies of the rulers of Gwynedd in the thirteenth century, which represented the background to the Edwardian Conquest and the consequent creation of the lordship. Retrospective information presented by the 1334 Survey of Denbigh was a major source for the discussion on bond communities and free descent groupings, together with efforts to establish a money economy and the establishment of a pre-conquest borough at Llanrwst.[1]

The first five individuals who served as lords of Denbigh in the period 1282–1344 were prominent figures in the English realm, with the first lord, Henry de Lacy, earl of Lincoln, surviving the rebellion that erupted in Denbigh in 1294–5. Prominent individuals in the lordship were actively involved in the political ambitions of the second lord, Thomas, earl of Lancaster, who was executed in 1322, as also were his successors, Thomas Despenser, the elder, earl of Winchester, in 1326, and Roger Mortimer, the first earl of March, in 1330. These three lords were involved in unsuccessful attempts to extend their authority in the English realm, while the fifth lord, William Montagu, the first earl of Salisbury, in contrast to his three predecessors, died from natural causes.[2]

Problems experienced in the early period with regard to the relationship between the lords of Denbigh and the principality of Wales, marcher lords and prominent inhabitants of the lordship again surfaced throughout the later history of the lordship. The involvement of several prominent individuals in the murder of

Henry Shaldeford in February 1345 attracted an angry local response, and counter-claims for possession of the lordship were presented by members of the Mortimer and Montagu families.[3]

Following his proclamation as Prince of Wales in September 1400, Owain Glyn Dŵr led a series of attacks on a number of towns in north-east Wales, including Denbigh, but the garrisoning of Denbigh castle in 1402 by members of prominent local families illustrated the continuing trust placed in these families. Glyn Dŵr's influence within the lordship survived the military defeat at the battle of Shrewsbury, fought in 1403. A number of sites within the lordship suffered from military attacks, but the payment of fines in 1407 and 1408 illustrated the success of some settler and native families to restore their fortunes after the rebellion.[4]

The lordship of Denbigh, together with the other parts of the extensive estates of Edmund Mortimer, the fifth earl of March, was inherited by his nephew, Richard, duke of York. The latter's death in December 1460 resulted in the accession of Edward IV and thereby the incorporation of the lordship into the kingdom of England, which represented its status until the formation of Denbighshire following the Union legislation of 1536-43.[5]

The 1334 Survey referred to activities at four manors that experienced difficulties in the period 1305-31. While an impression of deterioration was conveyed in the entries for Dinorben Fawr and Ystrad Owain in 1334, demesne cultivation had clearly ceased at the two recently established manors of Denbigh and Kilford. The financial problems of the lordship were reflected by the policy of total commutation of dues that accelerated the process set in motion in the pre-conquest period.[6]

A distinctive feature of the lordship of Denbigh was the adoption of a social policy, which involved the formation of a colony, comprising English settlers with territory that had been largely acquired by the process of escheat and re-location of local residents. Total control was thereby exerted over specific localities, with the five centres of English settlement surrounded by townships containing displaced Welsh tenants, but some prominent members of the local community were also rewarded by the grant of lands.[7]

An attempt therefore seems to have been made to replicate the distinction between Welshry and Englishry in the older marcher lordships, with the contrast here based largely on personal identity rather than economic grounds. Female tenants were identified in all five commotes and the extremely favourable tenurial terms offered to members of the settler community led to periodic outbreaks of conflict, as in 1294 and 1345. Family properties traced included those of male members of the Heton, Hulton, Pontefract and Swynemore families together with male and female members of the Pigot, Plesyngton, Salusbury and Wilberley families.[8]

Significant tenurial developments, recorded in the 1437 rental, and concentrating on the commotes of Ceinmeirch and Is Aled, were profitably compared with the information presented in the comprehensive 1334 Survey. Outbreaks of plague and rebellion had clearly provided opportunities for kindred members to evade restrictions on the acquisition and disposal of their lands, and the number of Welsh tenants had increased by 1437 with lands acquired in localities where they had not been present in 1334. The rentals of 1450/1, 1476/7 and 1491/2 contained information relating to the entire lordship, and numerous examples of leaseholders were identified together with several female and male members of Welsh and settler families who held individual plots of land.[9]

Following the creation of the lordship in 1282, its administration was competently organised with Denbigh utilised as the administrative centre. Detailed descriptions were provided of the castle built here in the post-conquest period. The most important officials of the central administration were identified as the steward, receiver and constable, and the continuing operation of the commote court, the basic judicial institution, and activities of the *ynad* ('legal official'), represented the survival of aspects of the pre-conquest administrative framework. The introduction of

English criminal law was accompanied by the continuing use of Welsh law in the commote courts, the operation of Welsh law in real actions dealing with property issues, and also the occasional use of Welsh law in civil and criminal cases by settler families when they considered that it would benefit them.[10]

Various sources of seignorial revenue and payments to the central receiver were identified and the lordship was a very lucrative financial unit throughout the fourteenth century. A detailed examination of the period 1334–1425 considered outbreaks of the Black Death, the delivery of substantial sums of money to the central receiver in a period of high seignorial profits, and the financial and economic impact of the Glyn Dŵr rebellion. The lordship, despite a decline in its value in this period, continued to be one of the most valuable financial assets in the extensive Mortimer estate.[11]

An examination of the lordship's three boroughs indicated that commercial activities centred on the borough of Denbigh contributed significantly to the policy of economic and social reconstruction adopted in the lordship. Problems encountered were illustrated by the award of two foundation charters, in 1285 and then between 1295 and 1305, with the latter representing a second and more successful attempt to establish a borough at the centre of the lordship. A number of shopkeepers and craftsmen were sustained here by the commercial monopoly enjoyed by the burgesses as inhabitants of the surrounding areas were required to trade within the borough.[12]

With regard to the other two boroughs Abergele was similar to Denbigh in that the low level of burgage rents attracted English settlers, On the other hand, in Llanrwst, burgage rents that varied from 1s. to 4s. seem to have been motivated by financial exploitation. Possible financial problems were probably caused by the plague, and again in the early fifteenth century as a result of the Glyn Dŵr rebellion, and Sir John Wynn commented on the damage caused to the boroughs of Llanrwst and Denbigh as a result of the fifteenth-century dynastic conflicts.[13]

On the other hand, the evidence relating to Denbigh in the sixteenth century suggests a healthy economy with the holding of a weekly market and biennial fairs, and the establishment of various specialist craft guilds. Favourable comments were also recorded in the writings of John Leland and Humphrey Llwyd, and the flourishing cattle market held at Denbigh is reputed to have attracted English buyers and drovers.[14]

A significant consequence of Henry Tudor's accession as king of England was the charter of privileges granted to the lordship of Denbigh in 1506. Prominent individuals favoured by the king included Rhys ap Maredudd whose sons Morys Gethin and Sir Robert ap Rhys, and grandson Dr Elis Prys, were significant landholders and officials in the lordship, with the two latter individuals also generous bardic patrons. Members of the Salusbury and Pigot families were notable patrons of Welsh literary traditions in the late fifteenth century and sixteenth century, and several important literary figures had close personal and family links with this area.[15]

Considerable efforts to improve the enforcement of law and order were undertaken during the eight-year tenure of Rowland Lee as President of the Council in the Marches (1534–42). This was followed by the Union legislation of 1536–43 that resulted in the creation of Denbighshire, the establishment at Denbigh of a chancery and exchequer responsible for the three shires of north-east Wales and the Court of Great Sessions. Local residents were clearly aware of the enhanced legal rights to which they were entitled, as illustrated in the incident at the Denbigh market-cross in May 1537.[16]

Later developments that illustrated the continued operation of the lordship of Denbigh included the activities of Robert Dudley, earl of Leicester, who was granted the lordship of Denbigh in June 1563,[17] Humphrey Foulkes and Edward Lhuyd, who were clearly aware of their family associations with prominent kindred groupings'.[18]

The locality's immense contribution to the literary traditions of Wales has attracted several favourable comments over the years, with several individuals commenting on its immense contribution to the cultural life of Wales. The Denbighshire Historical Society, since its establishment in 1952, has contributed significantly to ensuring a continuing awareness of the county's heritage. It was therefore extremely appropriate that the first volume of the annual transactions produced by the society contained a reference by the late Professor Gruffudd John Williams to the Vale of Clwyd and its surrounding area as the most important region in Wales for its literary activities from the early fifteenth century to the eighteenth century.[19]

Notes

1 See pp. 21–8..
2 See pp. 31–43, 231.
3 See pp. 113–23, 231–2.
4 See pp. 127–35, 232.
5 See pp. 187–90, 201–9, 232, 235.
6 See pp. 57–74, 232.
7 See pp. 77–92, 232–3.
8 See pp. 139–58, 191–8, 233, 235.
9 See pp. 47–54, 175–84, 233–4.
10 See pp. 161–72, 234.
11 See pp. 95–104, 110–12.
12 See pp. 104–7, 220–2, 234.
13 See pp. 222–4, 235.
14 See pp. 204–7, 235–6.
15 See pp. 227–8, 235.
16 G. J. Williams, 'Traddodiad llenyddol Dyffryn Clwyd a'r cyffiniau', *TDHS*, 1 (1952), 20.
17 R. Brinley Jones, *William Salesbury* (Cardiff), p. 3.
18 *Supra*, pp. 228–9, 235.
19 Williams, 'Traddodiad llenyddol Dyffryn Clwyd', 20.

APPENDIX

Devolution of the Lordship of Denbigh, 1282–1543

16 October 1282 to 5 February 1311	Henry de Lacy, earl of Lincoln
1 July 1311 to 22 March 1322	Thomas, earl of Lancaster
9 July 1322 to 27 October 1326	Hugh de Despenser, earl of Winchester
13 September 1327 to 29 November 1330	Roger Mortimer, 1st earl of March
18 January 1331 to 30 January 1344	William Montagu, 1st earl of Salusbury
8 April 1344 to 24 October 1353	Edward, Prince of Wales (The Black Prince)
24 October 1353 to 20 January 1355	William Montagu, 2nd earl of Salusbury
20 January 1355 to 26 February 1360	Roger Mortimer, 2nd earl of March
23 May 1360 to 10 February 1361	Edward, Prince of Wales (The Black Prince)
10 February 1361 to 15 November 1364	Isabel, Edward III's daughter
15 November 1364 to 6 January 1373	Philippa of Clarence, 5th Countess of Ulster (wife of Edmund Mortimer)

6 January 1373 to 27 December 1381	Edmund Mortimer, 3rd earl of March
27 December 1381 to 25 February 1394	Crown
25 February 1394 to 20 July 1398	Roger Mortimer, 4th earl of March
20 July 1398 to 6 November 1399	Crown
6 November 1399 to 21 July 1403	(custody: Henry Percy 'Hotspur')
21 July 1403 to 9 June 1413	Henry, Prince of Wales
9 June 1413 to 18 January 1425	Edmund Mortimer, 5th earl of March
18 January 1425 to 30 December 1460	Richard, 3rd duke of York
30 December 1460 to 4 March 1461	Edward, 6th earl of March
4 March 1461 to 3 October 1470	Edward IV
3 October 1470 to 11 April 1471	Henry VI
11 April 1471 to 9 April 1483	Edward IV
9 April 1483 to 25 June 1483	Edward V
26 June 1483 to 22 August 1485	Richard III
22 August 1485 to 21 April 1509	Henry VII
22 April 1509 to 28 January 1547	Henry VIII

BIBLIOGRAPHY

Primary sources: unpublished sources

The National Library of Wales, Aberystwyth
Bachymbyd Deeds and Documents
Cernioge Collection (A Schedule of Cernioge Deeds and Documents (1962))
Chirk Castle Manuscripts and Documents
Coedcae and Trofarth Deeds
Downing Deeds
Eriviat Estate Deeds
Gwydir Manuscripts
Gwysaney Deeds
Lleweni Deeds and Documents
Peniarth Manuscripts and Documents
Plas Iolyn Collection of Manuscripts and Documents
Plas-yn-Cefn Collection
Wigfair Deeds and Documents
Wynnstay Archives

The National Archives, Kew

Chancery
C 47 Chancery Miscellaneous
134 Inquisitions *post mortem* (Edward II)
135 Inquisitions *post mortem* (Edward III)
145 Miscellaneous Inquisitions

Duchy of Lancaster
DL 29 Ministers' accounts
DL 36 *Cartae* Miscellaneous
DL 43 Rentals and Surveys

Exchequer
E 40 Ancient Deeds
101 Accounts various
142 Ancient extents
149 Inquisitions *post mortem*
163 Exchequer miscellaneous
179 Subsidy rolls
317 Parliamentary surveys
321 Proceedings of the Court of Augmentations

Land Revenue
LR 2 Miscellaneous Books
LR 12 Receivers' Accounts, Series III

Special Collections
SC 2 Court Rolls
SC 6 Ministers' and Receivers' Accounts
SC 11 Rentals and Surveys (rolls)
SC 12 Rentals and Surveys (portfolios)

Bangor University Archives and Special Collections
Kinmel MSS
Mostyn MSS
Penrhyn MSS

North East Wales Archives (formerly Denbighshire Record Office, Ruthin)
DD/WY Wynnstay papers

Flintshire Record Office, Hawarden
D/GA Galltfaenan papers
D/GW Gwysaney papers

British Library
Egerton Roll

Bodleian Library, Oxford

Hatfield House Library
Cecil Papers
Montague Cartulary

Bodleian Library
Survey of Denbigh MS, 1334

Primary sources: published sources

[Adam Usk], *The Chronicle of Adam Usk, 1377–1421*, ed. and trans. by Chris Given-Wilson, (Oxford, 1997).
Ballard, A., and J. Tait (eds), *British Borough Charters, 1216–1397* (Cambridge, 1923).
Ballinger, J. (ed.), *Calendar of the Wynn (of Gwydir) Papers* (Aberystwyth, 1926).
Bartrum, Peter C. (ed.), *Welsh Genealogies, AD 300–1400* (Cardiff, 1974).
Bartrum, Peter C. (ed.), *Welsh Genealogies, AD 1400–1500* (Aberystwyth, 1983).
Beresford M. W., and Finberg, H. P. R. (eds), *Medieval English Boroughs: A Handlist* (1973).
Booth, P. H. W., and A. D. Carr (eds), *Account of Master John de Burnham the Younger, Chamberlain of Chester, of the Revenues of the Counties of Chester and Flint, 1361–2*, Record Society of Lancashire and Cheshire, vol. 125 (Gloucestershire, 1991).
Bowen, I. (ed.), *The Statutes of Wales* (London, 1908).
Calendar of Charter Rolls.

Calendar of Close Roll.
Calendar of Fine Rolls.
Calendar of Inquisitions Miscellaneous.
Calendar of Inquisitions Post Mortem.
Calendar of Patent Rolls.
Calendar of Recognizance Rolls of the Palatinate of Chester, Appendix ii to the Annual Report of the Deputy Keeper of the Public Records (London, 1875).
Calendar of Welsh Rolls, Calendar of Chancery Rolls Various.
Camden, William, *Britannia, Newly Translated into English*, published by E. Gibson (London, 1695).
Clancy, Joseph P. (trans.), *Medieval Welsh Poems* (Dublin, 2003).
Cokayne, George E. (comp.), *The Complete Peerage of England* (Gloucester, 1982).
Davies, Annie Mary (trans.) *Life and Letters of Henry Rees* (Bangor, 1904).
Davies, J. Conway (ed.), *The Welsh Assize Roll, 1277–1284* (Cardiff, 1940).
Davies, J. H., 'Owain Lawgoch', *Trans. Cymm* (1899–1900).
Dictionary of Welsh Biography to 1940 (London, 1959).
Dwnn, Lewis, *Heraldic Visitations of Wales and Part of the Marches*, 2 vols, ed. by S. R. Meyrick, (Llandovery, 1846).
Edwards, J. Goronwy (ed.), *Calendar of Ancient Correspondence Concerning Wales* (London, 1935).
Edwards, J. Goronwy (ed.), *Littere Wallie Preserved in Liber A in the Public Record Office* (Cardiff, 1940).
Ellis, R. (ed.), *Registrum vulgariter nuncupatum, 'The record of Caernarvon'*, Record Commission (London, 1838).
Ellis, T. P. (ed.), *The First Extent of Bromfield and Yale AD 1315*, Cymmrodorion Record Series, vol. 11 (London, 1924).
Evans, D. L. (ed.), *Flintshire Ministers' Accounts 1328–1353*, Flintshire Historical Society Record Series, vol. 2 (1929).
Evans, J. Gwenogvryn (ed.), *Oll synnwyr pen Kembero ygyd* (copied by William Salesbury from a collection by Gruffudd Hiraethog) (Bangor, 1902).
Farley, A, and H. Ellis (eds), *Domesday Book*, 4 vols (London, 1783–1816).
Fryde, E. B. (ed.), *Book of Prests of the King's Wardrobe for 1294–5* (Oxford, 1962).

Fryde, Natalie, *List of Welsh Entries in the Memoranda Rolls, 1282–1343* (Cardiff, 1974).

Gairdener, J. (ed.), *Paston Letters*, vol. 2 (London, 1872).

Gregory, William, *Historical Collections of a London Citizen, 1189–1469*, ed. by J. Gairdner, Camden Society, New Series, no. 18 (London, 1876).

Griffith, J. E., *Pedigrees of Anglesey and Caernarvonshire Families* (Horncastle, 1914).

Griffiths, G. Milwyn, 'Glimpses of Denbighshire in the Records of the Court of Great Sessions', *TDHS*, 22 (1973).

Gruffydd, Geraint, 'Humphrey Llwyd of Denbigh: Some Documents and a Catalogue', *TDHS*, 17 (1968).

Gruffydd, Geraint, 'Humphrey Llwyd of Denbigh: Some Documents and a Catalogue', *TDHS*, 18 (1969).

Haddan, A. W., and W. Stubb (eds), *Councils and Ecclesiastical Documents Relating to Great Britain and Ireland*, vol. 1 (Oxford, 1869).

Jack, R. I., 'Records of Denbighshire Lordships: The Lordship of Dyffryn Clwyd in 1324', *TDHS*, 17 (1968).

Jenkins, D. (ed.), *Llyfr Colan, Y Gyfraith Cymreig yn ôl hanner cyntaf Llawysgrif Peniarth 30* (Cardiff, 1963).

Jenkins, Geraint H., Richard Suggett and Eryn M. White, 'The Welsh Language in Early Modern Wales', in Geraint H. Jenkins (ed.), *The Welsh Language Before the Industrial Revolution* (Cardiff, 1997).

Johnston, D. R. (ed.), *Gwaith Iolo Goch* (Cardiff, 1988).

Johnstone, Dafydd (ed. and trans.), *Iolo Goch: Poems* (Llandysul, 1993).

Jones, Arthur (ed.), *Flintshire Ministers' Accounts 1301–1328*, Flintshire Historical Society Publications, vol. 3 (Prestatyn, 1913).

Jones, Elin M. (ed.), *Gwaith Llywarch ap Llywelyn 'Prydydd y Moch'* (Aberystwyth, 1991).

Jones, G. P., 'Rhos and Rhufoniog Pedigrees', *Arch. Camb.*, 80/5, 7th series (1925).

Jones, G. P. (ed.), *The Extent of Chirkland (1391–1393)* (Liverpool, 1933).

Jones, T. Gwynn (ed.), *Gwaith Tudur Aled* (Cardiff, 1926).

Jones, Thomas (ed.), *Brut y Tywysogion*, Peniarth MS 20 version (Cardiff, 1952).

Jones, Thomas (ed.), *Brut y Tywysogion*, Red Book of Hergest version (Cardiff, 1955).

Leland, John, *The Itinerary of Wales of John Leland in or About the Years 1536–1539*, ed. by Lucy Toulmin Smith (London, 1906).

Livingston, Michael, and John K. Bollard (eds), *Owain Glyndŵr: A Casebook* (Liverpool, 2013).

Llwyd, Humphrey, *The Breviary of Britayne ... written in Latin and lately published by Thomas Twyne, Gentleman* (1573).

Llwyd, Humphrey, *Cronica Walliae*, ed. by Ieuan M, Williams (Cardiff, 2002).

Llwyd, Humphrey, *'The Breviary of Britain' with Selections from 'The History of Cambria'*, ed. by Philip Schwyzer (London, 2011).

Luard, R. (ed.), *Matthaei Parisiensis Monachi Sancti Albani Chronica Majora*, Rolls Series (London, 1872–83).

Martin, C. T. (ed.), *Registrum Epistolarum Fratris Johannis Peckham Archiepiscopi Cantuarensis*, 3 vols, Rolls Series (London, 1882–5).

Matthew, H. C. G., and B. H. Harrison (eds), *The Oxford Dictionary of National Biography* (Oxford, 2004, 2008, 2014).

Morgan, Philip (ed.), *Domesday Book, 26: Cheshire* (Chichester, 1978).

Nicholas, H. (ed.), *Proceedings and Ordinances of the Privy Council of England*, 7 vols (London, 1834–7).

Owen, Edward, *A List of those who did Homage and Fealty to the First English Prince of Wales, AD 1301* (privately printed, 1901).

Palgrave, F. (ed.), *Parliamentary Writs and Writs of Military Summons*, 2 vols, Record Commission (London, 1822–34).

Parry, Glyn *A Guide to Records of the Great Session in Wales* (Aberystwyth, 1995).

Parry, Thomas, (ed.), *The Oxford Book of Welsh Verse* (Oxford, 1962).

Pryce, Huw (ed.), *The Acts of Welsh Rulers, 1120–1283* (Cardiff, 2005).

Pugh, T. B. (ed.), *The Marcher Lordships of South Wales, 1415–1536: Select Documents* (Cardiff, 1963).

Rees, William (ed.), *Calendar of Ancient Petitions Relating to Wales* (Cardiff, 1975).

Register of Edward, the Black Prince, 4 vols (London, 1930–3).

Richards, G. M. (trans.) *The Laws of Hywel Dda: The Book of Blegywryd* (Liverpool, 1954).

Richardson, H. G., and G. O. Sayles (eds), *Rotuli Parliamentorum Angliae hactenus inedita*, Camden Society, 3rd series li (London, 1935).

Riley, W. T. (ed.), *Thomas Walsingham, quondam Monachi S. Albani, Historia Anglicana, i, 1272–1381* (London, 1863).

Roberts, Enid (ed.), *Gwaith Siôn Tudur* (Caerdydd, 1978).

Roberts, Thomas (ed.), *Gwaith Tudur Penllyn ac Ieuan ap Tudur Penllyn* (Cardiff, 1958).

Rothwell, H. (ed.), *The Chronicle of Walter of Guisborough*, Camden Society, 3rd series (London, 1957).

Rowlands, Eurys I. (ed.), *Gwaith Lewys Môn* (Caerdydd, 1975).

Rymer, Thomas, *Foedera, conventiones, litterae, et euiuscunque generis acta publica*, 4 vols (London, 1816–69).

Smith, W. J. (ed.), *Calendar of Salusbury Correspondence 1553–circa 1700* (Cardiff, 1954).

Siddons, Michael P. (ed.) *Welsh Genealogies, AD 1500–1600* (Aberystwyth, 2017).

Speed, John, *The Theatre of the Empire of Great Britain* (1610).

Statutes of the Realm, 11 vols (London, 1810–28).

Stubbs, W. (ed.), *Chronicles of the Reigns of Edward I and Edward II*, vol. 2, Rolls Series (London, 1882).

Stubbs, W., *The Constitutional History of England in its Origin and Development*, vol. 1 (Oxford, 1897).

Thompson, E. M. (ed.), *Chronicon Galfridi le Baker de Swynebroke* (Oxford, 1889).

Thompson, E. M. (ed.), *Chronicon Adae de Usk, A.D. 1377–1421*, 2nd edn (London, 1904).

Trivet, Nicholas, *Annales sex regum Angliae … 1135–1307*, ed. by T. Hog (London, 1945).

Vinogradoff, P., and Morgan, F. (eds), *Survey of the Honour of Denbigh* (London, 1914).

Williams, Ifor, and J. Llywelyn Williams *Gwaith Guto'r Glyn*, 2nd edn (Cardiff,1969).

Williams-Jones, Keith, *The Merioneth Lay Subsidy Roll 1292–3* (Cardiff, 1976).

Wynn, Sir John, *The History of the Gwydir Family and Memoirs*, ed. by J. Gwynfor Jones (Llandysul, 1990).

Primary sources: online

DWB, *Welsh Biography Online*, Robert ap Rhys, Dr Elis Prys, Tomos Prys.

Secondary sources

Aaron, Jane, and Prescott, Sarah, *The Oxford Literary History of Wales, volume 3: Welsh Writing in English, 1536–1914* (Oxford, 2020).

Adams, S. L., 'The Gentry of North Wales and the Earl of Leicester's Expedition to the Netherlands, 1585–1586', *WHR*, 7/2 (December 1974).

Adams, S. L., 'Military Obligations of Leasehold Tenants in Leicesterian Denbigh: A Footnote', *TDHS*, 24 (1975).

Adams, S. L, 'The Composition of 1564 and the Earl of Lancaster's Reformation in the Lordship of Denbigh', *BBCS*, 26/4 (May 1976).

Adams, S. L, 'Office-holders of the Borough of Denbigh and the Stewards of the Lordships of Denbigh in the Reign of Elizabeth I', *TDHS*, 25 (1976).

Altschul, M., *A Baronial Family in Medieval England: The Clares, 1217–1314* (Baltimore MD, 1965).

Bailey, Mark, *After the Black Death: Economy, Society and the Law in Fourteenth-Century England* (Oxford, 2021).

Baker, A. R. H., and R. A. Butlin (eds), *Studies of Field Systems in the British Isles* (London, 1973).

Baldwin, J. F., 'The Household Administration of Henry Lacy and Thomas Lancaster', *EHR*, 42 (1927).

Ball, D. F., *Memoirs of the Soil Survey of Great Britain: The Soils and Land Use of the District around Rhyl and Denbigh* (London, 1960).

Barrell, A. D. M., and R. R. Davies, 'Land, Lineage and Revolt in North-East Wales, 1243–1441: A Case Study', *CMCS*, 29 (1995).

Barrell, A. D. M., and M. H. Brown, 'A Settler Community in Post-Conquest Rural Wales: The English of Dyffryn Clwyd, 1294–1399', *WHR*, 17/3 (June 1995).

Bartrum, P. C., 'Pedigrees of the Welsh Tribal Patriarchs', *NLW Journal*, 13 (1963–4).

Bean, J. M. W., *The Estates of the Percy family, 1416–1537* (London, 1958).

Bean, J. M. W., 'Henry IV and the Percies', *History*, 44 (1959).

Bell, Adrian R., and Anne Curry, with Adam Chapman, Andy Knight and David Simkins (eds), *The Soldier Experience in the Fourteenth Century* (Woodbridge, 2011).

Beresford, M. W., *New Towns of the Middle Ages: Town Plantation in England, Wales and Gascony* (Gloucester, 1967).

Booth, P. H. W., *The Financial Administration of the Lordship and County of Chester, 1272–1377* (Manchester, 1981).

Bowen, D. J., *Gruffudd Hiraethog a'i oes* (Caerdydd, 1958).

Bowen, D. J. (ed.), *Gwaith Gruffudd Hiraethog* (Cardiff, 1990).

Bowen, D. J., 'Beirdd a noddwyr y bedwaredd ganrif ar ddeg', *LlC*, 17 (1992).

Bowen, D. J., 'Beirdd a noddwyr y bymthegfed ganrif', *LlC*, 18–20 (1994–6).

Bowen, D. J., and Cledwyn Fychan, 'Cywydd gofyn Gruffudd Hiraethog', *TDHS*, 24, (1975).

Bowen E. G. (ed.), *Wales: A Physical, Historical and Regional Geography* (London, 1956).

Bowen, Geraint, *Y Traddodiad Rhyddiaith, Darlithiau Rhydychen* (Llandysul, 1970).

Bowen, Lloyd, *Early Modern Wales, c. 1536–c.1689* (Cardiff, 2022).

Bowsky, W. M. (ed.), *Studies in Medieval and Renaissance History*, vol. 2 (Lincoln NE, 1995).

Bradshaw, Brendan, and Peter R. Roberts (eds), *British Consciousness and Identity: The Making of Britain,1533–1707* (Cambridge, 1998).

Brooks, Simon, *Hanes Cymry, Lleiafrifoedd Ethnig a'r Gwareiddiad Cymraeg* (Cardiff, 2021).

Brough, G., *The Rise and Fall of Owain Glyndwr: England, France and the Welsh Rebellion in the Late Middle Ages* (London, 2017).
Browne, D., and Hughes, S. (eds), *The Archaeology of the Welsh Uplands* (Aberystwyth, 2003).
Burdett-Jones, Mary, 'Humphrey Foulkes: uchelgais heb ei gyflawni', *Y Traethodydd* (Ionawr, 2009).
Burdett-Jones, Mary, 'Humphrey Foulkes's Building the Palace, Dr Humphrey Foulkes's Attempt to Continue Edward Lhuyd's work', *TDHS*, 58 (2010).
Burnham, Helen, *A Guide to Ancient and Historic Wales, Clwyd and Powys* (London, 1995).
Burton, Janet, and Karen Stöber (eds), *The Abbeys and Priories of Medieval Wales* (Cardiff, 2015).
Burtscher, Michael, *The Fitzalans: Earls of Arundel and Surrey, Lords of the Welsh Marches (1267–1415)* (Logaston, 2011).
Butler, L. A. S., *Denbigh Castle: Town Walls ... Denbigh Friary* (Cardiff, 2007).
Carr, A. D., 'The Barons of Edeyrnion 1282–1485', *JMHRS*, 4 (1963–4).
Carr, A. D., 'Medieval Dinmael', *TDHS*, 13 (1964).
Carr, A. D. 'Welshmen and the Hundred Years War', *WHR*, 4 (1968).
Carr, A. D., 'An Aristocracy in Decline: The Native Welsh Lords After the Edwardian Conquest', *WHR*, 5 (1970).
Carr, A. D., 'Rhys ap Roppert', *TDHS*, 25 (1976).
Carr, A. D., 'The Last Days of Gwynedd', *TCHS*, 43 (1982).
Carr, A. D., 'Prydydd y Moch: ymateb hanesydd', *THSC* (1989).
Carr, A. D., *Owen of Wales: The End of the House of Gwynedd* (Cardiff, 1991).
Carr, A. D., 'The Medieval *Cantref* of Rhos', *TDHS*, 41 (1992).
Carr, A. D., *The Gentry of North Wales in the Later Middle Ages* (Cardiff, 2017).
Cathcart-King, D. J., *The Castle in England and Wales: An Interpretive History* (London, 1988).
Chaplais, Pierre, *Piers Gaveston, Edward II's Adoptive Brother* (Oxford, 1994).
Chapman, Adam, 'Rebels, Uchelwyr and Parvenus: Welsh Knights in the Fourteenth Century', in Adrian R. Bell and Anne Curry, with Adam Chapman, Andy Knight and David Simkins (eds), *The Soldier Experience in the Fourteenth Century* (Woodbridge, 2011).

Chapman, Adam, *Welsh Soldiers in the Later Middle Ages 1282–1422* (Woodbridge, 2015).

Chapman, T. Robin, and Bleddyn Owen Huws, *Penrhaith ein heniaith ni: Cyfrol Deyrnged Gruffydd Aled Williams* (Llanfihangel Genau'r Glyn, 2023).

Charles-Edwards T. M., *Early Irish and Welsh Kinship* (Oxford, 1993).

Charles-Edwards T. M., *Wales and the Britons, 350–1064*, (Oxford, 2014).

Charles-Edwards, T. M., and R. J. W. Evans (eds), *Wales and the Wider World: Welsh History in an International Context* (Donington, 2010).

Charles-Edwards, T. M., M. E. Owen and P. Russell (eds), *The Welsh King and His Court* (Cardiff, 2000).

Chrimes, S. B., *An Introduction to the Administrative History of Medieval England* (Oxford, 1952).

Chrimes, S. B., *Lancastrians, Yorkists and Henry VII* (London, 1964).

Chrimes, S. B., C. D. Ross and R. A. Griffiths, *Fifteenth-Century England 1399–1509: Studies in Politics and Society* (Manchester, 1972).

Colvin, H. M., *The History of the King's Works, volume 1: The Middle Ages* (London, 1963).

Davies, Ceri, *Latin Writers of the Renaissance* (Cardiff, 1981).

Davies, Elwyn, 'Hendre and Hafod in Denbighsire', *TDHS*, 26 (1977).

Davies, J. Conway, *The Baronial Opposition to Edward II* (Cambridge, 1914).

Davies, J. Conway, 'Felony in Edwardian Wales', *TCHS* (1916–17).

Davies, R. R., 'The Twilight of Welsh Law, 1284–1536', *History*, 51 (June 1966).

Davies, R. R., 'Owain Glyn Dŵr and the Welsh Squirearchy', *THSC* (1968).

Davies, R. R., 'Colonial Wales', *Past and Present*, 65 (1974).

Davies, R. R., 'Race Relations in Post-Conquest Wales: Confrontation and Compromise', *THSC* (1974–5).

Davies, R. R., *Lordship and Society in the March of Wales 1284–1400* (Oxford, 1978).

Davies, R. R., 'Buchedd a moes y Cymry', *WHR*, 12 (December 1984).

Davies, R. R., 'Dinbych yn oes Owain Glyndŵr', *TDHS*, 43 (1984).

Davies, R. R., 'The Administration of Law in Medieval Wales: The Role of the *Ynad Cwmwd (Judex Patriae)*', in T. M. Charles-Edwards, Morfydd E. Owen and D. B. Walters (eds) *Lawyers and Laymen: Studies in the History of Law presented to Professor Dafydd Jenkins on his Seventy-Fifth Birthday* (Cardiff, 1986).

Davies, R. R., *The Revolt of Owain Glyn Dŵr* (Oxford, 1995).

Davies, R. R., *The Age of Conquest: Wales, 1063–1415* (Oxford, 2000) [published originally as *Conquest, Coexistence and Change: Wales 1063–1415* (Oxford, 1987)].

Davies, R. R., 'Roger Mortimer, First Earl of March (1287–1330): Regent, Soldier and Magnate', in H. C. G. Matthew and B. H. Harrison (eds), *The Oxford Dictionary of National Biography* (Oxford, 2008).

Davies, R. R., 'Roger Mortimer, Second Earl of March (1328–1360) Magnate', in H. C. G. Matthew and B. H. Harrison (eds), *The Oxford Dictionary of National Biography* (Oxford, 2008).

Davies, R. R., and Geraint H. Jenkins (eds), *From Medieval to Modern: Historical Essays in Honour of Kenneth O. Morgan and Ralph A. Griffiths* (Cardiff, 2004).

Davies, Sean, 'The Teulu, c. 633–1283', *WHR*, 21 (2003).

Davies, Sean, *War and Society in Medieval Wales, 633–1283: Welsh Military Institutions* (Cardiff, 2014).

Davies, Wendy, *Wales in the Early Middle Ages* (Leicester, 1982).

Denholm-Young, N., *Seignorial Administration in England* (London, 1937).

Dodd, A. H., 'North Wales in the Essex revolt of 1601', *EHR*, 59 (1944).

Dodd, G., and D. Biggs (eds), *The Reign of Henry IV: Rebellion and Survival, 1403–1413* (Woodbridge, 2008).

Dodd, G., H. Lacey and A. Musson (eds), *People, Power and Identity in the Late Middle Ages: Essays in Memory of W. Mark Ormrod* (London, 2021).

Douch, R., 'The Career, Lands and Family of William Montagu, Earl of Salisbury, 1301–44', *Bulletin of the Institute of Historical Research*, 24/12 (May 1951).

Dryburgh, Paul, and Philip Hume (eds), *The Mortimers of Wigmore, 1066–1485: Dynasty of Destiny* (Eardisley, 2023).

Du Boulay, F. R. H., *The Lordship of Canterbury: An Essay on Medieval Society* (London, 1966).

Dunn, A., *The Politics of Magnate Power: England and Wales, 1389–1413* (Oxford, 2008).

Edgar, Iwan Rhys, 'William Salesbury: Cipolwg ar y dyn, ei feddwl a'i ddylanwad', *LlC*, 33 (2010), 61–79.

Edwards, J. Goronwy, 'Sir Gruffydd Llwyd', *EHR*, 30 (1915).

Edwards, J. Goronwy, 'Note on the Boundaries of Medieval Flintshire', in *Flint Pleas, 1283–1285, Flintshire Historical Society Publications*, 8 (1922).

Edwards, J. Goronwy, 'The Battle of Maes Madog and the Welsh War of 1294–5', *EHR*, 39 (1924).

Edwards, J. Goronwy, 'Edward I's Castle Building in Wales', *Proceedings of the British Academy*, 32 (1946).

Edwards, J. Goronwy, 'The Normans and the Welsh March', *Proceedings of the British Academy*, 42 (1956).

Edwards, J. Goronwy, *The Principality of Wales, 1267–1967: A Study in Constitutional History* (Caernarfon, 1969).

Edwards, Nancy (ed.), *Landscape and Settlement in Medieval Wales* (Oxford, 1997).

Ellis, T. P., 'The English Element in the Perfeddwlad', *Y Cymmrodor*, 35 (1925).

Ellis, T. P., *Welsh Tribal Law and Custom in the Middle Ages*, vol. 1 (Oxford, 1926).

Evans, Brian, 'Owain Glyn Dŵr's raid on Ruthin', *TDHS*, 49 (2000).

Evans, D. L., 'Some Notes on the History of the Principality in the Time of the Black Prince, 1343–76', *THSC* (1925–6).

Evans, D. S., (ed.), *Historia Gruffud vab Kenan* (Cardiff, 1977).

Evans, D. W, and Brynley. F. Roberts (eds), *Edward Lhwyd: Archaeologia Britannica, Texts and Translations* (Aberystwyth, 2008).

Evans, E. D., 'The Crown Lordships of Denbighshire, Part 1', *TDHS*, 50 (2001).

Evans, Gareth, and Arnold Hughes (eds), *The History of Ruthin* (Ruthin, 2014).

Evans, Geraint, 'Tudor London and the Origins of Welsh Writing in English', in Geraint Evans and Helen Fulton (eds), *The Cambridge History of Welsh Literature* (Cambridge, 2019).

Evans, Geraint, and Fulton, Helen (eds), *The Cambridge History of Welsh Literature* (Cambridge, 2019).

Evans, H. T., *Wales and the Wars of the Roses* (Stroud, 1998 [1915]).
Evans, J. Wyn, 'The Early Church in Denbighshire', *TDHS*, 35 (1986).
Evans, W. A., 'The Salusburies of Lleweni and the Carmelite friary in Denbigh' *TDHS*, 4 (1955).
Evans, W. A., 'The Four John Salusburys of Lleweni in the Sixteenth Century', *TDHS*, 12 (1963).
Fasti Ecclesiae Anglicanae 1300–1541: The Welsh Dioceses (London 1965).
Fielding, Susan, 'The Shire Hall, Denbigh', *Arch. Camb.*, 166 (2017).
Fox, Robin, *Kinship and Marriage* (Harmondsworth, 1967).
Fryde, Natalie, 'Welsh Troops in the Scottish Campaign of 1322', *BBCS*, 26 (1974).
Fryde, Natalie, *The Tyranny and Fall of Edward II, 1322–1326* (Cambridge, 1976).
Fulton, Helen, 'Owain Glyndŵr and the uses of prophecy', *SC*, 39, (2005).
Fulton, Helen, 'Owain Glyndŵr and the prophetic tradition', in Michael Livingston and John K. Bollard (eds), *Owain Glyndŵr: A Casebook* (Liverpool, 2013).
Fulton, Helen (ed.), *Urban Culture in Medieval Wales* (Cardiff, 2012).
Fychan, Cledwyn, 'William Salesbury a Llansannan', *TDHS*, 25 (1976).
Fychan, Cledwyn, 'Lewys Aled; Wiliam Byrcinsha', *TDHS*, 26 (1977).
Fychan, Cledwyn, 'Y canu i wŷr eglwysig gorllewin sir Ddinbych', *TDHS*, 28 (1979).
Fychan, Cledwyn, 'Tudur Aled: ailystyried ei gynefin', *NLW Journal*, 33 (1983–4).
Fychan, Cledwyn, 'Bleddyn Fychan a Gwrthryfel Madog ap Llywelyn, 1294–5', *TDHS*, 49 (2000).
Gardner, W., and H. N. Savory, *Dinorben: A Hill Fort Occupied in Early Iron Age and Roman Times* (Cardiff, 1964).
Giles, J. A. (ed.), *Incerti Scriptoria Chronicon Angliae* (London, 1848).

Given, J. B., *State and Society in Medieval Europe: Gwynedd and Languedoc under Outside Rule* (Ithaca NY, 1990).
Given-Wilson, Chris (ed. and trans.), *Chronicle of Adam of Usk, 1377–1421* (Oxford, 1977).

Given-Wilson, Chris, *The English Nobility in the Late Middle Ages* (London, 1987).
Given-Wilson, Chris, 'Chronicles of the Mortimer family, c. 1250–1450', in Richard Eales and Shaun Tyas (eds), *Family and Dynasty in Late-Medieval England: Proceedings of the 1997 Harlaxton Symposium* (Donington, 2003).
Given-Wilson, Chris, *Henry IV* (London, 2016).
Goodall, J. A. A., 'The Baronial Castles of the Welsh Conquest', in D. M. Williams and J. R. Kenyon, *The Impact of the Edwardian Castles in Wales* (Oxford, 2010).
Goodman, A., 'Owain Glyn Dŵr before 1400', *WHR*, 5/1 (1970–1).
Goody, Jack, Joan Thirsk and E. P. Thompson (eds), *Family and Inheritance: Rural Society in Western Europe, 1200–1800* (Cambridge, 1976).
Gresham, Colin A., 'The Aberconway Charter', *Arch. Camb.*, 94 (1939).
Gresham, Colin A., *Eifionydd* (Cardiff, 1973).
Gresham, Colin A., *Medieval Stone Carving in North Wales* (Cardiff, 1968).
Gresham, Colin A., 'The Aberconway Charter: Further Consideration', *BBCS*, 30 (1982–3).
Gresham, Colin A., W. J. Hemp and F. R. Thompson, 'Hen Ddinbych', *Arch. Camb.*, 108 (1959).
Griffiths, John, 'The Revolt of Madog ap Llywelyn, 1294–5', *TCHS*, 18 (1955).
Griffiths, Milwyn, 'Denbighshire in the Records of the Court of Great Sessions', *TDHS*, 22 (1973).
Griffiths, Ralph A., 'The Revolt of Rhys ap Maredudd, 1287–88', *WHR*, 3 (1966).
Griffiths, Ralph A., 'Wales and the Marches', in S. B. Chrimes, C. D. Ross and R. A. Griffiths, *Fifteenth-Century England 1399–1509: Studies in Politics and Society* (Manchester, 1972).
Griffiths, Ralph A., 'Richard, Duke of York and the Royal Household in Wales, 1449–1550', *WHR*, 8/1 (June 1976).
Griffiths, Ralph A. (ed.), *Boroughs of Mediaeval Wales* (Cardiff, 1978).
Griffiths, Ralph A., *The Reign of King Henry VI* (London, 1981).
Griffiths, Ralph A., *Conquerors and Conquered in Medieval Wales* (Stroud, 1995).

Griffiths, Ralph A., 'Edmund Mortimer, Fifth Earl of March and Seventh Earl of Ulster (1391–1425)', in *Oxford Dictionary of National Biography* (Oxford, 2008).

Griffiths, Ralph A., 'An Immigrant Elite in the Later Middle Ages: Locating the de Parys Family in North Wales and Chester', *WHR*, 25 (2012).

Griffiths, Ralph A., 'Herbert, William, First Earl of Pembroke (c. 1423–1469)', in *Oxford Dictionary of National Biography* (Oxford, 2014).

Griffiths, Ralph A., 'Patronage, politics and the principality of Wales 1413–1461', in H. Hearder and H. R. Loyn (eds), *British Government and Administration: Studies Presented to S. B. Chrimes* (Cardiff, 2018).

Griffiths, Ralph A., *The Principality of Wales in the Later Middle Ages: The Structure and Personnel of Government, volume 1: South Wales 1277–1536* (Cardiff, 2018).

Griffiths, Ralph A., and Thomas, Roger S., *The Making of the Tudor Dynasty* (Stroud, 1985).

Griffiths, Ralph A., and P. R. Schofield (eds), *Wales and the Welsh in the Middle Ages* (Cardiff, 2011).

Griffiths, W. R. M. 'Prince Henry', *BBCS*, 32 (1985).

Griffiths, W. R. M., 'Prince Henry's War', *BBCS*, 34, (1987).

Gruffydd, Geraint, *Y Ffordd Gadarn, ysgrifau ar ffydd a chrefydd* (Pen-y-bont, 2008).

Gruffydd, R. Geraint, 'William Morgan', in Geraint Bowen, *Y Traddodiad Rhyddiaith, Darlithiau Rhydychen* (Llandysul, 1970).

Guy, Ben, *Medieval Welsh Genealogy: An Introduction and Textual Study* (Woodbridge, 2020).

Hamilton, J. S., *Piers Gaveston, Earl of Cornwall, 1307–1312: Politics and Patronage in the Reign of Edward II* (London, 1988).

Hays, R. W., *The History of the Abbey of Aberconwy, 1186–1537* (Cardiff, 1963).

Hearder, H., and H. R. Loyn (eds), *British Government and Administration: Studies Presented to S. B. Chrimes* (Cardiff, 2018 [1974]).

Heaton, E. R., *The Heatons of Deane: The Varying Fortunes of a Lancashire Family Over 850 Years* (Aberystwyth, 2000).

de Hemmeon, M. W., *Burgage Tenure in Medieval England* (Harvard, 1914).

Hemp, W. J., 'Denbigh Castle', *Y Cymmrodor*, 36 (1925).
Hewitt, H. J., *The Black Prince's Expedition, 1355–57* (Barnsley, 2004).
Hewitt, H. J., *The Organisation of War in the Reign of Edward III, 1338–62* (Barnsley, 2005).
Henken, Elissa R., *National Redeemer: Owain Glyndŵr in Welsh Tradition* (Cardiff, 1996).
Hicks, Michael, *The Wars of the Roses* (New Haven CT, 2012).
Hilton, R. H., *Ministers' Accounts of the Warwickshire Estates of the Duke of Clarence* (Oxford, 1952).
Hilton, R. H., *Bond Men Made Free: Medieval Peasant Movements and the English Rising of 1381* (London, 2003).
Hislop, Malcolm, *Master James of St George: And the Castles of the Welsh Wars* (Barnsley, 2020).
Holmes, G. A., *The Estates of the Higher Nobility in Fourteenth-Century England* (Cambridge, 1957).
Holmes, G. A., 'Edmund Mortimer, Third Earl of March and Earl of Ulster (1352–1381)', *Oxford Dictionary of National Biography* (Oxford, 2004).
Hume, Philip, *The Welsh Marcher Lordships, vol. I: Central and North* (Eardisley, 2021).
Hume, Philip, *On the Trail of the Mortimers in the Welsh Marches* (Eardisley, 2022).
Hopkinson, Charles, and Martin Speight, *The Mortimers, Lords of the March* (Logaston, 2002).
Howard, Sharon, *Law and Disorder in Early Modern Wales* (Cardiff, 2008).
Howe, G. M., *Wales From the Air: A Survey of the Physical and Cultural Landscape* (Cardiff, 1957).
Hubbard, E., *The Buildings of Wales: Clwyd* (Harmondsworth, 1986).
Insley, Charles, 'Fact and Fiction in Thirteenth-Century Gwynedd', *SC*, 33 (1999).
Insley, Charles, 'Welsh and English in the Medieval Lordship of Ruthin', *TDHS*, 18 (1969).
Insley, Charles, 'Ruthin', in R. A. Griffiths (ed.), *Boroughs of Mediaeval Wales* (Cardiff, 1978).
Insley, Charles, 'The Cloth Industry in Medieval Ruthin', *WHR*, 10 (1980).

Insley, Charles 'Fulling Mills in Wales', *Arch. Camb.*, 130 (1981).
Jack, R. I., 'Glyn Dŵr and the Lordship of Ruthin', *WHR*, 2 (1965).
Jacob, E. F., *The Fifteenth Century, 1399–1485* (Oxford, 1961).
Jarman, A.O. H., and G. Hughes, *A Guide to Welsh Literature*, vol. 2 (Cardiff, 1992).
Jenkins, Dafydd, 'A Lawyer Looks at Welsh Land Law', *THSC* (1967).
Jenkins, Dafydd, *Celtic Law Papers* (Brussels, 1973).
Jenkins, Dafydd, 'Law and Government in Wales before the Acts of Union', in Dafydd Jenkins, *Celtic Law Papers* (Brussels, 1973).
Jenkins, Dafydd, *Hywel Dda: The Law* (Llandysul, 1986).
Jenkins, Geraint H. (ed.), *The Welsh Language Before the Industrial Revolution* (Cardiff, 1997).
Jenkins, Philip, *A History of Modern Wales, 1536–1990* (London, 1992).
Johnston, Dafydd, *Gwaith Iolo Goch* (Caerdydd, 1988).
Johnston, Dafydd, *Iolo Goch* (Caernarfon, 1989).
Johnston, Dafydd, *Llên yr Uchelwyr: Hanes Beirniadol Llenyddiaeth Cymraeg, 1300–1525* (Cardiff, 2005).
Johnstone, Neil, 'An Investigation into the Location of the Royal Courts of Thirteenth-Century Gwynedd', in Nancy Edwards (ed.), *Landscape and Settlement in Medieval Wales* (Oxford, 1997).
Jones, Craig Owen, *Llywelyn Bren* (Llanrwst, 2006).
Jones, Craig Owen, *The Revolt of Madog ap Llywelyn* (Pwllheli, 2008).
Jones, Francis, 'Welsh Bonds for Keeping the Peace, 1283 and 1295', *BBCS*, 13 (1950).
Jones, Francis, 'The Heraldry of Gwynedd', *TCHS*, 24 (1963).
Jones, Frank Price, *Crwydro Gorllewin Dinbych* (Llandybie, 1969).
Jones, Gareth Elwyn, *The Gentry and the Elizabethan State* (Swansea, 1977).
Jones, G. R. J., 'The Tribal System in Wales: A Reassessment in the Light of Settlement Studies', *WHR*, 1 (1961).
Jones, G. R. J., 'The Distribution of Bond Settlements in North-West Wales', *WHR*, 2/1 (1964).
Jones, G. R. J., 'The Defences of Gwynedd in the Thirteenth Century', *TCHS*, 30 (1969).

Jones, G. R. J., 'Post-Roman Wales', in H. P. R. Finberg (ed.), *The Agrarian History of England and Wales, volume 1, part 2, AD 45–1042* (Cambridge, 1972).

Jones, J. Gwynfor (ed.), 'The Welsh Poets and their Patrons', *WHR*, 9/1 (June 1979).

Jones, J. Gwynfor, 'Patrymau bonheddig uchelwrol yn sir Ddinbych, c.1540–1640: dehongliad y beirdd', *TDHS*, 29 (1980).

Jones, J. Gwynfor, *Class, Community and Culture in Tudor Wales* (Cardiff, 1989).

Jones, J. Gwynfor, *Early Modern Wales, c.1525–1640* (Basingstoke, 1994).

Jones, J. Gwynfor, *The Wynn Family of Gwydir: Origins, Growth and Development, c.1490–1674* (Aberystwyth, 1995).

Jones, R. Brinley, *William Salesbury* (Cardiff, 1994).

Jones, R. Brinley, 'Humphrey Llwyd (1527–1568)', in *Oxford Dictionary of National Biography* (Oxford, 2004).

Jones, Robin Gwyndaf, 'Sir Richard Clough of Denbigh, *c.* 1530–1570, Part 1', *TDHS*, 19 (1970).

Jones, Robin Gwyndaf, 'Sir Richard Clough of Denbigh, *c.* 1530–1570, Part 2', *TDHS*, 19 (1971).

Jones, Robin Gwyndaf, 'Sir Richard Clough of Denbigh, *c.* 1530–1570, Part 3', *TDHS*, 19 (1973).

Kenyon, John R., and Richard Avent (eds), *Castles in Wales and the Marches: Essays in Honour of D. J. Cathcart-King* (Cardiff, 1987).

Kenyon, John R., *The Medieval Castles of Wales* (Cardiff, 2010).

Korngiebel, Diane M., 'English Colonial Ethnic Discrimination in the Lordship of Dyffryn Clwyd: Segregation and Integration, 1282–c.1340', *WHR*, 23/2 (December 2006).

Langley, David, 'The Royal Courts of the Welsh Princes in Gwynedd', in Nancy Edwards (ed.), *Landscape and Settlement in Medieval Wales* (Oxford, 1997).

Lewis, Ceri W., 'The Treaty of Woodstock, 1247: Its Background and Significance', *WHR*, 2 (1964–5).

Lewis, E. A., *The Mediaeval Boroughs of Snowdonia* (London, 1912).

Lieberman, M., *The March of Wales, 1067–1300* (Cardiff, 2008).

Lieberman, M., *The Medieval March of Wales* (Cambridge, 2010).

Lloyd, J. E., 'Who was Gwenllian de Lacy?', *Arch. Camb.*, 6/19 (1919).
Lloyd, J. E., 'The Mother of Gruffudd ap Llywelyn', *BBCS*, 1/4 (1923).
Lloyd, J. E., *Owen Glendower* (Oxford, 1931).
Lloyd, J. E., *A History of Wales from the Earliest Times to the Edwardian Conquest*, vol. 2 (London, 1939).
Lloyd, J. Y. W., *History of Powys Fadog*, vol. 4 (London, 1884).
Lloyd, J. Y. W., *History of Powys Fadog*, vol. 5 (London, 1885)
Lockyer, Roger, and Gaunt, Peter, *Tudor and Stuart Britain, 1485–1714* (London, 2018).
Lord, Peter, *The Visual Culture of Wales: Medieval Vision* (Cardiff, 2003).
Lynch, Frances, 'Prehistoric Funerary and Ritual Sites in Denbighshire and East Conwy', *TDHS*, 51 (2002).
Lynch, Peredur, 'Court Poetry, Power and Politics', in T. M. Charles-Edwards, M. E. Owen and P. Russell (eds), *The Welsh King and His Court* (Cardiff, 2000).
Maddicott, J. R., *Thomas of Lancaster, 1307–1322: A study in the Reign of Edward II* (Oxford, 1970).
Maddicott, J. R., 'The English Peasantry and the Demands of the Crown, 1294–1341', *Past and Present Society*, 1 (1975).
Mathias, W. A., 'William Salesbury, ei fywyd a'i waith', in Geraint Bowen, *Y Traddodiad Rhyddiaith, Darlithiau Rhydychen* (Llandysul, 1970).
Matthews, E. Gwynn, '"Colofn dysg": Humphrey Lhwyd o Ddinbych', in E. Gwynn Matthews, *Genefa, Paris a Sir Ddinbych ac ysgrifau eraill* (Tal-y-bont, 2019).
Matthews, E. Gwynn, *Genefa, Paris a Sir Ddinbych ac ysgrifau eraill* (Tal-y-bont, 2019).
Matthews, E. Gwynn, 'Y Gair yn y Llan, William Salesbury ac Addoliad yr Eglwys', in E. Gwynn Matthews, *Genefa, Paris a Sir Ddinbych ac ysgrifau eraill* (Tal-y-bont, 2019).
Maund, K. L., *Ireland, Wales and England in the Eleventh Century* (Woodbridge, 1991).
Maund, K. L., *The Welsh Kings* (Stroud, 2006).
McKisack, M., *The Fourteenth Century, 1307–1399*, (Oxford, 1959).

Messham, J. E., 'The County of Flint and the Rebellion of Owen Glyndŵr in the Records of the Earldom of Chester', *Journal of the Flintshire Historical Society*, 23 (1967–8).

Miller, Edward (ed.), *The Agrarian History of England and Wales, volume 3: 1348–1500* (Cambridge, 1991).

Morgan, P. J., *War and Society in Late Medieval Cheshire, 1277–1403* (Manchester, 1987).

Morgan, Prys, 'Wild Wales: Civilizing the Welsh from the Sixteenth to the Nineteenth Centuries', in Peter Burke, Brian Harrison and Paul Slack (eds), *Civil Histories: Essays Presented to Sir Keith Thomas* (Oxford, 2000).

Morgan, R. 'The Barony of Powys, 1275–1360', *WHR*, 10/1 (1980).

Morrice, J. C. (ed.), *Barddoniaeth Wiliam Llŷn* (Bangor, 1908).

Morris, J. E., *The Welsh Wars of Edward I* (Oxford, 1901; Stroud, 1998).

Mortimer, I., *The Perfect King: The Life of Edward III, Father of the English Nation* (London, 2008).

Mortimer, I., *The Greatest Traitor: The Life of Sir Roger Mortimer, Ruler of England, 1327–1330* (London, 2010).

Newcombe, Richard, *An Account of the Castle and Town of Denbigh* (Denbigh, 1829).

Ormerod, G., *The History of the County Palatine and City of Chester*, 3 vols (London, 1875–82).

Ormrod, W. Mark, *Edward III* (New Haven CT, 2011).

Otway-Ruthven, A. J., *A History of Medieval Ireland* (London, 1980).

Owen, D. Huw, 'Tenurial and Economic Developments in North Wales in the Twelfth and Thirteenth Centuries', *WHR*, 6 (December 1972).

Owen, D. Huw, 'Treth and Ardreth: Some Aspects of Commutation in North Wales in the Thirteenth Century', *BBCS*, 25/4 (May 1974).

Owen, D. Huw, 'The Englishry of Denbigh: An English Colony in Medieval Wales', *THSC* (1974–5).

Owen, D. Huw, 'Denbigh', in Ralph A. Griffiths (eds), *Boroughs of Mediaeval Wales* (Cardiff, 1978).

Owen, D. Huw (ed.), *Settlement and Society in Wales* (Cardiff, 1989).

Owen, D. Huw, 'The Middle Ages', in D. Huw Owen (ed.), *Settlement and Society in Wales* (Cardiff, 1989).

Owen, D. Huw, 'Rural Life in Medieval Wales', *Studia Celtica Japonica*, 5 (December 1992).

Owen, D. Huw, 'Clans and Gentry Families in the Vale of Clwyd', in R. A. Griffiths and P. R. Schofield (eds), *Wales and the Welsh in the Middle Ages* (Cardiff, 2011).

Owen, D. Huw, and J. Beverley Smith, 'Government and Society 1283–1536', in J. Beverley Smith and Llinos Beverley Smith (eds), *History of Merioneth, volume 2: The Middle Ages* (Cardiff, 2001).

Owen, G. D., *Elizabethan Wales: The Social Scene* (Cardiff, 1964).

Owen, Nicholas, 'Memoirs of the Life of Edward Lhuyd', in *British Remains* (London, 1777).

Owen, R. M., 'The Street Names of Denbigh', *TDHS*, 28 (1979).

Owen, R. M., 'The Street Names of Denbigh, Part II', *TDHS*, 29, (1980).

Owen, R. M., 'The Street Names of Denbigh, Part III', *TDHS*, 29, (1981).

Palmer, A. N., and E. Owen, *A History of Ancient Tenures of Land in North Wales and the Marches* (printed privately, 1910).

Parry, Thomas, *A History of Welsh Literature*, trans. by H. Idris Bell (Oxford, 1955).

Parry, Thomas, *Hanes Llenyddiaeth Gymraeg hyd 1900* (Caerdydd, 1979).

Phillips, J. R. S., 'When Did Owain Glyndwr Die?', *BBCS*, 24 (1970).

Phillips, J. R. S., *Aymer de Valence, Earl of Pembroke, 1307–1324: Baronial Politics in the Reign of Edward II* (Oxford, 1972).

Phillips, J. R. S., *Edward II* (London, 2011).

Phillips, J. R. S., 'Some Afterthoughts on Edward II', in G. Dodd, H. Lacey and A. Musson (eds), *People, Power and Identity in the Late Middle Ages: Essays in Memory of W. Mark Ormrod* (London, 2021).

Pierce, J., *The Life and Work of William Salesbury: Rare Scholar* (Tal-y-bont, 2016).

Pierce, T. Jones, *Medieval Welsh Society*, ed. by J. Beverley Smith (Cardiff, 1972).

Pierce, T. Jones, 'The Growth of Commutation in Gwynedd During the Thirteenth Century', in T. Jones Pierce, *Medieval Welsh Society*, ed. by J. Beverley Smith (Cardiff, 1972).

Pierce, T. Jones, 'The "Gafael" in Bangor MS 1939', in T. Jones Pierce, *Medieval Welsh Society*, ed. by J. Beverley Smith (Cardiff, 1972).
Postan, M. M., *Medieval Trade and Finance* (Cambridge, 1973).
Powicke, F. M., *King Henry III and the Lord Edward* (Oxford, 1947).
Pratt, D., 'Bromfield and Yale in English Politics', *TDHS*, 30 (1981).
Pratt, D., 'The Marcher Lordship of Chirk, 1329–1330', *TDHS*, 39 (1990).
Pratt, D., 'The de Warenne Lords of Bromfield and Yale 1282–1353', *TDHS*, 62 (2014).
Prestwich, M., 'Edward I in Wales: A New Account of 1294–5', *WHR*, 6 (1972).
Prestwich, M., *War, Policy and Finance under Edward I* (London, 1972).
Prestwich, M., *Edward I* (London and New Haven CT, 1997).
Prestwich, M., *The Three Edwards: War and State in England, 1272–1377* (London, 2003).
Prestwich, M., 'Welsh Infantry in Flanders in 1297', in R. A. Griffiths and P. R Schofield (eds), *Wales and the Welsh in the Middle Ages* (Cardiff, 2011).
Pryce, Huw, *Native Law and the Church in Medieval Wales* (Oxford, 1993).
Pryce, Huw, 'Welsh Rulers and European Change, c.1100–1282', in Huw Pryce and John Watts (eds), *Power and Identity in the Middle Ages: Essays in Memory of Rees Davies* (Oxford, 2007).
Pryce, Huw, 'Anglo-Welsh Agreements, 1201–77', in R. A. Griffiths and P. R. Schofield (eds), *Wales and the Welsh in the Middle Ages* (Cardiff, 2011).
Pryce, Huw, *J. E. Lloyd and the Creation of Welsh History: Renewing a Nation's Past* (Cardiff, 2011).
Pryce, Huw, *Writing Welsh History. From the Early Middle Ages to the Twenty-First Century* (Oxford, 2022).
Pryce, Huw, and John Watts (eds), *Power and Identity in the Middle Ages: Essays in Memory of Rees Davies* (Oxford, 2007).
Pugh, T. B. (ed.), *Glamorgan County History, volume 3: The Middle Ages* (Cardiff, 1971).
Putnam, B., *The Place in Legal History of Sir William Shareshull* (Cambridge, 1950).

Redknap, Mark, *Discovered in Time: Treasures from Early Wales* (Cardiff, 2011).
Rees, E. A., *A Life of Guto'r Glyn* (Talybont, 2008).
Rees, William, *South Wales and the March* (Oxford, 1924).
Rees, William, *The Union of England and Wales* (Cardiff, 1947).
Reeves, A. C., *The Marcher Lords* (Llandybie, 1983).
Reynolds, S., *An Introduction to the History of English Medieval Towns* (Oxford, 1977).
Reynolds, S., *Fiefs and Vassals: The Medieval Evidence Reinterpreted* (Oxford, 1994).
Reynolds, S., *Kingdoms and Communities in Western Europe, 900–1300* (Oxford, 1997).
Richards, Melville, 'Prydydd y Moch', *TDHS*, 11 (1962).
Roberts, Brynley, *Edward Lhwyd, c.1660–1709: Naturalist, Antiquary, Philologist* (Cardiff, 2022).
Roberts, Enid Pierce, 'Siôn Tudur', *LlC*, 2 (1952–3).
Roberts, Enid Pierce, 'Wiliam Cynwal' *TDHS*, 12 (1963).
Roberts, Enid Pierce, 'Teulu Plas Iolyn', *TDHS*, 13 (1964).
Roberts, Enid Pierce, 'Cywyddau Marwnad Rhisiart Miltwn', in J. E. C. Williams (ed.), *Ysgrifau Beirniadol*, vol. 2 (Denbigh, 1966).
Roberts, Enid Pierce, 'Sion Salsbri, Lleweni', *TDHS*, 19 (1970).
Roberts, Enid Pierce, 'Uchelwyr y beirdd', *TDHS*, 25 (1976).
Roberts, Glyn, 'The Anglesey Submissions of 1406', *BBCS*, 15 (1952).
Roberts, Glyn, *Aspects of Welsh History* (Cardiff, 1969).
Roberts, Glyn, 'Wyrion Eden: The Anglesey Descendants of Ednyfed Fychan in the Fourteenth Century', in Glyn Roberts, *Aspects of Welsh History* (Cardiff, 1969).
Roberts, Michael, and Simone Clarke (eds), *Women and Gender in Early Modern Wales* (Cardiff, 2000).
Roberts, Peter R., 'The "Act of Union" in Welsh History', *THSC* (1974).
Roberts, Peter R., 'The Welsh Language, English Law and Tudor Legislation', *TCHS* (1989).
Roberts, Peter R., 'Tudor Legislation and the Political Status of 'The British Tongue', in Geraint H. Jenkins (ed.), *The Welsh Language Before the Industrial Revolution* (Cardiff, 1997).

Roberts, Sara Elin, 'Legal Practice in Fifteenth-Century Brycheiniog', *SC*, 35 (2001).
Roberts, Sara Elin, *Jasper, The Tudor Kingmaker* (Fonthill, 2015).
Roberts, Sara Elin, *The Growth of Law in Medieval Wales, c. 1100–c.1500* (Woodbridge, 2022).
Roderick, A. J., 'The Four Cantreds: A Study in Administration', *BBCS*, 10 (1939–41).
Roderick, A. J. (ed.), *Wales Through the Ages* (Llandybie, 1959).
Rosenthal, J. T., 'The Estates and Finances of Richard, Duke of York (1411–1460)', in W. M. Bowsky (ed.), *Studies in Medieval and Renaissance History*, vol. 2 (Lincoln NE, 1995).
Ross, C. D, *Edward IV* (London, 1997).
Ross, C. D., *Richard III* (New Haven CT, 2011).
Rowlands, Eurys I., 'Iolo Goch', in J. Carney and D. Greene (eds), *Celtic Studies: Essays in Memory of Angus Matheson 1912–1962* (London, 1968).
Rowlands, Eurys I. (ed.), *Gwaith Lewys Môn* (Cardiff, 1975).
Russell, J. C., *British Medieval Population* (London, 1948).
Saul, N. E., *Richard II* (London, 1997).
Seebohm, F., *The Tribal System in Wales* (London, 1904).
Sherborne, James, 'Richard II's Return to Wales, July 1399', *WHR*, 7/4 (December 1975).
Siddons, Michael P., 'Welshman in the Service of France', *BBCS*, 36 (1989).
Siddons, Michael P., *The Development of Welsh Heraldry* (Aberystwyth, 1991).
Simpson, A. W. B., *An Introduction to the History of the Land Law* (Oxford, 1986).
Skinner, Patricia (ed.), *The Welsh and the Medieval World: Travel, Migration and Exile* (Cardiff, 2018).
Smith, G. Rex, 'The Penmachno Letter Patent and the Welsh Uprising of 1294–95', *CMCS*, 58 (2009).
Smith, G. Rex, 'On the Extent of the Lordship of Chirk, 1332', *CMCS*, 63 (2012).
Smith, J. Beverley, 'Crown and Community in the Principality of North Wales in the Reign of Henry Tudor', *WHR*, 3 (1966).

Smith, J. Beverley, 'The Lordship of Senghennydd', in T. B. Pugh (ed.), *Glamorgan County History, volume 3: The Middle Ages* (London, 1971).

Smith, J. Beverley, 'Edward II and the Allegiance of Wales', *WHR*, 8 (1976).

Smith, J. Beverley, 'Gruffydd Llwyd and the Celtic Alliance, 1315–18', *BBCS*, 26 (1976).

Smith, J. Beverley, 'The Death of Llywelyn ap Gruffudd'; *WHR*, 11 (1983).

Smith, J. Beverley, 'Magna Carta and the Charters of the Welsh Princes', *EHR*, 99 (1984).

Smith, J. Beverley, 'The *Gravamina* of Llywelyn ap Gruffudd', *BBCS*, 31 (1984–5).

Smith, J. Beverley, *Llywelyn ap Gruffudd, Prince of Wales* (Cardiff, 1998).

Smith, J. Beverley, and Llinos Beverley Smith (eds), *History of Merioneth, volume 2: The Middle Ages* (Cardiff, 2001).

Smith, Llinos Beverley, 'The Arundel Charters of the Lordship of Chirk in the Fourteenth Century', *BBCS*, 23 (1968–7).

Smith, Llinos Beverley, 'The Gage and the Land Market in Late Medieval Wales', *Economic History Review*, 2/29 (1976).

Smith, Llinos Beverley, '*Tir Prid*: Deeds of Gage of Land in Late Medieval Wales', *BBCS*, 27 (1977).

Smith, Llinos Beverley, 'The *Gravamina* of the Community of Gwynedd Against Llywelyn ap Gruffydd', *BBCS*, 31 (1984).

Smith, Llinos Beverley, 'Disputes and Settlements on Medieval Wales: The Role of Arbitration', *EHR*, 106 (1991).

Smith, Llinos Beverley, 'The Welsh Language Before 1536', in Geraint H. Jenkins (ed.), *The Welsh Language Before the Industrial Revolution* (Cardiff, 1997).

Smith, Llinos Beverley, 'Towards a History of Women in Late Medieval Wales', in Michael Roberts and Simone Clarke (eds), *Women and Gender in Early Modern Wales* (Cardiff, 2000).

Smith, Llinos Beverley, 'On the Hospitality of the Welsh: A Comparative View', in Huw Pryce and John Watts (eds), *Power and Identity in the Middle Ages: Essays in Memory of Rees Davies* (Oxford, 2007).

Smith, Llinos Beverley, 'Family, Land and Inheritance in Late Medieval Wales: A Case Study of Llannerch in the Lordship of Dyffryn Clwyd', *WHR*, 27 (2015).

Smith, Peter, *Houses of the Welsh Countryside* (London, 1988).

Somerville. R., *The Duchy of Lancaster*, 2 vols (London, 1970).

Stephens, Meic, *The New Companion to the Literature of Wales* (Oxford, 1998).

Steel, Anthony, *Richard II* (Cambridge, 1941).

Stephenson, David, *Political Power in Medieval Gwynedd: Governance and the Welsh Princes* (Cardiff, 2014) [published originally as *The Governance of Gwynedd* (Cardiff, 1984) but with new introduction].

Stephenson, David, *Medieval Powys: Kingdom, Principality and Lordships, 1132–1293* (Woodbridge, 2016).

Stephenson, David, 'New Light on a Dark Deed: The Death of Llywelyn ap Gruffudd, Prince of Wales', *AC*, 166 (2017).

Stephenson, David, *Medieval Wales, c. 1050–1332* (Cardiff, 2019).

Stevens, Matthew Frank, *Urban Assimilation in Post-Conquest Wales, Ethnicity, Gender and Economy in Ruthin, 1282–1348* (Cardiff, 2010).

Stevens, Matthew Frank, 'The Great Famine in Dyffryn Clwyd', *TDHS*, 63 (2015).

Stevens, Matthew Frank, 'The Black Death in the Lordship of Ruthin', *TDHS*, 65 (2017).

Stevens, Matthew Frank, *The Economy of Medieval Wales, 1067–1536* (Cardiff, 2019).

Suggett, Richard, 'The Interpretation of Late Medieval Houses in Wales', in R. R. Davies and Geraint H. Jenkins (eds), *From Medieval to Modern: Historical Essays in Honour of Kenneth O. Morgan and Ralph A. Griffiths* (Cardiff, 2004).

Tait, J., *The Medieval English Borough* (Manchester, 1936).

Taylor, A. J., 'Conway', in *The King's Works in Wales, 1277–1330* (London, 1974).

Taylor, A. J., 'Master St James of St George', in *Studies in Castles and Castle-Building* (London and Ronceverte, 1985).

Taylor, A. J., *The Welsh Castles of Edward I* (London, 1986).

Thirsk, J., (ed.), *The Agrarian History of England and Wales, volume 4: 1500–1640* (Cambridge, 1967).

Thirsk, J., (ed.), *The English Rural Landscape* (Oxford, 2000).
Thomas, Graham C. G., 'Oswestry 1400, Glyndwr's supporters on trial', *SC*, 40 (2006).
Thomas, Rebecca, *History and Identity in Early Medieval Wales* (Woodbridge, 2022).
Thomas, W. S. K., *Tudor Wales* (Llandysul, 1983).
Tout, T. F., *Chapters in the Administrative History of Medieval England* (Manchester, 1920–3).
Tuck, A., *Crown and Nobility, 1272–1461* (Oxford, 1999).
Tupling, G., *The Economic History of Rossindale* (Manchester, 1927).
Turvey, Roger, *Llywelyn the Great, Prince of Gwynedd* (Llandysul, 2007).
Usher, G. A., 'The Extent of the Lordship of Denbigh, 1334', *TDHS*, 3 (1954).
Walker, David, *The Norman Conquerors* (Swansea, 1977).
Walker, David, *Medieval Wales* (Cambridge, 1990).
Waters, W. H., *The Edwardian Settlement of North Wales in its Administrative and Legal Aspects (1284–1343)* (Cardiff, 1935).
Watt, Diane (ed.), *Medieval Women in their Communities* (Cardiff, 1997).
Williams, C. R., *The History of Flintshire* (Denbigh, 1961).
Williams, David H., 'The Carmelites in Medieval Wales', *Arch. Camb.*, 167 (2018).
Williams, D. M., and J. R. Kenyon, *The Impact of the Edwardian Castles in Wales* (Oxford, 2010).
Williams, Glanmor, *The Welsh Church from Conquest to Reformation* (Cardiff, 1962).
Williams, Glanmor, *Owen Glendower* (London, 1966).
Williams, Glanmor, *Welsh Reformation Essays* (Cardiff, 1967).
Williams, Glanmor, *Religion, Language and Nationality in Wales* (Cardiff, 1979).
Williams, Glanmor, *Harri Tudur a Chymru/Henry Tudor and Wales* (Cardiff, 1985).
Williams, Glanmor, *Recovery, Reorientation and Reformation: Wales c.1415–1642* (Oxford, 1987).
Williams, Glanmor, *Wales and the Reformation* (Cardiff, 1997).
Williams Glanmor, *Cymru a'r Gorffennol, Côr o Leisiau* (Caerdydd, 2000).

Williams, Gruffydd Aled, 'Edmwnd Prys, un arall o enwogion Llanrwst', *TDHS*, 23 (1974).

Williams, Gruffydd Aled, 'Wiliam Midleton, bonheddwr, anturiwr a bardd', *TDHS*, 24 (1975).

Williams, Gruffydd Aled, 'Edmwnd Prys (1543/4–1623), Dyneiddiwr Protestannaidd', *JMHRS*, 8 (1980).

Williams, Gruffydd Aled, *Ymryson Edmwnd Prys a Wiliam Cynwal* (Cardiff, 1986).

Williams, Gruffydd Aled, *Dyffryn Conwy a'r Dadeni* (Llanrwst, 1989).

Williams, Gruffydd Aled, 'Dwy lenyddiaeth, dau fyd: diwylliant yn Llyweni yng nghyfnod y Dadeni', *LlC*, 40 (2017).

Williams, Gruffydd Aled, *The Last Days of Owain Glyn Dŵr* (Tal-y-bont, 2017).

Williams, Gruffydd Aled, 'Edmwnd Prys a'i salmau cain (1621)', *Y Traethodydd*, 176/740 (2021).

Williams, G. J., 'Traddodiad llenyddol Dyffryn Clwyd a'r Cyffiniau', *TDHS*, 1 (1952).

Williams, J., *Ancient and Modern Denbigh* (Denbigh, 1856; reprinted Mold, 1989).

Williams, J., *The Records of Denbigh and its Lordship* (Wrexham, 1860).

Williams, J. E. Caerwyn, 'Beirdd y Tywysogion: arolwg', *LlC*, 11 (1970).

Williams, Gwyn A., *When was Wales?* (London, 1982).

Williams-Jones, Keith, 'The Taking of Conwy Castle, 1401', *TCHS*, 39 (1978).

Wolffe, B. P., *The Royal Demesne in English History: The Crown Estate in the Governance of the Realm from the Conquest to 1509* (London, 2019).

Wolffe, B. P., *The Crown Lands 1461–1536, An Aspect of Yorkist and Early Tudor Government* (London, 2021).

Yorke, Philip, *The Royal Tribes of Wales* (Wrexham, 1799).

Unpublished University of Wales MA and PhD dissertations

Jones, G. R. J., 'The Military Geography of Gwynedd' (MA, 1949).

Owen, D. Huw, 'The Lordship of Denbigh, 1282–1425' (PhD, 1967).

INDEX

Aberconwy, abbey, abbot, 11–12, 21, 34, 190–1, 202
Aberconway, Treaty of 14–15
Abergele, 15, 25, 27, 39, 50, 53, 82, 84, 87, 92–3, 104–7, 109, 133 197, 220–1, 234
accounts
   (1297) 57, 59, 103
   (1305) 57, 59, 60–2, 101, 104
   (1311) 60–3
Alice, da. Henry, Earl of Lincoln; wife Thomas Earl of Lancaster, 36, 38, 43
Aled river, 8, 24, 37
Alltfaenan, 50, 63, 83, 87, 140–1, 153, 195
Alys, wife Wiliam Llywelyn, 193
amobr, amobrage, 53, 170, 179–81
Angharad, daughter of Dafydd, 193
Archwedlog, Forest of, township, 37, 71–2, 74, 83–4, 86, 88, 102, 153, 205
Arllwyd, 53, 196

Bachymbyd, 89, 91, 134–5, 143, 147, 151, 191–2, 201, 204
Backerne family, 215, 219
bailiff, of the English, 53, 164
Banastre Sir William, 177
Bannwr
   Efa, daughter of Dafydd (Bannwr), 146

Lleucu, daughter of Einion (Bannw), 147
Pannwr, Dafydd, 181, 192
Barrog, 70–1, 81, 162, 204
Berain, 39, 42, 65, 69–71, 74, 79, 84, 89, 92, 102, 132, 140, 142–3, 216
Berfeddwlad, Y *see* Perfeddwlad
Billyng family, 91, 132–4, 149, 216–17, 219
Birchinshaw family, 145, 193, 206, 228
Black Death, 161, 163–5, 234
Black Prince, Black Prince's Register, Council, 121, 164, 176–7, 184, 237
Blackburn family, 49, 103, 162
Blackheath, battle of, 183, 204
Bleddyn Fychan, 36–7, 207, 229
Bodeiliog, 66, 69, 74, 89, 96
Bodysgawen, 69–70, 74, 79, 81, 92, 96, 140, 142
Braint Hir, 24, 26, 140, 205
Bridlington family, 145,150
Bromfield and Yale, 3, 16, 32, 35, 39–40, 43, 52, 56, 113–14, 119
Brunham John, 121, 176–7
Brynffanugl, 65, 206

Cadwaladr ap Rhys, 183
Caernarfon, Caernarfonshire, 11–12, 34, 115, 117, 189

Caledan, 23, 67
Cambridge, Earl of, 135, 187
Camden William, 216, 225
Campaigns (military: 1277, 1282, 1294), 64, 66–7
Carwedfynydd, 71, 79
Castleford, family, 87, 106
Cegidog, 23, 60, 87, 106
Ceinmeirch, 3, 21, 23–4, 27, 50–1, 54, 58, 64–5, 67–8, 72, 74, 78, 86–9, 100, 116, 134, 139 144, 146, 150, 153, 156, 162, 164–7, 170, 180, 191–2, 199, 203, 223, 231, 233
Cernenyfed, 90, 133–4, 142–4, 146, 156, 191
Cernioge, 191, 202
Cernioge deeds, 210
Charter(s), 201, 216–17, 224, 226
Chaumbre, William de la, 39–42, 98
Cheshire, 130–31
Chester, Chamberlain, county, castles, Justice, 13–15, 31, 131, 134, 154, 164, 176
Chirk, Lordship of, 16, 31–2, 207, 228
Chwibren, 88, 196
Chwibren Isaf, 229
Cilcedig, 23, 50, 83, 87–8, 149
Cilcennis, 22, 198
Clan lands, 139–40
Clitheroe family, 47, 85, 88
Clough, Richard, 222
Clwyd mill/new mill, 132, 153, 171, 198
Clwyd river, vale of, 1, 7, 11, 32, 37, 207
Coed Godebog, 228–9
Colwyn, 23
commote court, 174–5, 179, 233
commutation of dues, 26–7, 63–4
constable, 48, 49, 50, 103, 174, 176, 215, 233
Conway, castle, 129, 137
Conway family, 132, 198

Conwy river, valley 1, 7, 11, 13, 16, 25, 31, 32, 222
Gorves, Llywelyn, 144, 145
Council of Marches, 224, 235
Court of Great Sessions, 224, 235
Creuddun, 12, 32–3
Cromwell, Thomas, 203
Curteys family, 39, 43, 50, 130, 153–5, 180, 194
Cynan ap Llywarch 13, 25–6, 65, 71, 73, 80
Cynwrig Routh family, 79–80, 179–80

Dafydd Chwith, 72–3, 116–17
Davies, Annie Mary, 229–30
Degannwy, 10–11, 13
Deicus Penllwyd, 135, 147
Delves John, 121, 176, 178, 184
demesne, 59, 60–1, 232
Denbigh, borough, burgesses, town, 27, 53, 72, 84, 86, 90, 92–110, 115, 117, 131–2, 163, 183, 189–90, 205, 209, 222–4, 213–20, 222–4, 233–5
Denbigh, castle, 34–5, 37, 40–1, 48, 50, 54, 65–6, 68, 73, 87, 92, 97, 100, 113, 117, 119, 129–32, 163, 180, 182–3, 188–9, 205, 214
Denbigh, court, 176–8
Denbigh, lordship of, lords, 1, 3, 7, 11–12, 16, 21–2, 25–6, 31–2, 34, 36–42, 47, 51, 57–9, 68, 77, 79, 96, 102, 104, 107, 113–15, 117–23, 127–32, 134–5, 139, 144, 148, 154, 158, 161, 164–5, 168, 171–2, 176, 181–3, 187–90, 201, 203–5, 207–8, 214, 222, 231–2, 235
Denbighshire, 189, 204, 208–9, 215, 224, 227–8, 232, 235–6
Despenser, Hugh de, elder, Earl of, 40–3, 119, 237

Dinbych/Denbigh, 14, 47, 66, 89, 95–6
Dincadfel, 13, 26, 73
Dinerth, 84, 202
Dinmael, 32, 33, 51, 122, 129
Dinorben, Fawr, Fychan, 10, 14–15, 22, 48–9, 59, 60–2, 82, 84, 87, 196–7, 227, 237
distain, 49
Dolben family, 130, 156–7, 214, 217, 219, 224
Duckworth family, 90, 101–2, 148
Dyffryn Clwyd, 184, 236

Edeirnion, 129
Ednyfed Fychan, and family, 15, 25, 36, 38, 40, 122, 124, 183, 207
Edrud ap Marchudd, 25
Edward I (Edward, lord), 7, 16, 31, 35–7, 101, 154
Edward II, 38, 42, 101
Edward III, 119
Edward IV, 189, 232, 238
Edward V, 238
Edward, Prince of Wales, 177
English colony, families, settlers, tenants, 3, 64, 66, 75, 84, 157, 162, 23
Englishry, 77–8, 84, 93, 97, 133–4, 157, 162–4, 176, 184, 232–3
Ereifiad, 32, 71, 81, 89, 92, 96, 140, 142, 193
Erethlyn, 198, 204
escheat, 64–6, 73, 96
escheator, 50, 55, 57, 78, 130, 177–9, 183, 215
Evyas, family, 143–4

Faenol 32–3
fine/fines, 169, 177
Fletcher family, 180, 196
Flint/Flintshire, 31, 36, 52, 122, 129, 154
Forest, forest court, 78, 178, 180
Fraunces family, 133–4, 220
Frodesham family, 155–6
Foulkes, Humphrey, 228, 230, 235

gafael (ion), 23, 26
Galghull, park, 54, 183
Garthmeilyr, 92, 129
Garsnodiog, 54, 90–1, 180
Garthewin, 99, 204
Gaveston, Piers, 38
Gwytherin, 70–1
Glyn Dŵr Owain, rebellion, 128–35, 139, 148, 153, 157, 161–3, 167–9, 171, 173, 180, 214–15, 218
Glyndyfrdwy, 129
Goronwy ap Ednyfed Fychan, 25
Goronwy ap Heilyn, 15, 16, 25, 26
Great Sessions, Court of, 178, 209, 235
Grey, John de, 13–14, 101, 119
Grey, Reginald, lord of Ruthin, 15, 31–2, 35–6, 130, 184
Gronw Gethyn, 132–3
Gruffudd Hiraethog, 1, 205, 210
Gruffudd ap Rhodri, 12, 68, 73
Grugor, 72, 88
gwely(au), 34, 24
Gwenllian de Lacy, 15, 32
Gwenllian Goch, 82
Gwenynog Cynon, 69, 70–1, 80, 88–9, 92, 145, 195
Gwenynog Wyntus, 66, 89, 142, 153, 195
Gwydir, family, 57, 68, 73
Gwynedd, 7, 10–11, 13, 22, 27
Gwynedd Is Conwy, 7, 11, 15, 27, 114
Gwynedd Uwch Conwy, 24–7
Gwytherin, 10, 25, 42, 53, 70–1, 204

Hawarden, 15–16
Heaton/Heton family, 85, 88–9, 217, 220
Hedd Molwynog, 24, 36, 207, 229
Henllan, and mill, 10, 21, 86, 205
Henbury family, 150, 153, 158, 171, 213, 219
Hendregyda, 50, 81, 87, 92
Henry III, 14
Henry IV, 130–1
Henry V, 135
Henry VI, 238
Henry VII, 235, 238
Henry VIII, 219
Henry, Prince of Wales, 131, 154
Herbert, Sir William, 182, 187, 189, 190
Hereford, 97
Herefordshire, 85
Hereford family, 85, 99, 100
Heton family, 85, 88–90, 150, 158, 194
Hiraethog, Mynydd, 8, 12, 190, 202
Hoghton family, 99, 155–6, 177–8
Holland family, 39, 49, 83, 121, 143, 150, 158, 183, 193, 195, 197–8, 227–8
Hospitallers, St John, 190, 202
Hulton family, 50, 85, 86, 99, 101–2, 150, 220
Huxley family, 192, 194, 217, 220
Hywel ap Gronw, 15, 124

Ieuan, son of Llywelyn Chwith, 181, 207
Ieuan Wyn, 121–2
Iolo Goch, 127, 136, 207
Iorwerth ap Llywarch of Lleweni, 39, 41–2, 58, 73, 79, 80, 194
see also Yerward de la Chaumbre
Is Aled, 3, 21, 23–4, 26–7, 42, 48, 50–2, 57–9, 65, 71, 74, 78, 86–9, 91, 139, 141, 153, 162–3, 165, 169, 223

Is Dulas, 3, 21–2, 27, 50–1, 53, 57–8, 62, 82, 84, 86–7, 92, 139, 162–4, 174, 196, 204

James of St George (Master), 35
Justice of North Wales, 43, 50, 131, 176

Kilford/fulling mill, manor, 23, 54, 61–2, 66, 102, 153, 193, 227, 232
Kilford family, 91, 145
kindred groupings, 64, 68, 235
Knowsely family, 140, 219, 220

Lacy, Henry Earl of Lincoln, 7, 16, 31–9, 41, 43, 47–8, 58, 68, 72–3, 85, 93, 97, 99, 100–1, 106, 111, 217, 231
Lancashire, 88, 90, 205
Lancaster, Duchy, 99
Lancaster, Thomas, Earl of, 36, 38–41, 43, 231, 237
Law (English/family), 178, 210, 233
Lawrence, family, 133, 146, 196
Lawton family, 143, 162–3
Lee, Rowland, 208, 235
Leicester, Earl of, 227, 229, 235
Leland John, 35, 216, 220, 223, 225, 234
Lewis Môn, 206, 210
Lhuyd, Edward 235
Llaethfan, 83
Llanefydd, 10, 26, 202, 207
Llanfair, Llanfair mill, 19, 204
Llangernyw, 10, 16, 21, 204
Llandyrnog, 16
Llannerch, family, 144–5, 149, 195
Llanrhaeadr, 21
Llanrwst, 27, 73–4, 79–81, 92–3, 104–8, 110, 121, 130, 153, 190, 204, 207, 221, 234
Llansannan, 10, 21, 23, 36, 206, 228

Llechryd, 70–1, 207
Lleucu, da. Llywarch, 82
Lleucu, wife Cynddelw ap Cynwrig, 82
Lleweni, Acre/Park, 39, 42, 50, 89–93, 102, 107–8, 132–4, 143, 145–6, 148–50, 152–4, 171, 193–5, 204–5, 207, 209
Lleweni, new borough, 205
Llewesog, 67, 87–8, 91, 99, 132, 140, 151–2
Lloyd family, 129–31, 149, 183, 193, 205, 228
Llwyd, Sir Gruffudd, 39, 40, 42, 101, 111
Llwyd Humphrey, 1, 48, 205, 211, 223, 235
Llwytgoed, 25, 84, 202
Llyn y Cymer, 12, 202
Llŷn, Wiliam, 206, 210
Llysfaen, 87, 154
Llys Gwenllian, 15, 23, 32
Llywarch Holbwrch, 154, 205
Llywarch ap Llywelyn (Prydydd y Moch), 12
Llywelyn Bottreys, 181
Llywelyn Chwith, 181
Llywelyn ap Gruffudd, 13–16
Llywelyn ap Gruffudd Chwith, 197
Llywelyn ap Iorwerth, 11–13, 15, 39

Madog ap Llywelyn, 35–6, 38, 49
Maenan, 21, 34
Maerdy, 22–3, 47
March, Welsh, 33, 39, 118, 119
marcher lords/lordships 33, 43, 122, 184–5, 233
Marchudd ap Cynan, 23, 207
Marchwethian, 23–4, 154, 204, 206–7, 228
master forester, 50–1, 53, 103, 177, 182
Mathebrwd, 68, 72
Middelton family *see* Myddelton family

ministers' accounts, 161–2, 164
Mochdre, 23
Mody family, 102, 143, 193
Moel-y-wig, 54, 180, 183
Montagu family/estate, 1st–2nd earls of Salisbury, 42–3, 113, 115, 118–20, 127, 163, 231–2, 237
Morgan, Bishop William, 207, 211
Mortimer, Roger, lord of Chirk, 31–2
Mortimer family/estate, 1st–5th earls of March, 31–2, 41–2, 115, 118–20, 122, 127–8, 130–1, 135–6, 138, 164, 168, 170–1, 177, 181–2, 187, 215, 231–2, 234, 237–8
Morys Gethin, 202, 235
Mostyn family, 98, 100, 102
Myddelton family, 207, 228
Mynydd Hiraethog, 8, 12, 21

Nantglyn Cynon, 25, 70–1, 74, 140, 181
Nantglyn 'Sanctorum', 25, 81, 140–1, 181

Oswestry, 43, 113, 182
Owain Lawgoch, 121–2

parker, parks, 54, 183
Peake family, 101, 151, 180, 194
Pennant Erethlyn, 93, 107–8, 110
Penporchell, 62, 69, 70, 74, 96
Percy, Henry (Hotspur), 168, 205
Petrual, 162–3
Pigot family, 45, 48, 80, 85, 152, 180, 205–7, 214, 233, 235
Pirye, John, 116, 162
Plas Iolyn, 202–3, 206–7
Plesyngton family, 99, 100, 151, 191–2, 233
Pontefract family, 47, 49, 83–7, 99, 101, 103, 106, 108, 155–6, 233

Postin, 23, 54, 67, 180, 183
Prince of Wales, and Principality
   of Wales, 14, 33, 38, 40,
   49–50, 114, 120, 154, 168
Prion, 23
Prys, 23–4, 70–1, 96, 202
Prys family, 203, 206–7, 235
Puleston family, 188–9

raglot/raglotry (rhaglaw), 15, 51–3,
   134, 174, 179–81
raglot advocariae, 51–3, 180
Ramsbothom family, 85, 90, 148,
   156
rebellion (1294/5), 83, 92, 99, 104,
   117, 233
receiver/receiver's accounts, 3, 47–8,
   50, 54, 129, 161–6, 182–3
Receiver-General, 164–5, 184
Rees, Henry, William (Gwilym
   Hiraethog), 229
Rental (1330), 3, 5
Rental (1437), 3, 131, 139–40, 142–4,
   149–54, 157–8, 161, 171
Rental (1450–1), 3, 191, 194, 216,
   233
Rental (1476–7), 3, 216–17, 219–20,
   224, 233
Rental (1491–2), 3, 191–2, 233
rhaglaw, 16, 183, 213
   see also raglot
Rhiw, 22, 64, 198
Rhos, 1, 7, 9–16, 21, 27, 31–3, 37,
   51, 68, 206
Rhuddlan, 10, 13, 16, 35, 115, 117,
   132, 214
Rhufoniog, 1, 9–16, 21, 27, 31–3,
   37, 51, 68, 206
Rhys ap Maredudd (Rhys Fawr),
   190–1, 202, 206, 235
Rhys ap Roppert, 121–2
Richard II, 127
Richard III, 190, 238
ringild, ringlildry, 51, 53, 129, 134,
   163, 165–7, 174, 179, 181
Robert ap Rhys, 201–3, 206–7, 235
Romworth family, 100, 138, 140,
   153, 193–4
Rossindale family, 85, 150, 157,
   205, 217
Ruthin, 3, 11, 32, 35, 40, 113, 127,
   130, 134, 163, 215, 227
Rybchester, Cecilia, 92, 109

Salusbury family, 50, 85, 90, 94,
   127, 134, 149–50, 152–4,
   171, 176–8, 180, 182–3, 192–5,
   197, 201–7, 209, 211, 214–16,
   219, 227–8, 233, 235
Schutlesworth family, 166, 179
Segrwyd, and Park of, 23, 43, 50,
   64, 80, 86, 89–91, 133–4,
   141–2, 144–7, 150, 153–7
sergeant of the peace, 51–3, 134,
   179
settler families, 3, 233
Seynpol family, 99, 100
Sgeibion, 67–8, 72–3, 81, 87–9, 91,
   116, 132, 134, 142, 144, 146,
   148, 181, 191
Shaldeford Henry de, and family,
   83, 115–17, 215, 232
Sharesuill, Sri William, 177, 179, 184
Shoresworth, 98–100
Shrewsbury, 127, 130–1, 136, 232
Sion Tudur, 205, 207, 210–11
Spenne family, 151, 191–2
Stafford family, 113, 115–16, 123
steward, 55, 182–3
St Asaph, Bishop, diocese, 14, 21,
   117, 202, 204
Survey of Denbigh (1334), 1–3,
   21–4, 26–7, 42, 57, 59–62,
   64, 80–1, 83, 85, 87, 95, 99,
   102, 104, 106, 108, 115–16,
   139–40, 142–3, 149, 151–2,
   154, 156–7, 161–2, 207, 213,
   217, 220, 231–2

Surrey, earl of, 32, 35–6, 39
Swynemore family, 83, 85, 87–9, 99, 101–2, 115–16, 133, 145, 151–2, 170, 176, 180, 195, 214–15, 220, 233
Symondstone family, 85, 91
Steynbourne family, 99, 105

Taldrach, 69–70, 74, 81, 96
Talhaearn, 53, 81
Tal-y-bryn, 39, 42, 74, 92
Tangwystl Goch, 13, 15, 26
Tegeingl (Englefield), 10, 13, 15, 31, 56
Tir prid, 25–2
Totenhale family, 83, 99
Trebwll, 68, 72
Treth, 62, 72, 74
Tudur ap Robert, Berain, 206
Tudor, Henry, 201
Tudor, Jasper, 182, 188–90
Tudur Aled, 202, 206–7, 210–11, 229
Tudur Penllyn, 190, 206
twnc, 27, 62, 72, 163, 167
Twynnan, 26, 82
Tŷ-brith, 84, 197–8
Tywysog, 69–70, 74, 81, 96, 129

Union, Acts of, 174, 189, 208–9, 211, 224, 227, 232, 235
Uwch Aled, 3, 21, 23–4, 27, 36–7, 53, 57–8, 67, 84, 86, 88, 130, 162–3, 165–7, 179–81, 196, 229
Uwch Dulas, 3, 21–2, 25–7, 68, 82, 84, 92, 108, 134, 139, 162–5, 167, 170, 180, 191–2, 194, 196–7, 221

Vale of Clwyd, 5, 7, 11, 32, 77

Warenne, John, Earl of Surrey, 32, 35–6, 39, 114
Warwick, Richard, Earl of, 187, 198
Welsh law/Welsh land law, 184, 234
Welshry, 77, 184, 233
Whiteacre family, 84, 90, 156
Wigfair, 100, 102, 115–16, 176, 197, 210
Wilberley family, 89, 233
Winchester, earl of 40–1
Wood, family, 155 ,157
Woodward, 53, 213
Wynn family, 4, 12, 57, 68, 190, 222, 234

Yankyn ap Bleddyn, 146, 150
York, Richard, Duke of, Yorkist cause, 188, 190, 206, 232
Ysbyty Ifan, 42, 190
Ystrad, manor, 14, 23, 48
Ystrad Cynan, 25, 43, 61, 65–6, 69–72, 74, 80, 87, 100, 102, 153, 195
Ystrad Owain, 15, 22–3, 59–61, 66, 232

Zusche, Alan la 14